EMT-BASIC
EXAM

EMT-BASIC
EXAM

3rd Edition

LEARNINGEXPRESS®

NEW YORK

Library of Congress Cataloging-in-Publication Data:
EMT-basic exam.—3rd ed.
    p. cm.
  ISBN 1-57685-487-6 (pbk.)
    1. Emergency medicine—Examinations, questions, etc. 2. Emergency medical
technicians—Examinations, questions, etc. I. LearningExpress (Organization)

RC86.7.E5915 2005
616.02'5'076—dc22

                                                        2005045162

Printed in the United States of America

9 8 7 6 5 4 3 2 1

Third Edition

For information or to place an order, contact LearningExpress at:
    55 Broadway
    8th Floor
    New York, NY 10006

Or visit us at:
    www.learnatest.com

List of Contributors

The following individuals contributed to the content of this book.

Virginia Brennan, PhD is a linguist and editor in Nashville, TN.

Angel Clark Burba, MS, EMT-P is on the faculty of the EMT–Paramedic Program at Howard Community College in Maryland. She serves on the Education Committee of the National Association of EMS Educators (NAEMSE).

Jan Gallagher, PhD is an editor and educator living and working in New Jersey.

Bill Garcia, EMT-P was a founding staff member of *Rescue* (now, *Fire-Rescue*) magazine and serves in the U.S. Navy Reserves. He has been in EMS for 28 years.

Art Hsieh has been in EMS since 1982, and he began teaching full time in 1996. He is a past president of the National Association of EMS Educators (NAEMSE). He currently directs an EMS education program in northern California.

Dawn S. Pakora, EMT-P is a part-time faculty member of EMS at the University of Maryland–Baltimore County and a full-time EMS provider. She has been in EMS for 23 years.

Elaine Silverstein is a writer and editor living and working in New Jersey.

Steven C. Wood is the EMS coordinator in charge of operations for the City of San Diego, Division of EMS. He has been in EMS for 18 years.

Contents

EMT-BASIC
EXAM

The EMT-Basic Exam

CHAPTER SUMMARY

This chapter tells you how to become certified as an Emergency Medical Technician-Basic (EMT-B). It outlines the certification requirements of the National Registry of Emergency Medical Technicians and tells you how to use this book to study for the written exam.

The National Registry of Emergency Medical Technicians (NREMT) was established in 1969 in response to a suggestion of the U.S. Committee on Highway Safety. Today, the NREMT is an independent, not-for-profit agency whose job is to certify that EMTs have the knowledge and skills to do their job—to save lives and preserve health. By setting uniform national standards for training, testing, and continuing education, the NREMT helps ensure patient safety throughout the United States.

In some states, the NREMT certification process is the only licensure process for EMTs. Other states have their own testing procedures. (A list of specific certification requirements for all 50 states, Washington D.C., Puerto Rico, and the U.S. Virgin Islands appears in Chapter 8.) Nearly all states and U.S. territories base their curriculum and tests on the U.S. Department of Transportation's 1994 National Standard Curriculum for EMT-Basics. The NREMT exam uses the same curriculum to guide the construction of exam questions. Therefore, whether you will be taking a state test or the NREMT test, you will be learning and studying similar material. This book is based on the NREMT written examination.

▶ Minimum Requirements

To apply for national registration as an EMT-Basic with the NREMT, you must meet the following requirements:

- You must be at least 18 years old.
- You must have successfully completed a state-approved National Standard EMT-B training program within the last two years.
- If your state does not require national EMT-B registration, you must obtain official documentation of your current state EMT-B certification.
- You must have successfully completed all sections of a state-approved EMT-B practical exam within the past 12 months. This exam must equal or exceed all the criteria established by the National Registry.
- You must complete the felony statement on the application and submit the required documentation.
- You must submit current cardiopulmonary resuscitation (CPR) credentials from either the American Heart Association or the American Red Cross.
- You must submit an acceptable application attesting to the satisfaction of the previous requirements.
- You must send a $20.00 nonrefundable/nontransferable application fee (money order only). All fees must be made payable to the National Registry of Emergency Medical Technicians and submitted with the application to cover processing of the application.
- You must successfully complete the National Registry EMT-Basic written examination.

▶ How to Apply

When you have met all the requirements outlined above and are ready to take the exam, contact the NREMT to obtain an application and to find out where you can take the test in your state. Write or call the NREMT at:

National Registry of Emergency
Medical Technicians
P.O. Box 29233
Columbus, OH 43229
614-888-4484

When you contact the National Registry, you will find out whether the examination is administered through your state EMT office or whether you need to make individual arrangements to take the exam.

Finally, you must submit an application to the National Registry stating that you have met all the requirements, accompanied by the registration fee.

You can also fill out an NREMT application online by going to http://www.nremt.org/EMT Services/candidate_application.asp. You can view a copy of the application on page 5.

▶ The EMT-B Written Exam

The National Registry's EMT-B written examination consists of 150 multiple-choice questions. Exam content is based on tasks identified in the EMT-Basic Practical Analysis conducted by the NREMT. The exam is then formatted based on the 1994 DOT national standard curriculum for EMT-Basics.

The exam consists of six content areas:

SUBTEST	# OF QUESTIONS
Airway and Breathing	25–31
Cardiology	24–30
Trauma	23–29
Medical	21–27
Obstetrics and Pediatrics	18–24
Operations	21–27
TOTAL	**150**

To pass the exam, you must obtain an overall score of at least 70%. In other words, you must answer 105 of the 150 questions correctly. You will learn your score approximately three to four weeks after you take the examination.

The NREMT offers accommodations on the written examination for candidates with learning disabilities. If you were diagnosed with a learning disability in reading, decoding, or reading comprehension, contact the NREMT for a copy of their Examination Accommodations Policy.

▶ The EMT-B Practical Examination

When you apply for National Registry EMT-B registration, you will fill out an application that consists of several sections. Section I requires verification of your CPR credentials from either the American Heart Association or the American Red Cross. The verification may be in the form of an instructor signature or a copy of your current card attesting to competency in the following skills:

- Adult 1 & 2 Rescuer CPR
- Child & Infant CPR
- Adult/Child/Infant obstructed airway maneuvers

Section II of the National Registry EMT-B application requires proof that you have successfully completed a state-approved practical examination within a 12-month period. At a minimum, the exam must evaluate your performance in the following skills. To pass the practical exam, you must meet or exceed the NREMT's criteria in the following six areas:

- **Station #1:** Patient Assessment/Management—Trauma
- **Station #2:** Patient Assessment/Management—Medical
- **Station #3:** Cardiac Arrest Management/AED

- **Station #4:** Spinal Immobilization (seated or supine patient)
- **Station #5:** Bag-Valve-Mask Apneic Patient with a Pulse
- **Station #6:** Random Skill Station. This will consist of one of the following skills:
  - Long bone immobilization
  - Joint dislocation immobilization
  - Traction splinting
  - Bleeding control/shock management
  - Upper airway adjuncts and suction
  - Mouth-to-mask with supplemental oxygen
  - Supplemental oxygen administration

Chapter 7 contains more detailed information about the NREMT practical exam.

▶ Using This Book to Prepare

The bulk of this book consists of four complete written practice tests, each containing 150 questions similar to those on the National Registry EMT-B written examination. The practice test items are grouped in content areas, just like the items on the NREMT-Basic examination. The table on page 4 shows the breakdown of content areas in each practice test in this book.

The first step in using this book to prepare for the EMT-Basic written examination is to read Chapter 2, which presents the nine-step LearningExpress Test Preparation System. Chapter 2 introduces essential test-taking strategies that you can practice as you take the exams in this book.

Next, take one complete practice test and score your answers using the answer key. Complete explanations for the answers are included. Remember, the passing score for the EMT-Basic written exam is 70%, or 105 correct answers. If you score over 70% on your first practice exam, congratulations! However, even if you do very well on the practice test, don't become over confident and simply assume that you'll pass the actual test easily—the items on that test will be different from those on the practice test. You'll still need to do some test preparation. No matter what your initial score, follow the suggestions in the next paragraphs.

If you score below 70% on your first practice test, don't panic, but do put in some concentrated study time. Begin your studying by determining your major areas of weakness. For example, perhaps you answered 50 items on the practice test incorrectly, giving you a score of 100, or approximately 67%. Upon rereading the questions you missed, you find that they break down into the following content areas: Cardiology: 12 questions missed; Airway and Breathing: 3 questions missed; Trauma: 13 questions missed; Medical: 4 questions missed; Obstetrics and Pediatrics: 12 questions missed; Operations: 6 questions missed.

This analysis tells you that you need to concentrate your study in the areas of Cardiology, Trauma, and Obstetrics and Pediatrics. Try putting in one or two concentrated evenings of study on each area. Review all the material on these topics in the textbook and printed materials from your EMS course. Then,

take a second practice test and check your total score and content area breakdown again. Chances are that your total will have improved.

In the time leading up to the EMT-Basic written exam, use the remaining practice tests to further pinpoint areas of weakness and to find areas to review. For example, suppose that after additional study sessions, you take the third practice test. You now do well on all the questions about circulation *except* the ones that ask you to recognize signs and symptoms of shock. This information tells you which specific pages of your textbook you should review.

Once you have worked on and improved your areas of weakness, use the final days before the test to do some general reviewing. Devote a short period of time each day to reviewing one or two chapters of your textbook. Then, use the fourth practice test to rehearse test-taking strategies and procedures.

After reading and studying this book, you'll be well on your way to obtaining certification as an EMT-Basic. Good luck as you enter this rewarding and worthwhile career!

CONTENT AREA	RANGE OF NUMBER OF QUESTIONS IN THE NREMT EXAM	NUMBER OF QUESTIONS IN EACH EXAM IN THIS BOOK			
		I	II	III	IV
Airway and Breathing	25–31	31	24	24	25
Cardiology	24–30	24	26	24	22
Trauma	23–29	24	24	26	28
Medical	21–27	25	29	27	28
Obstetrics and Pediatrics	18–24	24	24	24	21
Operations	21–27	21	21	22	22
	Total	150	150	150	150

EMT-Basic Application

The National Registry of Emergency Medical Technicians

I am submitting this application to test at

_____ in _____
Name of Facility   City

_____ on _____
State   Date (MM/DD/YY)

Application Date ☐☐ - ☐☐ - ☐☐☐☐

Social Security Number ☐☐☐ - ☐☐ - ☐☐☐☐

Have you ever applied for NREMT-B registration? ○ Yes ○ No

If you possess current state certification as an EMT, please list your current state EMT certification number in the space provided and attach a copy of your current EMT card

Current EMT Number
Please attach copy of card

Last Name

First Name

MI

Mailing Address

Program Code ☐☐☐ - ☐☐

City

State

Zip Code + 4

Gender
○ Male
○ Female

Date of Birth ☐☐ - ☐☐ - ☐☐☐☐

APPROVED EMT-B COURSE: Applicant must have completed an approved EMT-Basic Training Program that equals or exceeds the objectives of the National Standard EMT-Basic Curriculum. Attach a copy of your course completion certificate or a copy of your current EMT-B card. If your initial EMT-Basic training program is more than two years old or you hold current state certification as an EMT-Basic, you must document completion of 24 hours of approved EMT-B refresher training within the past two years and attach official documentation to this application.

Name of initial training institution or agency	Street Address	City	State	Zip Code

Initial Course Instructor/Course Coordinator	Course Completion Date ☐☐ - ☐☐ - ☐☐☐☐	Classroom Hours
Refresher Course Instructor/Course Coordinator	Refersher Completion Date ☐☐ - ☐☐ - ☐☐☐☐	Classroom Hours

What is the highest level of education you have completed?
○ Didn't complete high school
○ High school graduate/GED
○ Associate's degree
○ Bachelor's degree
○ Graduate degree

Please indicate the type of EMT-B service you are or will be affiliated with. (mark all that apply)
○ Fire Department
○ Private
○ Hospital-Based
○ 3rd-Service
○ Volunteer
○ Other
○ U.S. Government
○ Army
○ Navy
○ Air Force
○ Coast Guard

Will you be paid for your services as an EMT-B?
○ Yes
○ No
○ Not yet affiliated

Ethnic Origin
○ Native American
○ Asian
○ Black
○ Hispanic
○ White
○ Other

Licensing Action and Felony Statement

○ Yes ○ No   Have you ever been subject to limitation, suspension, or termination of your right to practice in a health care occupation or voluntarily surrendered a health care licensure in any state or to an agency authorizing the legal right to work?

○ Yes ○ No   Have you ever been convicted of a felony

If you answered "yes" to either question, you must provide official documentation that fully describes the offense, current status, and disposition of the case

Candidate Statement and Signature: I hereby affirm and declare that the above information on this application is true and correct and that any fraudulent entry may be considered a sufficient cause for rejection or subsequent revocation. I further agree to abide by all policies and procedures of the National Registry of EMTs, and hereby authorize the NREMT to release my examination scores to the teaching institution/agency, any state office of Emergency Medical Services, or any agency authorizing the legal right to practice. I further permit the NREMT to release my current status (registered or not registered) with the NREMT to the public 30 days following mailing of my test scores.

Applicant Signature

EMT-Basic Practical Examination Verification

This is to verify that on ☐☐ - ☐☐☐☐ , _____ completed a state-approved
                          Date (MM-YYYY)   Candidate's Name

practical examination at _____
                        Examination Site and State

equal to or exceeding the criteria established by the NREMT and performed satisfactorily so as to be deemed competent in the following skills:

Patient Assessment/Management - Trauma
Patient Assessment/Management - Medical
Cardiac Arrest Management/AED

Bag-Valve-Mask (Apneic Patient)
Spinal Immobilization (Seated or Supine Patient)
Random Skill Verification _____

Physician Name (Print or Type)

Agent or Assignee's Name (Print or Type)

Physician Signature

Agent or Assignee's Signature

License #

Agent or Assignee's Title

MM234771-2   6543   HR04

477121

Section I: CPR Credential

As the candidate's CPR instructor/training officer, I hereby verify the candidate has been examined and performed satisfactorily so as to be deemed competent in each of the following skills:

Adult 1 & 2 Rescuer CPR
Adult Obstructed Airway Maneuvers
Child CPR
Child Obstructed Airway Maneuvers
Infant CPR
Infant Obstructed Airway Maneuvers

_____
Verifying Signature   Date

CPR Expiration Date

☐☐ - ☐☐ - ☐☐☐☐

Please submit a copy of your current CPR card and/or ensure the appropriate verification signatures are affixed to this section of the application

Section II: Statement of Competency in EMT-Basic Skills

As the EMT-Basic Training Program Director or service director of training/operations, I verify that _____
has been examined and performed satisfactorily so as to be deemed competent in each of the following skills: (Candidate's Name)

Patient Assessment/Management - Trauma
Patient Assessment/Management - Medical
Cardiac Arrest Management/AED
Bleeding Control/Shock Management
Bag-Valve-Mask Apneic Patient
Supplemental Oxygen Administration
Upper Airway Adjuncts and Suction

Mouth-to-Mask with Supplemental Oxygen
Spinal Immobilization Supine Patient
Spinal Immobilization Seated Patient
Long Bone Immobilization
Joint Dislocation Immobilization
Traction Splinting

Signature: _____   Date: _____

Name (Please Print) _____

Title (Please Print) _____   Telephone # _____

Character Reference

Name	Street Address	City	State	Zip Code

National Registry EMT-Basic Application Information

Entry Requirements:

1. Successful completion of a state-approved EMT-Basic training program within the past 24 months, that equals or exceeds the behavioral objectives of the EMT-Basic National Standard Curriculum as developed and promulgated by the U.S. Department of Transportation.
2. If the candidate's initial EMT-Basic training completion date is beyond 24 months and the candidate has maintained state certification as an EMT-Basic, the candidate must document completion of 24 hours of state-approved EMT-Basic refresher training that meets all objectives of the current EMT-Basic National Standard Refresher Curriculum. Program completion date can be no older than 24 months from the date of testing.
3. Current CPR credential verifying competence in the skills listed in the "**CPR Credential**" section of this application.
4. The **EMT-Basic Practical Examination Verification** section of the application must be signed by the Physician Medical Director or the agent or assignee of the physician attesting to the candidates successful completion, within the past 12 months, of a practical examination that meets or exceeds the criteria established by the NREMT.
5. **Section II : Statement of Competency in EMT-Basic Skills** (above) must be signed by the EMT-Basic Training Program Director or the Director of Training/Operations. **Applications submitted for each re-examination must also be completed in their entirety and signed in an original fashion**.
6. Submission of a completed application and official course completion documentation attesting to the above requirements as well as all other published entry requirements of the National Registry of EMTs.
7. A non-refundable, non-transferable application fee of $20.00, payable to the National Registry of Emergency Medical Technicians, must be submitted with this application. Each attempt of the written examination requires submission of an application and a $20.00 non-refundable, non-transferable application fee.
8. Successful completion of the National Registry EMT-Basic written examinations.

Checklist for Submitting an Application for the National Registry EMT-Basic Examination Process:

1. Have you, your Physician Medical Director, and/or your training director or service director of training/operations signed the application? **Applications submitted for each re-examination must also be completed in their entirety and signed in an original fashion**.
2. Have you attached a copy of your CPR card which will be current and valid at the time of the examination or has your CPR instructor affixed his or her signature to the appropriate space in the "**CPR Credential**" section of this application?
3. Have you or your program director attached to this application official documentation of successful completion of state-approved EMT-Basic training which meets or exceeds the bahavioral objectives of the current EMT-Basic National Standard Curriculum?
4. Have you filled in all of the information requested on the application, including the felony statement?
5. Have you attached a check or money order in the appropriate amount to this application. Each attempt of the written examination requires submission of an application and a $20.00 non-refunable, non-transferable application fee.
6. Be sure to bring an official photo identification (driver's license) and two #2 pencils to the examination site.
7. For more information please visit our homepage at http://www.nremt.org or contact us via telephone at (614) 888-4484.

Payments or contributions to the NREMT are not deductible as charitable contributions for Federal Income Tax purposes. Payments may be deductible as a business expense. If in doubt, please contact your tax advisor.

477122

2 ▶ The LearningExpress Test Preparation System

CHAPTER SUMMARY

Taking the EMT-Basic exam can be tough. It demands a lot of preparation if you want to achieve a top score. Your career in emergency medical services depends on your passing the exam. The Learning-Express Test Preparation System, developed exclusively for Learning-Express by leading test experts, gives you the discipline and attitude you need to be a winner.

First, the bad news: Taking the EMT-Basic exam is no picnic, and neither is getting ready for it. Your future career as an EMT depends on passing, but there are all sorts of pitfalls that can keep you from doing your best on this all-important exam. Here are some of the obstacles that can stand in the way of your success:

- being unfamiliar with the format of the exam
- being paralyzed by test anxiety
- leaving your preparation to the last minute
- not preparing at all!
- not knowing vital test-taking skills: how to pace yourself through the exam, how to use the process of elimination, and when to guess
- not being in tip-top mental and physical shape
- arriving late at the test site, working on an empty stomach, or shivering through the exam because the room is cold

What's the common denominator in all these test-taking pitfalls? One thing: *control*. Who's in control, you or the exam?

Now, the good news: The LearningExpress Test Preparation System puts *you* in control. In just nine easy-to-follow steps, you will learn everything you need to know to ensure that you are in charge of your preparation and your performance on the exam. Other test takers may let the test get the better of them; other test takers may be unprepared or out of shape, but not you. You will have taken all the steps you need to get a high score on the EMT-Basic exam.

Here's how the LearningExpress Test Preparation System works: Nine easy steps lead you through everything you need to know and do to get ready to master your exam. Each of the following steps includes both reading about the step and one or more activities. It's important that you do the activities along with the reading, or you won't get the full benefits of the system. Each step tells you approximately how much time that step will take you to complete.

Step 1. Get Information	50 minutes
Step 2. Conquer Test Anxiety	20 minutes
Step 3. Make a Plan	30 minutes
Step 4. Learn to Manage Your Time	10 minutes
Step 5. Learn to Use the Process of Elimination	20 minutes
Step 6. Know When to Guess	20 minutes
Step 7. Reach Your Peak Performance Zone	10 minutes
Step 8. Get Your Act Together	10 minutes
Step 9. Do It!	10 minutes
TOTAL	**3 HOURS**

We estimate that working through the entire system will take you approximately three hours, though it's perfectly OK if you work more quickly or slowly than the time estimates assume. If you have a whole afternoon or evening free, you can work through the whole LearningExpress Test Preparation System in one sitting. Otherwise, you can break it up and do just one or two steps a day for the next several days. It's up to you—remember, *you're* in control.

▶ Step 1: Get Information

Time to complete: 50 minutes
Activities: Read Chapter 1, "The EMT-Basic Exam"
and Chapter 8, "State Certification
Requirements"

Knowledge is power. The first step in the LearningExpress Test Preparation System is finding out everything you can about the EMT-Basic exam. Once you have your information, the next steps in the LearningExpress Test Preparation System will show you what to do about it.

Part A: Straight Talk about the EMT-Basic Exam

Why do you have to take this exam anyway? Simply put, because lives depend on your performance in the field. The EMT-Basic written exam is just one part of a whole series of evaluations you have to go through to show that you can be trusted with the health and safety of the people you serve. The written exam attempts to measure your knowledge of your trade. The practical skills exam attempts to measure your ability to apply what you know.

It's important for you to remember that your score on the EMT-Basic written exam does not determine how smart you are or even whether you will make a good EMT. There are all kinds of things a written exam like this can't test: whether you are likely to frequently show up late or call in sick, whether you can keep your cool under the stress of trying to revive a victim of cardiac arrest, whether you can be trusted with confidential information about people's health, etc. Those kinds of things are hard to evaluate, while whether you can fill in the right little circles on a bubble answer sheet is easy to evaluate.

This is not to say that filling in the right little circles is not important. The knowledge tested on the written exam is knowledge you will need to do your job. Furthermore, your ability to enter the profession you've trained for depends on your passing this exam. And that's why you're here—using the LearningExpress Test Preparation System to achieve control over the exam.

Part B: What's on the Test

If you haven't already done so, stop here and read Chapter 1 of this book, which gives you an overview of EMT-Basic written exams in general and the National Registry of Emergency Medical Technicians (NREMT) exam in particular.

Many states use the NREMT exam, but others do not. Turn to Chapter 8 for a state-by-state overview of certification requirements. If you haven't already gotten the full rundown on certification procedures as part of your training program, you can contact your state's EMT agency listed in Chapter 8 for details.

▶ Step 2: Conquer Test Anxiety

Time to complete: 20 minutes
Activity: Take the Test Stress Exam

Having complete information about the exam is the first step in getting control of it. Next, you have to overcome one of the biggest obstacles to test success: anxiety. Test anxiety can not only impair your performance on the exam itself, it can even keep you from preparing! In Step 2, you'll learn stress management techniques that will help you succeed on your exam. Learn these strategies now, and practice them as you work through the exams in this book, so they'll be second nature to you by exam day.

Combating Test Anxiety

The first thing you need to know is that a little test anxiety is a good thing. Everyone gets nervous before a big exam—and if that nervousness motivates you to prepare thoroughly, so much the better. It's said that Sir Laurence Olivier, one of the foremost British actors of the twentieth century, felt sick before every performance. His stage fright didn't impair his performance; in fact, it probably gave him a little extra edge—just the kind of edge you need to do well, whether on a stage or in an examination room.

The Test Stress Exam is on page 11. Stop here and answer the questions on that page to find out whether your level of test anxiety is cause for worry.

Stress Management before the Test

If you feel your level of anxiety is getting the best of you in the weeks before the test, here is what you need to do to bring the level down again:

- **Get prepared.** There's nothing like knowing what to expect and being prepared for it to put you in control of test anxiety. That's why you're reading this book. Use it faithfully, and remind yourself that you're better prepared than most of the people taking the test.

- **Practice self-confidence.** A positive attitude is a great way to combat test anxiety. This is no time to be humble or shy. Stand in front of the mirror and say to your reflection, "I'm prepared. I'm full of self-confidence. I'm going to ace this test. I know I can do it." Say it into a tape recorder and play it back once a day. If you hear it often enough, you'll believe it.
- **Fight negative messages.** Every time someone starts telling you how hard the exam is or how it's almost impossible to get a high score, start telling them your self-confidence messages. If that someone with the negative messages is *you*, telling yourself *you don't do well on exams, you just can't do this*, don't listen. Turn on your tape recorder and listen to your self-confidence messages.
- **Visualize.** Imagine yourself reporting for duty on your first day as an EMT. Think of yourself responding to calls, interacting with patients, preserving health, and saving lives. Visualizing success can help make it happen—and it reminds you of why you're doing all this work preparing for the exam.
- **Exercise.** Physical activity helps calm your body and focus your mind. Besides, being in good physical shape can actually help you do well on the exam. Go for a run, lift weights, go swimming—and do it regularly.

Stress Management on Test Day

There are several ways you can lower your anxiety on test day. They'll work best if you practice them in the weeks before the test, so you know which ones work best for you.

- **Deep breathing.** Take a deep breath while you count to five. Hold it for a count of one, then let it out for a count of five. Repeat several times.

- **Move your body.** Try rolling your head in a circle. Rotate your shoulders. Shake your hands from the wrist. Many people find these movements very relaxing.
- **Visualize again.** Think of the place where you are most relaxed: lying on the beach in the sun, walking through the park, or whatever. Now close your eyes and imagine you're actually there. If you practice in advance, you'll find that you only need a few seconds of this exercise to experience a significant increase in your sense of well-being.

When anxiety threatens to overwhelm you right there during the exam, there are still things you can do to manage the stress level.

- **Repeat your self-confidence messages.** You should have them memorized by now. Say them quietly to yourself, and believe them!
- **Visualize one more time.** This time, visualize yourself moving smoothly and quickly through the test answering every question correctly and finishing just before time is up. Like most visualization techniques, this one works best if you've practiced it ahead of time.
- **Find an easy question.** Skim over the test until you find an easy question, and answer it. Getting even one circle filled in helps get you into the test-taking groove.
- **Take a mental break.** Everyone loses concentration once in a while during a long test. It's normal, so you shouldn't worry about it. Instead, accept what has happened. Say to yourself, "Hey, I lost it there for a minute. My brain is taking a break." Put down your pencil, close your eyes, and do some deep breathing for a few seconds. Then, you're ready to go back to work.

Try these techniques ahead of time, and watch them work for you!

You only need to worry about test anxiety if it is extreme enough to impair your performance. The following questionnaire will diagnose your level of test anxiety. In the blank before each statement, write the number that most accurately describes your experience.

0 = Never   1 = Once or twice   2 = Sometimes   3 = Often

_____ I have gotten so nervous before an exam that I simply put down the books and didn't study for it.

_____ I have experienced disabling physical symptoms such as vomiting and severe headaches because I was nervous about an exam.

_____ I have simply not shown up for an exam because I was scared to take it.

_____ I have experienced dizziness and disorientation while taking an exam.

_____ I have had trouble filling in the little circles because my hands were shaking too hard.

_____ I have failed an exam because I was too nervous to complete it.

_____ **Total: Add up the numbers in the blanks above.**

Your Test Stress Score

Here are the steps you should take, depending on your score. If you scored:

- **Below 3,** your level of test anxiety is nothing to worry about; it's probably just enough to give you that little extra edge.
- **Between 3 and 6,** your test anxiety may be enough to impair your performance, and you should practice the stress management techniques listed in this section to try to bring your test anxiety down to manageable levels.
- **Above 6,** your level of test anxiety is a serious concern. In addition to practicing the stress management techniques listed in this section, you may want to seek additional, personal help. Call your local high school or community college and ask for the academic counselor. Tell the counselor that you have a level of test anxiety that sometimes keeps you from being able to take the exam. The counselor may be willing to help you or may suggest someone else with whom you should talk.

▶ Step 3: Make a Plan

Time to complete: 30 minutes
Activity: Construct a study plan

Maybe the most important thing you can do to get control of yourself and your exam is to make a study plan. Too many people fail to prepare simply because they fail to plan. Spending hours on the day before the exam poring over sample test questions not only raises your level of test anxiety, it also is simply no substitute for careful preparation and practice over time.

Don't fall into the cram trap. Take control of your preparation time by mapping out a study schedule. On the following pages are two sample schedules, based on the amount of time you have before you take the EMT-Basic written exam. If you're the kind of person who needs deadlines and assignments to motivate you for a project, here they are. If you're the kind of person who doesn't like to follow other people's plans, you can use the following suggested schedules to construct your own.

Even more important than making a plan is making a commitment. You can't review everything you learned in your EMT course in one night. You have to set aside some time every day for study and practice. Try for at least 20 minutes a day. Twenty minutes daily will do you much more good than two hours on Saturday.

Don't put off your studying until the day before the exam. Start now. A few minutes a day, with half an hour or more on weekends, can make a big difference in your score.

Schedule A: The 30-Day Plan

If you have at least a month before you take the EMT-Basic exam, you have plenty of time to prepare—as long as you don't waste it! If you have less than a month, turn to Schedule B.

TIME	PREPARATION
Days 1–4	Skim over the written materials from your training program, particularly noting 1) areas you expect to be emphasized on the exam and 2) areas you don't remember well. On Day 4, concentrate on those areas.
Day 5	Take the first practice exam in Chapter 3.
Day 6	Score the first practice exam. Use the outline of skills on the test given in Chapter 1 to reveal your strongest and weakest areas. Identify two areas that you will concentrate on before you take the second practice exam.
Days 7–10	Study the two areas you identified as your weak points. Don't worry about the other areas.
Day 11	Take the second practice exam in Chapter 4.
Day 12	Score the second practice exam. Identify one area to concentrate on before you take the third practice exam.
Days 13–18	Study the one area you identified for review. In addition, review both practice exams you've already taken, with special attention to the answer explanations.
Day 19	Take the third practice exam in Chapter 5.
Day 20	Once again, identify one area to review, based on your score on the third practice exam.
Days 20–21	Study the one area you identified for review.
Days 22–25	Take an overview of all your training materials, consolidating your strengths and improving on your weaknesses.
Days 26–27	Review all the areas that have given you the most trouble in the three practice exams you've already taken.
Day 28	Take the fourth practice exam in Chapter 6 and score it. Note how much you've improved!
Day 29	Review one or two weak areas.
Day before the exam	Relax. Do something unrelated to the exam, and go to bed at a reasonable hour.

Schedule B: The 10-Day Plan

If you have two weeks or less before you take the exam, you have your work cut out for you. Use this 10-day schedule to help you make the most of your time.

TIME	PREPARATION
Day 1	Take the first practice exam in Chapter 3 and score it using the answer key at the end. Turn to the list of subject areas on the exam in Chapter 1 and find out which areas need the most work based on your exam score.
Day 2	Review one area that gave you trouble on the first practice exam.
Day 3	Review another area that gave you trouble on the first practice exam.
Day 4	Take the second practice exam in Chapter 4 and score it.
Day 5	If your score on the second practice exam doesn't show improvement on the two areas you studied, review them. If you did improve in those areas, choose a new weak area to study.
Day 6	Take the third practice exam in Chapter 5 and score it.
Day 7	Choose your weakest area from the third practice exam to review.
Day 8	Review any areas that you have not yet reviewed in this schedule.
Day 9	Take the fourth practice exam in Chapter 6 and score it. Brush up on any remaining trouble areas.
Day before the exam	Relax. Do something unrelated to the exam, and go to bed at a reasonable hour.

▶ Step 4: Learn to Manage Your Time

Time to complete: 10 minutes to read, many hours of practice!
Activities: Practice these strategies as you take the sample tests in this book

Steps 4, 5, and 6 of the LearningExpress Test Preparation System put you in charge of your exam by showing you test-taking strategies that work. Practice these strategies as you take the sample tests in this book, and then you'll be ready to use them on test day.

First, you'll take control of your time on the exam. Most EMT-Basic exams have a time limit of three hours, which may give you more than enough time to complete all the questions—or may not. It's a terrible feeling to hear the examiner say, "Five minutes left," when you're only three-quarters through the test. Here are some tips to avoid that happening to *you*.

- **Follow directions.** If the directions are given orally, listen to them. If they're written on the exam booklet, read them carefully. Ask questions *before* the exam begins if there's anything you don't understand. If you're allowed to write in your exam booklet, write down the beginning and ending time of the exam.
- **Pace yourself.** Glance at your watch every few minutes, and compare the time to how far you've gotten in the test. When one-quarter of the time

has elapsed, you should be one-quarter through the test, and so on. If you're falling behind, pick up the pace a bit.

- **Keep moving.** Don't dither around on one question. If you don't know the answer, skip the question and move on. Circle the number of the question in your test booklet in case you have time to come back to it later.
- **Keep track of your place on the answer sheet.** If you skip a question, make sure you skip on the answer sheet too. Check yourself every 5–10 questions to make sure the question number and the answer sheet number are still the same.
- **Don't rush.** Though you should keep moving, rushing won't help. Try to keep calm and work methodically and quickly.

▶ Step 5: Learn to Use the Process of Elimination

Time to complete: 20 minutes
Activity: Complete worksheet on Using the Process of Elimination

After time management, the next most important tool for taking control of your exam is using the process of elimination wisely. It's standard test-taking wisdom that you should always read all the answer choices before choosing your answer. This helps you find the right answer by eliminating wrong answer choices. And, sure enough, that standard wisdom applies to your exam, too.

Let's say you're facing a question that goes like this:

13. Which of the following lists of signs and symptoms indicates cardiac compromise?
   a. headache, dizziness, nausea, confusion
   b. dull chest pain, sudden sweating, difficulty breathing
   c. wheezing, labored breathing, chest pain
   d. difficulty breathing, high fever, rapid pulse

You should always use the process of elimination on a question like this, even if the right answer jumps out at you. Sometimes the answer that jumps out isn't right after all. Let's assume, for the purpose of this exercise, that you're a little rusty on your signs and symptoms of cardiac compromise, so you need to use a little intuition to make up for what you don't remember. Proceed through the answer choices in order.

Start with answer **a.** This one is pretty easy to eliminate; none of these signs and symptoms is consistent with cardiac compromise. Mark an X next to choice **a** so you never have to look at it again.

On to the next. "Dull chest pain" looks good, though if you're not up on your cardiac signs and symptoms you might wonder if it should be "acute chest pain" instead. "Sudden sweating" and "difficulty breathing"? Check. And that's what you write next to answer **b**—a check mark, meaning, "Good answer, I might use this one."

Choice **c** is a possibility. Maybe you don't really expect wheezing in cardiac compromise, but you know "chest pain" is right, and let's say you're not sure whether "labored breathing" is a sign of cardiac difficulty. Put a question mark next to **c,** meaning, "Well, maybe."

Choice **d** strikes you about the same; "difficulty breathing" is a good sign of cardiac compromise. But wait a minute. "High fever"? Not really. "Rapid pulse"? Well, maybe. This doesn't really sound like cardiac compromise, and you've already got a better answer picked out in choice **b.** If you're feeling sure of yourself, put an X next to this one. If you want to be careful, put a question mark.

Now, your question looks like this:

13. Which of the following lists of signs and symptoms indicates cardiac compromise?
   X **a.** headache, dizziness, nausea, confusion
   ✔ **b.** dull chest pain, sudden sweating, difficulty breathing
   ? **c.** wheezing, labored breathing, chest pain
   ? **d.** difficulty breathing, high fever, rapid pulse

You've got just one check mark, for a good answer. If you're pressed for time, you should simply mark answer **b** on your answer sheet. If you've got the time to be extra careful, you could compare your check-mark answer to your question-mark answers to make sure that it's better.

It's good to have a system for marking good, bad, and maybe answers. We're recommending this one:

X = bad

✔ = good

? = maybe

If you don't like these marks, devise your own system. Just make sure you do it long before test day (while you're working through the practice exams in this book) so you won't have to worry about it during the test.

Even when you think you're absolutely clueless about a question, you can often use the process of elimination to get rid of one answer choice. If so, you're better prepared to make an educated guess, as you'll see in Step 6. More often, the process of elimination helps you get down to only *two* possibly right answers. Then you're in a strong position to guess. And sometimes, even though you don't know the right answer, you find it simply by getting rid of the wrong ones, as you did in the previous example.

Try using your powers of elimination on the questions in the worksheet "Using the Process of Elimination" beginning on the next page. The questions aren't about EMT work; they're just designed to show you how the process of elimination works. The answer explanations for this worksheet show one way you might use the process to arrive at the right answer.

The process of elimination is your tool for the next step, which is knowing when to guess.

Using the Process of Elimination

Use the process of elimination to answer the following questions.

1. Ilsa is as old as Meghan will be in five years. The difference between Ed's age and Meghan's age is twice the difference between Ilsa's age and Meghan's age. Ed is 29. How old is Ilsa?
   a. 4
   b. 10
   c. 19
   d. 24

2. "All drivers of commercial vehicles must carry a valid commercial driver's license whenever operating a commercial vehicle." According to this sentence, which of the following people need NOT carry a commercial driver's license?
   a. a truck driver idling his engine while waiting to be directed to a loading dock
   b. a bus operator backing her bus out of the way of another bus in the bus lot
   c. a taxi driver driving his personal car to the grocery store
   d. a limousine driver taking the limousine to her home after dropping off her last passenger of the evening

3. Smoking tobacco has been linked to
   a. increased risk of stroke and heart attack.
   b. all forms of respiratory disease.
   c. increasing mortality rates over the past ten years.
   d. juvenile delinquency.

4. Which of the following words is spelled correctly?
   a. incorrigible
   b. outragous
   c. domestickated
   d. understandible

Answers

Here are the answers, as well as some suggestions on how you might have used the process of elimination to find them.

1. d. You should have eliminated answer **a** off the bat. Ilsa can't be four years old if Meghan is going to be Ilsa's age in five years. The best way to eliminate other answer choices is to try plugging them in to the information given in the problem. For instance, for answer **b,** if Ilsa is 10, then Meghan must be 5. The difference in their ages is 5. The difference between Ed's age, 29, and Meghan's age, 5, is 24. Is 24 two times 5? No. Then answer **b** is wrong. You could eliminate answer **c** in the same way and be left with answer **d.**

2. c. Note the word *not* in the question, and go through the answers one by one. Is the truck driver in choice **a** "operating a commercial vehicle"? Yes, idling counts as "operating," so he needs to have a commercial driver's license. Likewise, the bus operator in answer **b** is operating a commercial vehicle; the question doesn't say the operator must be on the street. The limo driver in **d** is operating a commercial vehicle, even if it doesn't have a passenger in it. However, the cabbie in answer **c** is *not* operating a commercial vehicle, but his own private car.

3. a. You could eliminate answer **b** simply because of the presence of *all.* Such absolutes hardly ever appear in correct answer choices. Choice **c** looks attractive until you think a little about what you know—aren't *fewer* people smoking these days, rather than more? So how could smoking be responsible for a higher mortality rate? (If you didn't know that *mortality rate* means the rate at which people die, you might keep this choice as a possibility, but you'd still be able to eliminate two answers and have only two to choose from.) And choice **d** is plain silly, so you could eliminate that one, too. And you're left with the correct choice, **a.**

4. a. How you used the process of elimination here depends on which words you recognized as being spelled incorrectly. If you knew that the correct spellings were *outrageous, domesticated,* and *understandable,* then you were home free. Surely you knew that at least one of those words was wrong!

▶ Step 6: Know When to Guess

Time to complete: 20 minutes
Activity: Complete worksheet on Your Guessing
  Ability

Armed with the process of elimination, you're ready to take control of one of the big questions in test taking: Should I guess? The first and main answer is "Yes." Some exams have what's called a "guessing penalty," in which a fraction of your wrong answers is subtracted from your right answers—but EMT-Basic exams don't often work that way. The number of questions you answer correctly yields your raw score, so you have nothing to lose and everything to gain by guessing.

The more complicated answer to the question "Should I guess?" depends on you—your personality and your "guessing intuition." There are two things you need to know about yourself before you go into the exam:

- Are you a risk-taker?
- Are you a good guesser?

You'll have to decide about your risk-taking quotient on your own. To find out if you're a good guesser, complete the worksheet "Your Guessing Ability" that begins on page 19. Frankly, even if you're a play-it-safe person with lousy intuition, you're probably still safe in guessing every time. The best thing would be if you could overcome your anxieties and go ahead and mark an answer. But you may want to have a sense of how good your intuition is before you go into the exam.

▶ Step 7: Reach Your Peak Performance Zone

Time to complete: 10 minutes to read; weeks to
  complete!
Activity: Complete the Physical Preparation
  Checklist

To get ready for a challenge like a big exam, you have to take control of your physical as well as your mental state. Exercise, proper diet, and rest will ensure that your body works with your mind, rather than against it, on test day, as well as during your preparation.

Exercise

If you don't already have a regular exercise program going, the time during which you're preparing for an exam is actually an excellent time to start one. And if you're already keeping fit—or trying to get that way—don't let the pressure of preparing for an exam fool you into quitting now. Exercise helps reduce stress by pumping wonderful good-feeling hormones called endorphins into your system. It also increases the oxygen supply throughout your body, including your brain, so you'll be at peak performance on test day.

A half hour of vigorous activity—enough to raise a sweat—every day should be your aim. If you're really pressed for time, every other day is OK. Choose an activity you like and get out there and do it. Jogging with a friend always makes the time go faster, or take a radio.

But don't overdo it. You don't want to exhaust yourself. Moderation is the key.

The following are ten really hard questions. You're not supposed to know the answers. Rather, this is an assessment of your ability to guess when you don't have a clue. Read each question carefully, just as if you did expect to answer it. If you have any knowledge at all of the subject of the question, use that knowledge to help you eliminate wrong answer choices. Use this answer grid to fill in your answers to the questions.

ANSWER GRID

1. (a) (b) (c) (d)   5. (a) (b) (c) (d)   9. (a) (b) (c) (d)
2. (a) (b) (c) (d)   6. (a) (b) (c) (d)   10. (a) (b) (c) (d)
3. (a) (b) (c) (d)   7. (a) (b) (c) (d)
4. (a) (b) (c) (d)   8. (a) (b) (c) (d)

1. September 7 is Independence Day in
  a. India.
  b. Costa Rica.
  c. Brazil.
  d. Australia.

2. Which of the following is the formula for determining the momentum of an object?
  a. $p = mv$
  b. $F = ma$
  c. $P = IV$
  d. $E = mc^2$

3. Because of the expansion of the universe, the stars and other celestial bodies are all moving away from each other. This phenomenon is known as
  a. Newton's first law.
  b. the big bang.
  c. gravitational collapse.
  d. Hubble flow.

4. American author Gertrude Stein was born in
  a. 1713.
  b. 1830.
  c. 1874.
  d. 1901.

5. Which of the following is NOT one of the Five Classics attributed to Confucius?
  a. the *I Ching*
  b. the *Book of Holiness*
  c. the *Spring and Autumn Annals*
  d. the *Book of History*

6. The religious and philosophical doctrine that holds that the universe is constantly in a struggle between good and evil is known as
  a. Pelagianism.
  b. Manichaeanism.
  c. neo-Hegelianism.
  d. Epicureanism.

7. The third Chief Justice of the U.S. Supreme Court was
  a. John Blair.
  b. William Cushing.
  c. James Wilson.
  d. John Jay.

8. Which of the following is the poisonous portion of a daffodil?
  a. the bulb
  b. the leaves
  c. the stem
  d. the flowers

9. The winner of the Masters golf tournament in 1953 was
   a. Sam Snead.
   b. Cary Middlecoff.
   c. Arnold Palmer.
   d. Ben Hogan.

10. The state with the highest per capita personal income in 1980 was
   a. Alaska.
   b. Connecticut.
   c. New York.
   d. Texas.

Answers

Check your answers against the correct answers below.

1. c.	**5.** b.	**9.** d.
2. a.	**6.** b.	**10.** a.
3. d.	**7.** b.	
4. c.	**8.** a.	

How Did You Do?

You may have simply gotten lucky and actually known the answer to one or two questions. In addition, your guessing was more successful if you were able to use the process of elimination on any of the questions. Maybe you didn't know who the third Chief Justice was (question 7), but you knew that John Jay was the first. In that case, you would have eliminated answer **d** and therefore improved your odds of guessing right from one in four to one in three.

According to probability, you should get $2\frac{1}{2}$ answers correct, so getting either two or three right would be average. If you got four or more right, you may be a really terrific guesser. If you got one or none right, you may be a really bad guesser.

Keep in mind, though, that this is only a small sample. You should continue to keep track of your guessing ability as you work through the sample questions in this book. Circle the numbers of questions you guess on as you make your guess; or, if you don't have time while you take the practice tests, go back afterward and try to remember on which questions you guessed. Remember, on a test with four answer choices, your chances of getting a correct answer is one in four. So keep a separate "guessing" score for each exam. How many questions did you guess on? How many did you get right? If the number you got right is at least one-fourth the number of questions you guessed on, you are at least an average guesser, maybe better—and you should always go ahead and guess on the real exam. If the number you got right is significantly lower than one-fourth of the number you guessed on, you would, frankly, be safe in guessing anyway, but maybe you'd feel more comfortable if you guessed only selectively, when you can eliminate a wrong answer or at least have a good feeling about one of the answer choices.

Diet

First of all, cut out the junk. Go easy on caffeine and nicotine, and eliminate alcohol and any other drugs from your system at least two weeks before the exam. Promise yourself a binge the night after the exam, if need be.

What your body needs for peak performance is simply a balanced diet. Eat plenty of fruits and vegetables, along with protein and carbohydrates. Foods high in lecithin (an amino acid), such as fish and beans, are especially good brain foods.

The night before the exam, you might "carbo-load" the way athletes do before a contest. Eat a big plate of spaghetti, rice and beans, or your favorite carbohydrate.

Rest

You probably know how much sleep you need every night to be at your best, even if you don't always get it. Make sure you do get that much sleep, though, for at least a week before the exam. Moderation is important here, too. Extra sleep will just make you groggy.

If you're not a morning person and your exam will be given in the morning, you should reset your internal clock so that your body doesn't think you're taking an exam at 3 A.M. You have to start this process well before the exam. The way it works is to get up half an hour earlier each morning, and then go to bed half an hour earlier that night. Don't try it the other way around; you'll just toss and turn if you go to bed early without having gotten up early. The next morning, get up another half an hour earlier, and so on. How long you will have to do this depends on how late you're used to getting up. Use the "Physical Preparation Checklist" on page 22 to make sure you're in tip-top form.

▶ Step 8: Get Your Act Together

Time to complete: 10 minutes to read; time to complete will vary

Activity: Complete "Final Preparations" worksheet
You're in control of your mind and body; you're in charge of test anxiety, your preparation, and your test-taking strategies. Now it's time to take charge of external factors, such as the testing site and the materials you need to take the exam.

Find Out Where the Test Center Is and Make a Trial Run

The testing agency or your EMS instructor will notify you when and where your exam is being held. Do you know how to get to the testing site? Do you know how long it will take to get there? If not, make a trial run, preferably on the same day of the week at the same time of day. On the "Final Preparations" worksheet on page 23, note the amount of time it will take you to get to the exam site. Plan on arriving 10 to 15 minutes early so you can get the lay of the land, use the bathroom, and calm down. Then figure out how early you will have to get up that morning, and make sure you get up that early every day for a week before the exam.

Gather Your Materials

The night before the exam, lay out the clothes you will wear and the materials you have to bring with you to the exam. Plan on dressing in layers; you won't have any control over the temperature of the examination room. Have a sweater or jacket you can take off if it's warm. Use the checklist on the "Final Preparations" worksheet on page 23 to help you pull together what you'll need.

Don't Skip Breakfast

Even if you don't usually eat breakfast, do so on exam morning. A cup of coffee doesn't count. Don't eat doughnuts or other sweet foods either. A sugar high will leave you with a sugar low in the middle of the exam. A mix of protein and carbohydrates is best: Cereal with milk and just a little sugar, or eggs with toast, will do your body a world of good.

Physical Preparation Checklist

For the week before the test, write down 1) what physical exercise you engaged in and for how long and 2) what you ate for each meal. Remember, you're trying for at least half an hour of exercise every other day (preferably every day) and a balanced diet that's light on junk food.

Exam minus 7 days

Exercise: _____ for _____ minutes

Breakfast: _____

Lunch: _____

Dinner: _____

Snacks: _____

Exam minus 6 days

Exercise: _____ for _____ minutes

Breakfast: _____

Lunch: _____

Dinner: _____

Snacks: _____

Exam minus 5 days

Exercise: _____ for _____ minutes

Breakfast: _____

Lunch: _____

Dinner: _____

Snacks: _____

Exam minus 4 days

Exercise: _____ for _____ minutes

Breakfast: _____

Lunch: _____

Dinner: _____

Snacks: _____

Exam minus 3 days

Exercise: _____ for _____ minutes

Breakfast: _____

Lunch: _____

Dinner: _____

Snacks: _____

Exam minus 2 days

Exercise: _____ for _____ minutes

Breakfast: _____

Lunch: _____

Dinner: _____

Snacks: _____

Exam minus 1 day

Exercise: _____ for _____ minutes

Breakfast: _____

Lunch: _____

Dinner: _____

Snacks: _____

▶ Step 9: Do It!

Time to complete: 10 minutes, plus test-taking time

Activity: Ace the EMT-Basic exam!

Fast-forward to exam day. You're ready. You made a study plan and followed through. You practiced your test-taking strategies while working through this book. You're in control of your physical, mental, and emotional state. You know when and where to show up and what to bring with you. In other words, you're better prepared than most other people taking the EMT-Basic exam with you. You're psyched.

Just one more thing. When you're done with the exam, you will have earned a reward. Plan a celebration. Call up your friends and plan a party, have a nice dinner for two, or go see a good movie—whatever your heart desires. Give yourself something to look forward to.

And then do it. Go into the exam, full of confidence, armed with test-taking strategies you've practiced till they became second nature. You're in control of yourself, your environment, and your performance on the exam. You're ready to succeed. So do it. Go in there and ace the exam. And look forward to your career as an EMT!

Final Preparations

Getting to the MEPS Pickup Site

Location of pickup site: _____

Date: _____

Departure time: _____

Do I know how to get to the pickup site?   Yes ___   No ___

If no, make a trial run.

Time it will take to get to the pickup site: _____

Things to Lay Out the Night Before

Clothes I will wear   ____

Sweater/jacket   ____

Watch   ____

Photo ID   ____

4 No. 2 pencils   ____

Other   ____

3 ▶ EMT-Basic Practice Exam 1

CHAPTER SUMMARY

This is the first of four practice exams in this book based on the National Registry EMT-Basic written exam.

ike the other tests in this book, this test is based on the National Registry's written exam for EMT-Basics. See Chapter 1 for a complete description of this exam.

Take this first exam in as relaxed a manner as you can, and don't worry about timing. You can time yourself on the other three exams. You should, however, allow sufficient time to take the entire exam at one sitting, at least two hours. Find a quiet place where you can work without being interrupted.

The answer sheet you should use is on page 27, followed by the exam itself. The correct answers, each fully explained, come after the exam. Once you have read and understood the answer explanations, turn to Chapter 1 for an explanation of how to assess your score.

1.	ⓐ	ⓑ	ⓒ	ⓓ
2.	ⓐ	ⓑ	ⓒ	ⓓ
3.	ⓐ	ⓑ	ⓒ	ⓓ
4.	ⓐ	ⓑ	ⓒ	ⓓ
5.	ⓐ	ⓑ	ⓒ	ⓓ
6.	ⓐ	ⓑ	ⓒ	ⓓ
7.	ⓐ	ⓑ	ⓒ	ⓓ
8.	ⓐ	ⓑ	ⓒ	ⓓ
9.	ⓐ	ⓑ	ⓒ	ⓓ
10.	ⓐ	ⓑ	ⓒ	ⓓ
11.	ⓐ	ⓑ	ⓒ	ⓓ
12.	ⓐ	ⓑ	ⓒ	ⓓ
13.	ⓐ	ⓑ	ⓒ	ⓓ
14.	ⓐ	ⓑ	ⓒ	ⓓ
15.	ⓐ	ⓑ	ⓒ	ⓓ
16.	ⓐ	ⓑ	ⓒ	ⓓ
17.	ⓐ	ⓑ	ⓒ	ⓓ
18.	ⓐ	ⓑ	ⓒ	ⓓ
19.	ⓐ	ⓑ	ⓒ	ⓓ
20.	ⓐ	ⓑ	ⓒ	ⓓ
21.	ⓐ	ⓑ	ⓒ	ⓓ
22.	ⓐ	ⓑ	ⓒ	ⓓ
23.	ⓐ	ⓑ	ⓒ	ⓓ
24.	ⓐ	ⓑ	ⓒ	ⓓ
25.	ⓐ	ⓑ	ⓒ	ⓓ
26.	ⓐ	ⓑ	ⓒ	ⓓ
27.	ⓐ	ⓑ	ⓒ	ⓓ
28.	ⓐ	ⓑ	ⓒ	ⓓ
29.	ⓐ	ⓑ	ⓒ	ⓓ
30.	ⓐ	ⓑ	ⓒ	ⓓ
31.	ⓐ	ⓑ	ⓒ	ⓓ
32.	ⓐ	ⓑ	ⓒ	ⓓ
33.	ⓐ	ⓑ	ⓒ	ⓓ
34.	ⓐ	ⓑ	ⓒ	ⓓ
35.	ⓐ	ⓑ	ⓒ	ⓓ
36.	ⓐ	ⓑ	ⓒ	ⓓ
37.	ⓐ	ⓑ	ⓒ	ⓓ
38.	ⓐ	ⓑ	ⓒ	ⓓ
39.	ⓐ	ⓑ	ⓒ	ⓓ
40.	ⓐ	ⓑ	ⓒ	ⓓ
41.	ⓐ	ⓑ	ⓒ	ⓓ
42.	ⓐ	ⓑ	ⓒ	ⓓ
43.	ⓐ	ⓑ	ⓒ	ⓓ
44.	ⓐ	ⓑ	ⓒ	ⓓ
45.	ⓐ	ⓑ	ⓒ	ⓓ
46.	ⓐ	ⓑ	ⓒ	ⓓ
47.	ⓐ	ⓑ	ⓒ	ⓓ
48.	ⓐ	ⓑ	ⓒ	ⓓ
49.	ⓐ	ⓑ	ⓒ	ⓓ
50.	ⓐ	ⓑ	ⓒ	ⓓ
51.	ⓐ	ⓑ	ⓒ	ⓓ
52.	ⓐ	ⓑ	ⓒ	ⓓ
53.	ⓐ	ⓑ	ⓒ	ⓓ
54.	ⓐ	ⓑ	ⓒ	ⓓ
55.	ⓐ	ⓑ	ⓒ	ⓓ
56.	ⓐ	ⓑ	ⓒ	ⓓ
57.	ⓐ	ⓑ	ⓒ	ⓓ
58.	ⓐ	ⓑ	ⓒ	ⓓ
59.	ⓐ	ⓑ	ⓒ	ⓓ
60.	ⓐ	ⓑ	ⓒ	ⓓ
61.	ⓐ	ⓑ	ⓒ	ⓓ
62.	ⓐ	ⓑ	ⓒ	ⓓ
63.	ⓐ	ⓑ	ⓒ	ⓓ
64.	ⓐ	ⓑ	ⓒ	ⓓ
65.	ⓐ	ⓑ	ⓒ	ⓓ
66.	ⓐ	ⓑ	ⓒ	ⓓ
67.	ⓐ	ⓑ	ⓒ	ⓓ
68.	ⓐ	ⓑ	ⓒ	ⓓ
69.	ⓐ	ⓑ	ⓒ	ⓓ
70.	ⓐ	ⓑ	ⓒ	ⓓ
71.	ⓐ	ⓑ	ⓒ	ⓓ
72.	ⓐ	ⓑ	ⓒ	ⓓ
73.	ⓐ	ⓑ	ⓒ	ⓓ
74.	ⓐ	ⓑ	ⓒ	ⓓ
75.	ⓐ	ⓑ	ⓒ	ⓓ
76.	ⓐ	ⓑ	ⓒ	ⓓ
77.	ⓐ	ⓑ	ⓒ	ⓓ
78.	ⓐ	ⓑ	ⓒ	ⓓ
79.	ⓐ	ⓑ	ⓒ	ⓓ
80.	ⓐ	ⓑ	ⓒ	ⓓ
81.	ⓐ	ⓑ	ⓒ	ⓓ
82.	ⓐ	ⓑ	ⓒ	ⓓ
83.	ⓐ	ⓑ	ⓒ	ⓓ
84.	ⓐ	ⓑ	ⓒ	ⓓ
85.	ⓐ	ⓑ	ⓒ	ⓓ
86.	ⓐ	ⓑ	ⓒ	ⓓ
87.	ⓐ	ⓑ	ⓒ	ⓓ
88.	ⓐ	ⓑ	ⓒ	ⓓ
89.	ⓐ	ⓑ	ⓒ	ⓓ
90.	ⓐ	ⓑ	ⓒ	ⓓ
91.	ⓐ	ⓑ	ⓒ	ⓓ
92.	ⓐ	ⓑ	ⓒ	ⓓ
93.	ⓐ	ⓑ	ⓒ	ⓓ
94.	ⓐ	ⓑ	ⓒ	ⓓ
95.	ⓐ	ⓑ	ⓒ	ⓓ
96.	ⓐ	ⓑ	ⓒ	ⓓ
97.	ⓐ	ⓑ	ⓒ	ⓓ
98.	ⓐ	ⓑ	ⓒ	ⓓ
99.	ⓐ	ⓑ	ⓒ	ⓓ
100.	ⓐ	ⓑ	ⓒ	ⓓ
101.	ⓐ	ⓑ	ⓒ	ⓓ
102.	ⓐ	ⓑ	ⓒ	ⓓ
103.	ⓐ	ⓑ	ⓒ	ⓓ
104.	ⓐ	ⓑ	ⓒ	ⓓ
105.	ⓐ	ⓑ	ⓒ	ⓓ
106.	ⓐ	ⓑ	ⓒ	ⓓ
107.	ⓐ	ⓑ	ⓒ	ⓓ
108.	ⓐ	ⓑ	ⓒ	ⓓ
109.	ⓐ	ⓑ	ⓒ	ⓓ
110.	ⓐ	ⓑ	ⓒ	ⓓ
111.	ⓐ	ⓑ	ⓒ	ⓓ
112.	ⓐ	ⓑ	ⓒ	ⓓ
113.	ⓐ	ⓑ	ⓒ	ⓓ
114.	ⓐ	ⓑ	ⓒ	ⓓ
115.	ⓐ	ⓑ	ⓒ	ⓓ
116.	ⓐ	ⓑ	ⓒ	ⓓ
117.	ⓐ	ⓑ	ⓒ	ⓓ
118.	ⓐ	ⓑ	ⓒ	ⓓ
119.	ⓐ	ⓑ	ⓒ	ⓓ
120.	ⓐ	ⓑ	ⓒ	ⓓ
121.	ⓐ	ⓑ	ⓒ	ⓓ
122.	ⓐ	ⓑ	ⓒ	ⓓ
123.	ⓐ	ⓑ	ⓒ	ⓓ
124.	ⓐ	ⓑ	ⓒ	ⓓ
125.	ⓐ	ⓑ	ⓒ	ⓓ
126.	ⓐ	ⓑ	ⓒ	ⓓ
127.	ⓐ	ⓑ	ⓒ	ⓓ
128.	ⓐ	ⓑ	ⓒ	ⓓ
129.	ⓐ	ⓑ	ⓒ	ⓓ
130.	ⓐ	ⓑ	ⓒ	ⓓ
131.	ⓐ	ⓑ	ⓒ	ⓓ
132.	ⓐ	ⓑ	ⓒ	ⓓ
133.	ⓐ	ⓑ	ⓒ	ⓓ
134.	ⓐ	ⓑ	ⓒ	ⓓ
135.	ⓐ	ⓑ	ⓒ	ⓓ
136.	ⓐ	ⓑ	ⓒ	ⓓ
137.	ⓐ	ⓑ	ⓒ	ⓓ
138.	ⓐ	ⓑ	ⓒ	ⓓ
139.	ⓐ	ⓑ	ⓒ	ⓓ
140.	ⓐ	ⓑ	ⓒ	ⓓ
141.	ⓐ	ⓑ	ⓒ	ⓓ
142.	ⓐ	ⓑ	ⓒ	ⓓ
143.	ⓐ	ⓑ	ⓒ	ⓓ
144.	ⓐ	ⓑ	ⓒ	ⓓ
145.	ⓐ	ⓑ	ⓒ	ⓓ
146.	ⓐ	ⓑ	ⓒ	ⓓ
147.	ⓐ	ⓑ	ⓒ	ⓓ
148.	ⓐ	ⓑ	ⓒ	ⓓ
149.	ⓐ	ⓑ	ⓒ	ⓓ
150.	ⓐ	ⓑ	ⓒ	ⓓ

► **EMT-Basic Practice Exam 1**

1. EMTs should wear high-efficiency particulate air (HEPA) respirators when they are in contact with patients who have which of the following?
   a. HIV or AIDS
   b. tuberculosis
   c. open wounds
   d. hepatitis B

2. In which of these situations should you wear a gown over your uniform?
   a. A 55-year-old man is suspected of having a myocardial infarction.
   b. The victim of a fall has no obvious wounds but is still unresponsive.
   c. A full-term pregnant woman is experiencing crowning with contractions.
   d. A 72-year-old woman is experiencing dizziness and difficulty breathing.

3. You are called to assist a 60-year-old woman who complains of a severe headache. Upon entering the home, you smell a strong odor of natural gas. What is your first action?
   a. Check the patient's airway, breathing, and circulation.
   b. Insert a nasopharyngeal airway and assess vital signs.
   c. Remove the patient from the house to your ambulance.
   d. Open all windows and determine the source of the gas leak.

4. The most common electrical rhythm disturbance that results in sudden cardiac arrest is called
   a. pulseless electrical activity.
   b. ventricular fibrillation.
   c. ventricular tachycardia.
   d. asystole.

5. Which of the following is the highest priority patient?
   a. 57-year-old man with chest pain and systolic blood pressure of 80
   b. 40-year-old woman with moderate pain from a leg injury
   c. 75-year-old man who appears confused but responds to commands
   d. 25-year-old woman in labor with contractions six minutes apart

6. Which patient should receive high-flow oxygen via a nonrebreather mask?
   a. distraught and upset 45-year-old woman breathing very shallowly and rapidly
   b. nonresponsive 25-year-old man with a gurgling sound when he breathes
   c. responsive 60-year-old man breathing at the rate of eight breaths per minute
   d. responsive 3-year-old child breathing at the rate of 28 breaths per minute

7. Your patient is 11 months old. How can you determine if she has a decreased mental status and is responsive to verbal stimuli?
   a. She will be upset when you take her from her mother's arms.
   b. She will be unable to tell you how old she is if you ask her.
   c. She will attempt to locate her parents' voices when they speak.
   d. She will try to pull away from a painful stimulus on her toe.

8. What is the best method to assess circulation in an infant?
   a. palpate the carotid pulse
   b. palpate the brachial pulse
   c. palpate the radial pulse
   d. observe capillary refill time

9. A 45-year-old male patient is experiencing chest discomfort. After placing him in his position of comfort, your next action should be to
   a. ventilate the patient with a nonrebreather mask at 15 liters per minute.
   b. ventilate the patient with the bag-valve mask at 15 liters per minute.
   c. administer oxygen by nonrebreather mask at 15 liters per minute.
   d. administer oxygen by the nasal cannula at 6 liters per minute.

10. Which patient is at highest risk for hidden injury?
   a. 9-year-old child who fell seven feet off a swing set onto mulch-covered ground
   b. 30-year-old woman who got out of her car after a low-speed collision
   c. 45-year-old man who was ejected from his car after a high-speed collision
   d. 25-year-old man who fell 12 feet from a low angle roof onto the grass

11. Which patient should receive a rapid trauma survey to determine hidden injuries?
   a. an alert 2-year-old child in a car seat who was in a medium-speed crash
   b. an alert 20-year-old man who fell ten feet and is complaining of leg pain
   c. an alert 65-year-old woman who fell in the bathtub and is complaining of wrist pain
   d. an alert 11-year-old girl who tripped while roller-skating and fell down three steps

12. Which of the following is a sign of increased pressure in the circulatory system?
   a. flat neck veins
   b. palpable carotid pulse
   c. distended jugular veins
   d. decreased radial pulse

13. An AED will shock which of the following rhythms?
   a. sinus rhythm
   b. asystole
   c. ventricular fibrillation
   d. pulseless electrical activity

14. When performing the rapid trauma assessment, what is the next step after assessing the neck?
   a. Assess the clavicles, scapula, and chest.
   b. Clear the airway and administer oxygen.
   c. Assess the head, eyes, ears, and nose.
   d. Apply a cervical immobilization device.

15. To assess the motor function in the lower extremities of a responsive patient, you would
   a. ask the patient to bend his knees.
   b. ask the patient to wiggle his toes.
   c. carefully move the patient's leg.
   d. touch the skin of the patient's foot.

16. Which patient can safely receive only a focused physical examination rather than a rapid trauma assessment?
   a. 10-year-old child with a deformed right lower leg who is responsive after falling off his bicycle
   b. 20-year-old woman who complains of severe pain in her ankle after stepping off a curb
   c. 70-year-old man who complains of neck pain after a medium-speed car collision
   d. 30-year-old man who is unresponsive but has only minor cuts on the extremities

17. You are using the OPQRST acronym to assess a responsive medical patient. What question would you ask to assess the P component?
   a. What were you doing when the pain started?
   b. Can you describe the character of the pain for me?
   c. What makes the pain feel worse or better?
   d. On a scale of 1 to 10, how would you rank the pain?

18. What is the first step in the physical assessment of an unresponsive medical patient?
a. Perform the initial assessment.
b. Assess a complete set of vital signs.
c. Position the patient to protect the airway.
d. Obtain SAMPLE history from a family member.

19. Which patient needs a detailed physical examination?
a. 48-year-old man with a history of heart disease who is complaining of chest pain
b. 35-year-old woman who has been in a single-car collision and who briefly lost consciousness
c. full-term pregnant woman whose water has broken and who is having contractions every two minutes
d. 53-year-old woman with a history of smoking who is distressed and short of breath

20. Where is a detailed physical exam typically performed?
a. at the scene of the accident or injury
b. in the hospital emergency department
c. in the ambulance during transport
d. in the triage area of the trauma center

21. When using an automated external defibrillator (AED), all of the following are appropriate methods for minimizing inappropriate shocks EXCEPT
a. practicing frequently.
b. annual replacement of the AED.
c. following local protocols.
d. moving patient out of the rain.

22. The purpose of the ongoing assessment is to re-evaluate the patient's condition and to
a. find any injuries missed during the initial assessment.
b. reassure the patient that you are still caring for him or her.
c. check the adequacy of each intervention performed.
d. protect the EMT against liability from malpractice.

23. When performing an ongoing assessment, what is the next step after reassessing the components of the initial assessment?
a. re-establish patient priority
b. record the vital signs
c. repeat the focused assessment
d. evaluate all interventions

24. The EMT-Basic may sometimes enlist bystanders to assist by
a. communicating with central dispatch.
b. administering medications.
c. administering oxygen.
d. placing the patient on a stretcher.

25. Your patient tells you that he just can't seem to catch his breath. You would describe the nature of the illness as
a. chest pain.
b. respiratory distress.
c. apnea.
d. emphysema.

26. You should apply an automated external defibrillator to
a. adult patients experiencing chest discomfort.
b. adult patients with significant traumatic injuries.
c. adult patients without respirations or a pulse.
d. adult patients with low blood pressure.

27. In which of the following situations should you call for immediate assistance?
   a. You must care for two critical patients with gunshot wounds.
   b. Your patient is a 26-year-old woman in active labor.
   c. Your patient is a child with fever who has had a brief seizure.
   d. Your partner is needed to stabilize the cervical spine.

28. The trachea divides into two
   a. carina.
   b. bronchi.
   c. alveoli.
   d. lungs.

29. What is the structure that prevents food and liquid from entering the trachea during swallowing?
   a. larynx
   b. cricoid cartilage
   c. epiglottis
   d. diaphragm

30. The air sacs in the lungs where oxygen–carbon dioxide exchange occurs are the
   a. bronchioles.
   b. bronchi.
   c. epiglottis.
   d. alveoli.

31. Air flow from the mouth and nose toward the lungs is known as
   a. exhalation.
   b. inhalation.
   c. alveolar/capillary exchange.
   d. capillary/cellular exchange.

32. The normal rate of breathing for an adult is how many breaths per minute?
   a. 12–20
   b. 15–30
   c. 25–50
   d. 8–12

33. Which occurs during capillary/cellular exchange?
   a. Oxygen enters the capillaries as carbon dioxide enters the alveoli.
   b. Oxygen-poor blood from the capillaries passes into the alveoli.
   c. Body cells give up carbon dioxide and capillaries give up oxygen.
   d. Body cells obtain nourishment from the capillaries.

34. Cardiac arrest in children is most often caused by
   a. chest trauma.
   b. respiratory compromise.
   c. hypovolemia.
   d. irregular rhythm.

35. Which of the following is a sign of inadequate breathing?
   a. warm, dry skin
   b. no audible sounds
   c. equal chest expansion
   d. accessory muscle use

36. The most reliable sign that you are ventilating a patient adequately is that
   a. gastric distention is present during BVM ventilation.
   b. you are ventilating over 20 times per minute for an adult.
   c. the chest rises and falls with each BVM ventilation.
   d. agonal sounds are heard during auscultation of the lung.

37. A gurgling sound heard with artificial ventilation is a sign that
   a. the patient must be suctioned immediately.
   b. supplemental oxygen should be added to the BVM.
   c. the airway is most likely open, patent, and clear.
   d. the patient is trying to communicate with you.

38. The first step in artificial ventilation with a bag-valve-mask unit in patients with no suspected trauma is to
   a. position the mask correctly on the face using both hands.
   b. place the patient's head in a hyperextended, sniffing position.
   c. insert an airway adjunct and select the correct mask size.
   d. have an assistant squeeze the bag until the patient's chest rises.

39. What is the preferred method for BLS ventilation of a patient?
   a. one-person bag-valve mask
   b. mouth-to-mask ventilation
   c. two-person bag-valve mask
   d. flow-restricted, oxygen-powered ventilation device

40. When suctioning a patient, how far should you insert a soft suction catheter?
   a. as far as you can see
   b. as far as the base of the tongue
   c. until resistance is encountered
   d. past the vocal cords

41. What is the correct procedure for a patient who has secretions or emesis that suctioning cannot easily remove?
   a. insert an oropharyngeal or nasopharyngeal airway immediately
   b. suction for 15 seconds, ventilate for two minutes, and then repeat
   c. logroll the patient and clear the oropharynx and nasopharynx
   d. hyperventilate the patient with a bag-valve-mask unit

42. During active inhalation, the diaphragm
   a. contracts and flattens, increasing the size of the chest cavity.
   b. relaxes, decreasing the size of the thoracic cavity.
   c. moves upward, forcing the lungs to contract.
   d. moves upward, forcing the ribs to move downward and inward.

43. What is the purpose of the head-tilt/chin-lift technique?
   a. to position the patient for insertion of an airway adjunct
   b. to remove foreign bodies from the upper airway
   c. to help the rescuer better visualize the larynx and vocal cords
   d. to lift the tongue and epiglottis out of their obstructing position

44. After opening the airway, the next step in patient management is to
   a. insert an endotracheal tube.
   b. assess adequacy of respirations.
   c. begin mouth-to-mouth ventilation.
   d. apply bag-valve-mask ventilation.

45. The flow rate of a nonrebreather mask should normally be set at rate?
   a. 20 L/min.
   b. 15 L/min.
   c. 10 L/min.
   d. 5 L/min.

46. A patient should receive high-flow oxygen if he or she exhibits
   a. fever.
   b. anxiety.
   c. dehydration.
   d. cyanosis.

47. The first step in the delivery of high-flow oxygen via a nonrebreather mask is to
   a. select the correct size mask.
   b. regulate the flow of oxygen.
   c. inflate the reservoir bag with oxygen.
   d. turn on the oxygen source.

48. When providing mouth-to-mask ventilation with supplementary oxygen, what is the first step after sealing the mask to the patient's face?
   a. Follow body substance precautions before touching the patient.
   b. Connect the one-way valve and filter (if available) to the mask.
   c. Exhale slowly over the ventilation port for 1.5 to two seconds.
   d. Attach oxygen tubing to the mask and set the flow rate at 15–30 L/min.

49. The correct rate of artificial ventilations for an adult patient is
   a. 3 ventilations per minute.
   b. 5 ventilations per minute.
   c. 10 ventilations per minute.
   d. 12 ventilations per minute.

50. When using the two-person bag-valve-mask procedure, one EMT ventilates the patient while the other
   a. suctions the patient and administers CPR.
   b. administers mouth-to-mask ventilation.
   c. inserts the oral or nasopharyngeal airway.
   d. maintains the mask seal and monitors chest rise.

51. Where is the cricoid cartilage located?
   a. inferior to the larynx
   b. superior to the epiglottis
   c. at the carina
   d. in the oropharynx

52. To perform the head-tilt/chin-lift, you place one hand on the patient's forehead and the fingers of your other hand are placed
   a. in the patient's mouth.
   b. on the patient's throat.
   c. under the patient's chin.
   d. under the patient's ears.

53. A bulb syringe is used to suction infants up to the age of
   a. one month.
   b. three to four months.
   c. six to eight months.
   d. one year.

54. The right ventricle pumps blood into the
   a. body, via the aorta.
   b. lungs, via the pulmonary vein.
   c. lungs, via the pulmonary artery.
   d. left atrium.

55. A 56-year-old female patient complains of mild chest discomfort. You should
   a. decide what type of heart problem it might be.
   b. decide whether the patient has a heart problem.
   c. maintain a high index of suspicion for cardiac compromise.
   d. apply the AED.

56. If a patient's blood pressure drops after administering nitroglycerin, you should
   a. assist the patient to lie down, and transport him or her immediately.
   b. administer a second dose of nitroglycerin and reassess again.
   c. place the patient supine and monitor her or his vital signs closely.
   d. administer oxygen and elevate the patient's legs.

57. Your patient is a 62-year-old man with a history of heart disease. He is experiencing chest pain. Your first action should be to
   a. place the pads for the automated external defibrillator on his chest.
   b. begin CPR while preparing the automated external defibrillator.
   c. ask him if he has taken his nitroglycerin, and if not, offer to assist him.
   d. place him in a comfortable position and administer high-flow oxygen.

58. Your patient is a 78-year-old woman with a history of heart disease. While you are transporting to the hospital, her level of consciousness decreases. You now feel a carotid pulse, but no radial pulse. What should you do?
   a. Request permission to administer nitroglycerin.
   b. Begin CPR and request ACLS services.
   c. Defibrillate the patient with an AED.
   d. Assess her ABCs and maintain her airway.

59. The EMT-B should request prehospital advanced cardiac life support for the care of the cardiac arrest patient
   a. because ACLS intervention provides higher survival rates.
   b. because EMT-Bs must have prehospital ACLS present to perform defibrillation.
   c. because only paramedics can transport cardiac arrest patients.
   d. because the EMT-B is not adequately trained to manage cardiac arrest.

60. Your patient is a 29-year-old man who has fallen off a ladder. He is bleeding profusely from a wound on his right forearm and has severe pain in his left thigh. Which of the following is an appropriate initial treatment for this patient?
   a. Perform a quick initial assessment to assess his ABCs.
   b. Stop the bleeding by applying a tourniquet near the elbow.
   c. Maintain an open airway and ventilate the patient with a BVM.
   d. Elevate the patient's legs 20 to 30 cm to treat him for shock.

61. Touching the patient when the semiautomatic external defibrillator is analyzing the rhythm
   a. is acceptable with today's modern defibrillators.
   b. is indicated to maintain cardiac compressions.
   c. is indicated to maintain artificial ventilation.
   d. can cause the AED to misinterpret a rhythm.

62. What should you do for the cardiac arrest patient found in the rain?
   a. Perform one rapid defibrillation, then move patient inside.
   b. Defibrillate three times, then move patient inside.
   c Move patient inside, away from the rain.
   d. Perform one rapid defibrillation, then start CPR if pulseless.

63. Your patient is bleeding profusely from a wound on her right forearm. Where is the pressure point for this injury?
  a. carotid artery
  b. ulnar artery
  c. brachial artery
  d. femoral artery

64. You suspect that your patient, who has a pelvic injury, is in shock. You must receive specific medical direction before you perform which of the following procedures?
  a. Use a pneumatic antishock garment.
  b. Stabilize the legs with a blanket and cravats.
  c. Elevate the lower end of the long board.
  d. Control external bleeding with direct pressure.

65. A bystander is performing CPR when you arrive. You evaluate the scene, practice body substance isolation, and begin your initial assessment by having the bystander
  a. verify pulselessness.
  b. continue CPR.
  c. stop CPR.
  d. provide a history of cardiac arrest.

66. Your patient is bleeding from a wound to the forearm. The blood flows in a steady, dark-red stream. What type of bleeding should you suspect?
  a. venous
  b. arterial
  c. capillary
  d. internal

67. Your patient is restless, anxious, and complaining of thirst. She exhibits increased heart rate and pale, clammy skin. You should do all the following EXCEPT
  a. maintain an open airway and provide oxygen.
  b. elevate her legs if not contraindicated.
  c. cover the patient with a blanket to keep her warm.
  d. give the patient small amounts of liquid to drink.

68. After early access to the EMS system, the next step in the chain of survival in cardiac care is
  a. early CPR.
  b. early defibrillation.
  c. early ACLS.
  d. cardiac medication.

69. Which of the following patients should be connected to the automatic external defibrillator?
  a. a 70-year-old man with a history of angina and a prescription for nitroglycerin; he is experiencing mild chest pain on exertion
  b. a 68-year-old woman experiencing severe, crushing chest pain; she is breathing on her own and has an irregular pulse
  c. a 56-year-old man who suddenly collapsed; he is not breathing on his own, and there is no carotid pulse
  d. an 80-year-old woman who suddenly collapsed; her breathing is shallow, and there is a weak carotid pulse

70. Which heart rhythm often converts to ventricular fibrillation?
  a. asystole
  b. ventricular tachycardia
  c. atrial fibrillation
  d. atrial tachycardia

71. What is the reason for stopping CPR before applying the automatic external defibrillator?
- **a.** to give the patient a chance to breathe on his or her own
- **b.** to allow the ACLS system to take over patient care
- **c.** to allow the EMT to verify pulselessness and apnea
- **d.** to allow other rescuers to get out of the way

72. The automatic external defibrillator advises you that no shock is indicated. What is the first thing you should do?
- **a.** Check the patient's carotid pulse.
- **b.** Turn the AED off and on again.
- **c.** Continue CPR and BVM ventilation.
- **d.** Remove and reattach the AED leads.

73. After receiving three consecutive "no shock indicated" messages on the AED, you should do which of the following?
- **a.** Consult medical control for direction.
- **b.** Check the AED battery/power supply.
- **c.** Check for a pulse and begin CPR.
- **d.** Begin transporting to the hospital.

74. You are transporting a patient who has been resuscitated but is still unresponsive. You should check the patient's pulse
- **a.** every 30 seconds.
- **b.** every minute.
- **c.** every 5 minutes.
- **d.** every 10 minutes.

75. The medical direction physician orders you to deliver additional shocks to a patient in cardiac arrest while en route to the hospital. What is the correct procedure to follow?
- **a.** Wait for the arrival of the ACLS team.
- **b.** Deliver the shocks without stopping CPR.
- **c.** Stop the vehicle before reanalyzing the rhythm.
- **d.** Refuse to defibrillate the patient while en route.

76. What is the primary action of nitroglycerin?
- **a.** lower the blood pressure
- **b.** contract the heart muscles
- **c.** slow the heart rate down
- **d.** dilate the coronary vessels

77. Patients commonly describe heart attack pain as which of the following characteristic?
- **a.** like "pins and needles"
- **b.** crushing or squeezing
- **c.** intermittent (comes and goes)
- **d.** less severe than indigestion

78. Hemorrhagic shock is caused by
- **a.** dehydration.
- **b.** diarrhea.
- **c.** bleeding.
- **d.** vomiting.

79. Your patient is a 19-year-old man with a severe nosebleed and no other signs of trauma. In what position should you place him?
- **a.** flat on his back, with lower extremities elevated
- **b.** sitting up and leaning forward
- **c.** prone
- **d.** supine

80. Your patient has profuse bleeding from a wound on her lower leg, but no signs of skeletal injury. The steps you should take to stop the bleeding, in the correct order, are
- **a.** direct pressure, elevation, pressure dressing, and pressure point.
- **b.** pressure point, tourniquet, and concentrated or diffuse direct pressure.
- **c.** PASG, lower extremity elevation, and diffuse direct pressure.
- **d.** elevation, pressure point, pressure dressing, and PASG.

81. Where should you place your hands when using the head-tilt/chin-lift maneuver to open an unconscious patient's airway?
    a. on the nose, with the fingertips pinching it closed, and under the neck
    b. on the nose, with the fingertips pinching it closed, and on the forehead
    c. on the forehead, with the other hand under the neck
    d. on the forehead, with the fingertips of the other hand under the lower jaw

82. Your patient is found lying on the ground after falling off a roof. She is unconscious and apneic. Which method should you use to open the patient's airway?
    a. head-tilt/chin-lift
    b. modified jaw thrust
    c. head-tilt only
    d. head-tilt/neck-lift

83. Which type of splint is the best to use for an angulated injury?
    a. rigid splint
    b. traction splint
    c. PASG
    d. pneumatic splint

84. When splinting an injured limb, you should assess pulse, motor function, and sensation distal to the injury
    a. after applying the splint.
    b. before applying the splint.
    c. while applying the splint.
    d. before and after applying the splint.

85. When performing the modified jaw-thrust maneuver to open your patient's airway, which of the following steps is NOT correct?
    a. Stabilize the patient's cervical spine with your forearms.
    b. Rest your elbows on the same surface as the patient.
    c. Tilt the head by applying gentle pressure to the forehead.
    d. Use your index fingers to push the angles of the lower jaw forward.

86. To support a patient's hand in a position of function, you would
    a. place a roll of gauze in his or her hand.
    b. lay the hand flat on a padded board.
    c. bend the wrist at a 90-degree angle.
    d. splint the lower arm with the hand dangling.

87. All of the following are risk factors for suicide EXCEPT
    a. recent death of a loved one.
    b. alcohol dependence.
    c. age younger than 20.
    d. age older than 40.

88. Your unconscious patient has blood in his airway. You should
    a. use a suction unit to immediately clear the airway.
    b. apply oxygen using a nonrebreather mask at 15 liters per minute.
    c. use a bag-valve mask to clear the airway.
    d. perform a finger sweep to remove the blockage.

89. Your patient is behaving abnormally but refuses treatment after falling down a flight of stairs. Before transporting the patient without consent, you should
  a. document the presence of any injury.
  b. ask bystanders to serve as witnesses.
  c. have bystanders help talk him into care.
  d. contact medical direction for advice.

90. You should not suction a patient's airway for more than 15 seconds because
  a. the patient's tongue may be injured.
  b. the suction unit's battery may drain too quickly.
  c. the patient will become hypoxic during this time.
  d. you may cause the patient to vomit.

91. Which of the following is true regarding using a pocket mask to ventilate a nonbreathing patient?
  a. There is direct contact between the rescuer and the patient's mouth.
  b. Oxygen cannot be connected to the mask.
  c. A one-way valve prevents exhaled air from contacting the rescuer.
  d. Oxygen levels of 100% may be achieved.

92. You are ventilating an apneic trauma patient using the jaw-thrust maneuver and a bag-valve mask. You should
  a. tilt the head as far as it can go.
  b. use your ring and little fingers to lift the jaw upward.
  c. kneel at the patient's side.
  d. do nothing. Use of airway adjuncts is not necessary.

93. To which patient should you administer oral glucose?
  a. a 60-year-old woman behaving as if she is intoxicated, and whose daughter informs you that she takes insulin by injection
  b. a 45-year-old man with a history of diabetes behaving erratically after falling and hitting his head in the bathtub
  c. a 70-year-old man with a long history of diabetes who is unconscious and cannot swallow
  d. a 52-year-old woman who tells you that she is feeling dizzy and has "low blood sugar"

94. The focused history for patients with altered mental status should include questions about a history of trauma, diabetes, seizures, and which of the following?
  a. heart disease
  b. pregnancy
  c. fever
  d. stress

95. Using a reservoir with a bag-valve-mask system will allow oxygen levels to increase to nearly
  a. 70%.
  b. 90%.
  c. 80%.
  d. 100%.

96. All of the following may be signs of allergic reaction EXCEPT
  a. headache and dizziness.
  b. rapid, labored breathing.
  c. decreased blood pressure.
  d. decreased heart rate.

97. Under medical direction, the EMT-Basic may administer epinephrine to a patient with respiratory distress or hypoperfusion resulting from an allergic reaction if the
   a. patient has no history of heart disease.
   b. patient is in severe respiratory distress or arrest.
   c. medication has been prescribed for this patient.
   d. medication has been stored in the refrigerator.

98. Which patient is most likely to benefit from receiving activated charcoal?
   a. a child who has ingested blood-pressure medication
   b. a child who has ingested drain cleaner containing lye
   c. an 18-year-old woman who was bitten by a spider
   d. a 24-year-old man who has inhaled carbon monoxide gas

99. Your patient is a 25-year-old woman who is severely hypothermic after having plunged into an icy river. Although she was rescued after only a few minutes in the water, she is showing a diminished level of responsiveness. Your care should include
   a. encouraging the patient to walk in order to improve her circulation.
   b. covering the patient in blankets and turning up the heat in the ambulance.
   c. giving her hot coffee or tea to drink and massaging her extremities.
   d. beginning active rewarming measures under direct medical direction.

100. Predisposing factors for hypothermia include all the following EXCEPT
   a. age.
   b. depression.
   c. exposure to cold.
   d. alcohol.

101. A sign of generalized cold emergency, or hypothermia, is cool skin on the
   a. feet or hands.
   b. ears.
   c. face.
   d. abdomen.

102. Two important principles in the emergency treatment of local cold injuries are to remove the patient from the cold environment and to
   a. rewarm the cold extremity quickly.
   b. warm the whole body as soon as possible.
   c. prevent further tissue damage.
   d. prevent or treat pain.

103. Which of the following indicates that a patient with hyperthermia is in serious danger?
   a. hot skin
   b. moist skin
   c. muscle cramps
   d. dizziness

104. When resuscitating a near-drowning victim, you should attempt to relieve gastric distention only if
   a. you have been specially trained in this procedure.
   b. you are acting under the orders of medical direction.
   c. the patient complains of stomach pains.
   d. it interferes with artificial ventilation.

105. Your patient has been stung by a bee, and the stinger is present in the wound. You should attempt to remove it by
   a. grabbing it with sterile tweezers.
   b. cutting around it with a knife.
   c. scraping it away with a rigid object.
   d. grabbing it with your fingers.

106. You adequately ventilate a patient with a bag-valve mask after the patient's
   a. skin color turns cyanotic.
   b. chest rises.
   c. abdomen rises.
   d. pulse rate decreases.

107. Your patient is a frightened 4-year-old girl who strongly resists receiving oxygen by mask. What should you do?
   a. Hold the mask firmly over the child's face and order her to breathe.
   b. Do not administer oxygen because you do not want to agitate her.
   c. Have a parent calm the child and hold the blow-by device for her.
   d. Call an ALS unit to the scene to sedate the child so you can oxygenate her.

108. Which of the following are the signs of early respiratory distress in children and infants?
   a. breathing rate of less than ten per minute, limp muscle tone, slow or absent heart rate, weak or absent distal pulses
   b. increased rate of breathing, nasal flaring, intercostal or supraclavicular retractions, mottled skin color, abdominal muscle use
   c. altered mental status, respiratory rate of over 60 or under 20 breaths per minute, severe retractions, severe use of accessory muscles
   d. inability to cough, crying with tears but no sounds, cyanosis, abdominal or chest wall movements with absent breath sounds

109. Your patient is an 8-year-old girl who had a single, brief seizure at school. Her mother arrives at the same time you do and reports that she has seizures often, and is under medical treatment. What should you do?
   a. Request ALS and law enforcement backup so you can transport the child.
   b. Administer a dose of the child's prescribed seizure control medication.
   c. Maintain ABCs, monitor vital signs, and transport the patient immediately.
   d. Ensure a patent airway and request medical direction regarding transport.

110. All of the following are signs of possible child abuse EXCEPT
   a. the presence of multiple bruises in various stages of healing.
   b. a single, severe traumatic event that occurred for no reason.
   c. injuries inconsistent with the mechanism described.
   d. conflicting histories of the injury from the guardians/parents.

111. The head of a newborn infant has just delivered. You should
   a. suction the baby's mouth and nostrils with a bulb syringe.
   b. push down on the baby's upper shoulder to facilitate the rest of the delivery.
   c. push up on the baby's lower shoulder to facilitate the rest of the delivery.
   d. ventilate the baby with a pediatric bag-valve mask and high-flow oxygen.

112. Emergency care for a responsive 7-year-old child with a foreign-body airway obstruction includes
- **a.** holding the child on your knee and performing back blows.
- **b.** standing behind the child and performing sub-diaphragmatic thrusts.
- **c.** placing the child supine on the floor and attempting to see the obstruction.
- **d.** placing the child supine on the floor and performing abdominal thrusts.

113. A 2-year-old is in respiratory failure when he has
- **a.** altered mental status and breathing rate of 68 per minute.
- **b.** limp muscle tone and weak or absent distal pulses.
- **c.** nasal flaring and mottled skin color.
- **d.** breathing rate of six per minute and heart rate of 50 per minute.

114. A sign or symptom of a predelivery emergency is
- **a.** the mother's skin is dry.
- **b.** profuse vaginal bleeding.
- **c.** the presence of a "bloody show."
- **d.** a contraction every 20 minutes.

115. Select the correct-size oral airway for a small child by measuring from the corner of the patient's mouth to what structure?
- **a.** central incisor
- **b.** angle of the jaw
- **c.** tip of the nose
- **d.** pinnea of the ear

116. Your patient is a 9-year-old girl who has cut her face. You can best comfort her and enlist her cooperation by
- **a.** allowing her to play with your equipment as you treat her injury.
- **b.** sitting her on her mother's lap during assessment and treatment.
- **c.** examining a teddy bear before you begin assessing her injury.
- **d.** explaining what you are doing and reassuring her about her recovery.

117. You are assisting with childbirth in the field. As the infant's head is delivered, you discover that the umbilical cord is wrapped tightly around the neck. You should immediately
- **a.** place the mother on her side and transport rapidly.
- **b.** deliver the infant with the cord wrapped around its neck.
- **c.** clamp the cord in two places and cut it between clamps.
- **d.** suction the infant's mouth and nose to clear secretions.

118. You have just assisted in delivering an infant with a pink body, a pulse rate of 106 per minute, and good muscle tone. The infant is crying lustily. How should you care for this newborn?
- **a.** Wrap the newborn in clean towels and give it to the mother to hold during transport.
- **b.** Provide positive pressure ventilations at the rate of 60 per minute with a bag-valve mask.
- **c.** Monitor the infant for one minute and reassess vital signs to see if the heart rate increases.
- **d.** Administer free-flow oxygen by holding an oxygen mask or tubing over the newborn's face.

119. Asking all of the following questions will help you decide whether delivery is imminent EXCEPT
   a. when is the baby due?
   b. do you feel increasing pressure in your vaginal area?
   c. do you feel the urge to move your bowels?
   d. when did you last eat or drink?

120. Seizures related to pregnancy generally occur during the
   a. first trimester.
   b. second trimester.
   c. third trimester.
   d. active part of labor.

121. The presence of a bloody show during the first stage of labor is a sign that
   a. the delivery of the infant is imminent.
   b. the newborn is in danger of respiratory distress.
   c. labor is progressing normally.
   d. the second stage of labor has begun.

122. Your patient has experienced a spontaneous abortion or miscarriage. You should
   a. remove any tissues from the vagina.
   b. discard any expelled tissues.
   c. place a sanitary napkin in the vagina.
   d. treat the patient for shock.

123. What is the first treatment when a mother bleeds excessively from her vagina after delivery?
   a. Massage her abdomen gently.
   b. Administer oxygen.
   c. Transport her immediately.
   d. Treat her for shock.

124. Emergency care for an infant when meconium is present in the amniotic fluid includes
   a. stimulating the infant to cough to expel the meconium.
   b. performing BVM ventilation to improve lung compliance.
   c. performing back blows and chest thrusts to remove the meconium.
   d. suctioning and notifying the hospital that meconium was present.

125. In addition to caring for injuries, emergency care for a rape victim should focus on which of the following?
   a. performing a pelvic or rectal exam on the patient
   b. collecting evidence of the rape and bagging it in plastic
   c. allowing the patient to shower and change clothes
   d. preserving evidence in a paper bag and reassuring the victim

126. The reason to position a pregnant woman on her left side is to
   a. reduce the pressure of the fetus on maternal circulation.
   b. make labor proceed more slowly by slowing down contractions.
   c. help turn a breech fetus in the birth canal to the vertex position.
   d. ensure that there is sufficient blood flow to the placenta.

127. The patient is a 29-year-old woman pregnant with her second child. She is 39 weeks pregnant and saw a bloody show approximately four hours ago. Her contractions are two minutes apart and lasting 60 seconds. Transport time is approximately 45 minutes. You should
   a. protect the airway and monitor vital signs while transporting.
   b. prepare for an imminent on-scene delivery.
   c. position the mother on her left side and begin transport.
   d. notify dispatch of the need for ALS assistance.

128. The average length of labor for a woman's first baby is
   a. 45 to 60 minutes.
   b. 2 to 3 hours.
   c. 12 to 18 hours.
   d. more than 24 hours.

129. The patient is said to be "crowning" when the
   a. placenta separates from the uterine wall.
   b. placenta is formed in an abnormal location.
   c. umbilical cord presents at the vaginal opening.
   d. baby's head is visible at the vaginal opening.

130. When arriving at the scene of a possible hazardous materials incident, you would identify hazards by
   a. thoroughly investigating the scene yourself.
   b. interviewing victims and bystanders.
   c. scanning with binoculars from a safe distance.
   d. assisting law enforcement officers in the search.

131. For which of these procedures should you wear gloves, gown, mask, and protective eyewear?
   a. performing endotracheal intubation
   b. performing oral/nasal suctioning
   c. cleaning contaminated instruments
   d. bleeding control with spurting blood

132. Which of the following situations represents your abandonment of a patient?
   a. You begin assessing a patient, but turn responsibility for that patient over to a first responder.
   b. You begin CPR on a cardiac arrest patient, but stop when the ALS team takes over care.
   c. With the approval of medical direction, you do not transport a patient who feels fine after having a seizure.
   d. You refuse to help a patient administer nitroglycerin that has been prescribed for someone else.

133. You are called to a store where a holdup has been committed. Police are already on the scene, searching for the gunman. Through the store window, you see the store manager, who has been shot. You should
   a. enter the store immediately to care for the manager.
   b. leave immediately and seek cover a distance away.
   c. wait until the police tell you it is safe to enter the scene.
   d. request medical direction to determine if you can enter.

134. A 30-year-old female is experiencing labor. Which of the follow questions should you ask when deciding whether to begin immediate transport or prepare for imminent delivery?
   a. How close are your labor contractions?
   b. What do your contractions feel like?
   c. Are you taking prenatal vitamins?
   d. Who is your doctor?

135. What is the first thing you should do after receiving orders from the medical direction physician?
   a. Carry out the orders immediately.
   b. Repeat the orders exactly as you heard them.
   c. Question anything you did not understand.
   d. Document the orders in your report.

136. Which of the following represents proper communication with the patient?

a. When talking to a 12-year-old: "Do you want to hold your Mommy's hand while I bandage you?"

b. When talking to an intoxicated 27-year-old man: "Get up. You are intoxicated and are not injured."

c. When talking to a 75-year-old woman: "Ma'am, we think you should go to the hospital to make sure you're OK. Will you come with us?"

d. When talking to a 4-year-old child: "I think you've fractured your femur. We'll stabilize you here and transport you to the hospital for surgery."

137. Your pregnant patient is experiencing contractions. She feels like she needs to move her bowels. This may indicate that

a. birth is still some time away.

b. birth is imminent.

c. she is going into shock.

d. the baby is still very high in the birth canal.

138. Which statement about a patient's right to refuse care is correct?

a. A child who is old enough to understand danger is old enough to refuse care and transport.

b. An adult patient who is of sound mind and understands the consequences can refuse treatment.

c. No one can authorize treatment or transport for any other individual, regardless of his or her age.

d. EMTs should leave immediately whenever a patient says that he or she will refuse care.

139. Which situation requires that an emergency patient be moved?

a. Your patient has undergone cardiac arrest while seated in a chair.

b. Your patient is found on the ground, unresponsive and alone.

c. Your patient is found in her bed, displaying early symptoms of shock.

d. Your patient is showing signs of inadequate breathing and shock.

140. What is the correct procedure for handling a used airway?

a. Discard it in a biohazard trash container.

b. Clean it with alcohol foam and dry it off.

c. Disinfect it with bleach and water solution.

d. Sterilize it in an autoclave or boiling water.

141. You can assess a pregnant patient's uterine contractions by placing your gloved-hand on

a. her abdomen, below the naval.

b. her abdomen, above the naval.

c. the right side of her abdomen.

d. the left side of her abdomen.

142. The purpose of incident management systems is to provide

a. a clear chain of command in case of legal liability.

b. a means of evaluating the EMS system's response to an event.

c. an orderly method for communications and decision making.

d. a training program for First Responders.

143. A 23-year-old pregnant female is bleeding profusely from her vagina. All of the following actions are appropriate EXCEPT

a. providing high-concentration oxygen.

b. placing a sanitary napkin in the vagina.

c. replacing pads as they become soaked.

d. rapid transport to the hospital.

144. In a multiple-casualty situation, which patient should be assigned the highest priority?
  a. adequate breathing, responsive, venous bleeding
  b. adequate breathing, responsive, suspected spine injury
  c. inadequate breathing, responsive, suspected broken tibia
  d. inadequate breathing, unresponsive, suspected internal bleeding

145. In a multiple-casualty situation, the lowest priority would be assigned to a patient who
  a. has moderate burns.
  b. is in respiratory distress.
  c. has died.
  d. is in shock.

146. Your patient is 84 years old and having difficulty breathing. Her daughter, age 45, is with her. When communicating with this patient, you should assume that she is
  a. incompetent; speak directly with the daughter.
  b. hard of hearing; speak extremely slowly and loudly.
  c. competent and able to understand; speak respectfully.
  d. confused; explain your treatment clearly to the daughter.

147. Which statement about patient confidentiality is correct?
  a. Patients who are cared for in a public place lose their right to confidentiality.
  b. The right to confidentiality does not apply to minors or to wards of the state.
  c. The patient who signs a statement releasing confidential information relinquishes all rights to privacy.
  d. A patient must sign a written release before any confidential information can be disclosed.

148. A pregnant female who is about to deliver a baby should be positioned
  a. on her right side with legs apart.
  b. in a sitting position on the stretcher.
  c. in the knee-chest position.
  d. supine with knees drawn up and spread apart.

149. Your patient, a 69-year-old man, is in cardiac arrest. His wife informs you that their physician has written a Do Not Resuscitate order for the patient, but she does not have the written order. You should
  a. provide all necessary care to save the patient's life.
  b. obey the Do Not Resuscitate order and leave immediately.
  c. leave right after documenting the wife's statement.
  d. call the patient's doctor and try to confirm the order.

150. Your patient is a 6-year-old child who fell off her bicycle. She has a suspected broken ankle, no respiratory compromise, and no suspected internal injuries. After providing necessary care at the scene, you are transporting the child and her father to the hospital. The father loudly insists that you use your siren and lights en route. You should
  a. request medical direction in dealing with the father.
  b. request permission from dispatch to use lights and siren.
  c. refuse, because it may cause an unnecessary hazard.
  d. comply, it will relax the father and comfort the patient.

► Answers

1. b. High-efficiency particulate air (HEPA) respirators are worn when in contact with patients who have airborne infections, such as tuberculosis. HIV/AIDS and hepatitis B are both blood borne pathogens. Contaminants from open wounds would also be blood borne.

2. c. Gowns should be worn when you expect to be exposed to large amounts of blood or body fluids, such as when assisting with childbirth.

3. c. Your first action should be to remove your crew and the patient from the possible noxious gas and to notify the gas company of the leak. You may also be required to alert the hazardous materials response team. You should not attempt to locate the gas leak yourself. Treatment for the patient will begin with an ABC assessment and management of any problems you might encounter.

4. b. Because ventricular fibrillation is the most common cause of sudden cardiac arrest, it is critical to apply an automated external defibrillator on an unconscious apneic and pulseless patient as quickly as possible. The other rhythms can also cause a patient to be in cardiac arrest, but they do not occur as frequently as "V-fib".

5. a. The patient with chest pain and systolic blood pressure less than 100 is the highest priority patient of the four. A leg injury may be life threatening if the femoral artery is injured, but most often, a single extremity injury is not a threat to life. The elderly gentleman may be exhibiting his normal mental status, or he may be having problems due to an ongoing health problem. You need more information before you can make that determination, but he is not in any imminent danger right now. Labor with contraction six minutes apart is not considered imminent delivery. If you have any questions, however, you should continue assessing this patient as well by asking pertinent questions and checking for crowning.

6. b. The patient should be suctioned to clear the airway before receiving high concentrations of oxygen. Patient A should be assessed to determine if she is hyperventilating and be treated accordingly. Patient C is breathing at a rate that is too slow, and he should be assisted with a BVM unit. Patient D is breathing at the correct rate for a child of his age.

7. c. An infant who is alert to verbal stimuli will still try to locate the parents' voices; choice **a** describes an alert infant; choice **d** describes an infant who is responsive to painful stimuli; choice **b** is incorrect because infants of this age are not developed enough to tell you their age regardless of their mental status.

8. b. Assess circulation in an infant by palpating the brachial pulse in the upper arm. The carotid and radial pulses are difficult to locate in infants. Capillary refill time shows that patients have impaired circulation, but it is not the first tool to use in assessing circulation because it is affected by external factors (like the environment) as well as internal factors like poor perfusion.

9. c. There is no information to indicate that the patient requires ventilatory support. Any patient experiencing chest discomfort should receive the highest possible concentration of oxygen.

10. c. A person who is ejected from a vehicle after a collision is at highest risk for hidden injury and death. In fact, ejected patients have a 300 times greater chance of dying than patients who remain inside the vehicle during a crash. Regarding falls, patients are considered to be at risk for hidden injury if they fall a distance greater than three times their height. The surface they land on is also considered with falls. Both patients A and D have falls two times their height and have landed on relatively soft surfaces.

11. a. The rapid trauma survey is used when you are unsure of the presence of hidden injuries or if the mechanism of injury (MOI) is unclear or severe enough to suggest the need for a rapid assessment. A 2-year-old child could be severely injured by a medium-speed collision, even if he or she appears alert and was properly restrained. The other choices do not represent MOIs considered to be high risk for hidden injury.

12. c. A supine patient may or may not have jugular veins that are prominent enough to palpate. However, even if the neck veins are normally present when an individual is supine, they will not be engorged in blood and overly firm to the touch. This is what is meant by the phrase "distended neck veins." Distended neck veins (in any position) are a sign of increased circulatory pressure. The carotid pulse should always be palpable. A decreased radial pulse may indicate hypovolemic shock or an injured extremity.

13. c. The other rhythms do not benefit from an electrical shock. The purpose of early defibrillation is to stop a highly chaotic, disorganized electrical rhythm such as ventricular fibrillation, with the hope that an organized rhythm will begin and generate a pulse.

14. d. The rapid trauma assessment starts with the top of the head and proceeds downward. You should immobilize the spine as soon as you have finished assessing the neck.

15. b. Assess motor function by asking the patient to wiggle his or her toes; moving the leg or having the patient bend the knee can compromise spinal stability; option **d** describes assessment of sensation, not motor function.

16. b. Patient **b** is the only one both responsive and who has no significant mechanism of injury.

17. c. The P component of the OPQRST acronym refers to provocation or palliation, or what makes the pain feel worse or better.

18. a. You should perform the initial assessment first, because the unresponsive patient cannot direct you to the specific complaint. Vital signs are completed during your second phase of patient assessment after you determine treatment priority and have a baseline ABC assessment. You cannot determine the appropriate course of treatment of any airway problem (including the need for positioning—choice **c**) until you have first assessed the airway. The SAMPLE history is important information to gather, but it should never come before any treatment that may be needed to correct an ABC abnormality.

19. b. Trauma and medical patients who are unresponsive, and all patients who have altered mental status, should receive a detailed physical assessment. It is easy to overlook something when the patient is not conscious enough to tell you what hurts or if the MOI and nature of illness (NOI) are unclear.

20. c. The detailed physical assessment is usually performed in the back of the ambulance during transport; its purpose is to reveal hidden injuries that escaped the initial rapid assessment.

21. b. AEDs are well-built, reliable devices that, when serviced and checked regularly, should last for quite some time. They do not require annual replacement.

22. c. The purpose of ongoing assessment is to check the adequacy of your initial interventions. The detailed examination is designed to find missed injuries.

23. b. The second step in the ongoing assessment is to record vital signs. Choice **a**, re-establishing patient priority, should be part of Step 1, repeating the initial assessment. Choices **c** (repeat the focused assessment) then **d** (evaluate all interventions) follow **b**.

24. d. Moving the patient under the EMT's guidance is an appropriate role for bystanders when there is not enough trained help present. The EMT should remember that the safety of the bystander assisting in moving the patient is also their responsibility. Provide BSI (gloves) and clear directions.

25. b. The nature of illness is the chief complaint, or the reason the patient called the ambulance.

26. c. Only those patients who are unresponsive, pulseless, and apneic should have the AED applied.

27. a. You could make the argument that you need additional help in the management of each of these situations; however, the one with the most critical need is when you must care for more than one critical patient. Both patients with gunshot wounds need immediate attention, so you should call for backup. In the other three situations, you should not require assistance unless some complicating factor presents itself. Patient **b** may or may not require ALS assistance, but most (over 80%) deliveries are simple and uncomplicated and can be easily managed by BLS providers. Patient **c** is having a febrile seizure, which is managed by stabilizing the ABCs and transporting. In patient **d**, even if your partner is required to stabilize the C-spine, you should be able to manage the patient for the time being until other assistance arrives to assist with packaging and moving the patient.

28. b. The trachea divides into the right and left bronchi; the carina is the point at which the division takes place; the alveoli are the minute air sacs in the lungs; and the lungs are the organs of air exchange.

29. c. The epiglottis is the leaf-shaped structure that closes off the trachea during swallowing. The larynx is the voice box, the structure that produces speech vibrations; the cricoid cartilage forms the lower portion of the larynx; the diaphragm is a large muscle that contracts to initiate inhalation.

30. d. The alveoli are the numerous minute air sacs that make up the lungs; bronchioles are small branches of the bronchi, which are the two main tubes branching from the trachea; the epiglottis is the structure that closes off the trachea during swallowing.

31. b. Inhalation is the flow of air into the lungs; exhalation is the flow of air out of the lungs; alveolar/capillary exchange and capillary/cellular exchange are two phases of respiratory physiology.

32. a. Normal breathing rate for an adult is 12–20 breaths per minute; 15–30 per minute is normal for a child, 25–50 for an infant; 8–12 is the range where you should be considering managing the patient with BVM ventilation, and below eight per minute, you should absolutely assist the adult patient's breathing with a BVM.

33. c. During capillary/cellular exchange, oxygen enters the body cells and carbon dioxide enters the capillaries; choices **a** and **b** describe alveolar/capillary exchange; choice **d** describes cellular digestion.

34. b. The most common complication causing pediatric cardiac arrest is inadequate breathing or other respiratory compromise.

35. d. Accessory muscles may be seen in use in the neck and as retractions above the clavicles and/or between the ribs. These muscles are used when greater than normal inspiratory and/or expiratory pressures are needed to move air. Normal breathing does not produce any audible sounds, but it will produce auscultatory sounds (heard with a stethoscope). Warm, dry skin and equal chest expansion are both signs of adequate breathing.

36. c. Choice **a** is a sign of inadequate ventilation. The rate (**b**) you are ventilating a person does not indicate adequacy, however, you are using the high end of normal when you are ventilating 20 times per minute; **d** (agonal sounds) is a sign that death is near.

37. a. A gurgling sound means that the patient needs to be suctioned immediately; ventilation cannot be adequate when the airway is blocked from mucous, blood, or other secretions.

38. b. Correct order of steps would be **b**, **c**, **a**, **d**.

39. c. As long as two responders are available, two-person bag-valve mask is the preferred method.

40. b. Choice **b** is the correct procedure. Choice **a** is correct for a rigid catheter, choice **c** is the correct method for inserting an oropharyngeal airway, and choice **d** is applicable only to endotracheal intubation.

41. c. Choice **c** is the correct procedure for clearing the airway when simple suctioning is not working. Choice **b** is appropriate for a patient with copious frothy secretions like the kind produced with pulmonary edema. Choices **a** and **d** are inappropriate without first clearing the airway.

42. a. Choice **a** describes what happens during active inhalation; choices **b**, **c**, and **d** describe what happens during exhalation.

43. d. The purpose of the head-tilt/chin-lift is to move the tongue and epiglottis out of the way of the airway; it is not useful for intubation (use the sniffing position), to remove foreign bodies, or to visualize the larynx.

44. b. After opening the airway, the EMT should assess the rate and depth of ventilations; choices **a**, **c**, and/or **d** would occur only after respiratory adequacy has been assessed and they are appropriate to use.

45. b. Fifteen liters per minute is the correct flow rate regardless of mask size; at this flow rate, a non-rebreather mask will deliver up to 90% oxygen.

46. d. Cyanosis, or a bluish coloration of the mucus membranes and skin, is caused by inadequate oxygen supply to the body tissues; the other choices are unrelated to oxygen supply.

47. a. Masks come in adult and pediatric sizes. In order to deliver the highest possible concentration of oxygen to the patient, you must have a properly fitting mask. Steps **d**, **b**, and **c** must then be completed (in that order) before placing the mask on the patient's face.

48. c. After sealing the mask to the patient's face, you should begin mouth-to-mask ventilation with a long, slow breath; steps **a**, **b** and **d** should be done before applying the mask.

49. d. The correct rate is 12 ventilations per minute for an adult (one breath every five seconds), and the correct rate for a child is 20 ventilations per minute.

50. d. During a two-person bag-valve-mask procedure, one EMT ventilates the patient while the other maintains the airway and monitors the patient's chest rise.

51. a. The cricoid cartilage forms a ring of firm cartilage and is located inferior to (below) the larynx.

52. c. You perform the head-tilt/chin-lift by pressing back on the patient's forehead with one hand while raising the chin with the fingers of the other hand.

53. b. A bulb syringe is used to suction an infant's nasal passage or mouth and is generally used with infants up to age 3–4 months. If you are using mechanical or hand-powered suction equipment in infants of this age, be very careful to use the lowest possible pressures needed to accomplish the job.

54. c. The right ventricle receives oxygen-poor blood from the right atrium. It then pumps the blood to the lungs via the pulmonary artery where it receives oxygen and releases carbon dioxide.

55. c. The role of the EMT-Basic is not to diagnose the exact cause of the patient's chief complaint. Maintaining a high suspicion for a cardiac emergency will guide your next step in managing this patient appropriately.

56. c. A drop in blood pressure is expected after nitroglycerin is administered, but you should reassess to make sure the systolic pressure does not fall below 100 mm Hg.

57. d. Your first action would be to administer oxygen and place the patient in a comfortable position; next, if not contraindicated, you would request permission to administer nitroglycerin. You should first obtain a set of vital signs to ensure he is not in cardiogenic shock. Never put defibrillator pads onto a conscious patient with a pulse; this procedure is contraindicated. AED pads are not serving the same function as the electrodes used by ALS providers to monitor the heart rhythm.

58. d. Any change in a patient's mental status should result in immediate assessment of the ABCs. If not already done, place this patient on supplemental oxygen and ventilate as needed. Neither CPR nor defibrillation (AED use) is appropriate for a patient with a pulse. Nitroglycerin is not administered to patients with altered levels of consciousness or in the absence of chest pain. You should first know the patient's blood pressure before assisting him or her in self-administering nitroglycerine.

59. a. Prehospital ACLS provides additional medications and other therapies that may help either terminate the cardiac arrest state or help prevent the patient who has regained a pulse from going back into cardiac arrest.

60. a. Although you note several injuries, you still need to perform a rapid initial assessment to determine if any problems with the ABCs that you have not noted may be more life threatening than what you can obviously see. Stop the bleeding (but do not use a tourniquet) and treat the patient for shock, but do not elevate the patient's legs if there is an injury to the legs, pelvis, head, neck, chest, abdomen, or spine. There is no indication that this patient needs ventilation at this time.

61. d. When the AED is attempting to analyze the patient's electrical rhythm, any movement of the patient or the unit could cause the machine to misinterpret the signal.

62. c. Safety is critical when performing defibrillation. Any defibrillation attempt in the rain may possibly harm anyone near the patient during the discharge of the unit.

63. c. The pressure point for wounds of the forearm arm is the brachial artery.

64. a. Always consult with medical direction before using PASG. You do not need medical direction to stabilize the legs (**b**), treat for shock (**c**), or control bleeding (**d**).

65. c. Having the bystander to stop CPR will allow you to reassess the patient's ventilatory and circulatory status. This will tell you whether you need to continue CPR or whether the patient has regained a pulse or is breathing.

66. a. Venous bleeding flows in a steady, dark-red stream. Arterial bleeding is bright red and spurts from the wound, while capillary bleeding oozes. Internal bleeding may or may not present externally recognizable signs or symptoms.

67. d. This patient has the classic signs and symptoms of shock. Do not offer anything to eat or drink to the patient you suspect of being in shock, since surgery may be necessary later.

68. a. The first step in the chain of survival is early access to EMS; the following steps, in order, are early CPR (**a**), early defibrillation (**b**), and early access to ACLS (**c** and **d**). Choice **d** is not actually a part of the chain of survival but is a subcomponent of ACLS level care.

69. c. The automatic external defibrillator (AED) should be used only on patients who are not breathing and have no carotid pulse.

70. b. Ventricular tachycardia often converts to ventricular fibrillation, a life-threatening heart rhythm that the AED is designed to correct.

71. c. Stop CPR briefly to verify pulselessness and apnea. Once you have the leads ready for placement on the chest wall, you should stop CPR, clear away from the patient, attach the AED leads, and perform the initial analysis. Resume CPR after the first round of shocks if they were unsuccessful and the patient persists in pulselessness. Stop CPR again every time you deliver shocks.

72. a. If the AED advises that no shock is indicated, check the patient's pulse. If there is no pulse, resume CPR for one minute before rechecking the pulse and reanalyzing the rhythm.

73. d. After three consecutive "no shock indicated" messages, you should make sure to begin transporting the patient while continuing CPR. Some jurisdictions may adopt a protocol or standing order that requires you to consider transporting following the first or second set of AED rounds, regardless of whether you shock. At the minimum, you should begin your transport by the third time you perform an analysis.

74. a. If the patient has been resuscitated but is still unresponsive, check the pulse every 30 seconds during transport and keep the AED leads attached to the patient.

75. c. If it becomes necessary to deliver shocks while en route with the patient, the proper procedure is to stop the vehicle before reanalyzing the rhythm because the AED has a motion detector sensor in place that will not allow the unit to operate in the presence of motion.

76. d. The primary action of nitroglycerin is to dilate the myocardial (coronary) arteries, therefore easing the heart's workload by increasing the blood flow. Lowering of blood pressure is a secondary effect seen with vessel dilation. Reflex tachycardia, not bradycardia, may occur as a result of nitroglycerine administration. It does not have any direct effects on the muscles of the heart.

77. b. Myocardial pain is often difficult to determine because it can take on many different characters; however, patients most commonly (over 40% of the time) describe the pain of a myocardial infarction as a crushing, squeezing, pressure that radiates outward to the arms and upper back.

78. c. Hemorrhagic (bleeding) shock is caused by internal or external blood loss. Hypovolemic (low volume) shock is caused by bleeding, dehydration, vomiting, or diarrhea.

79. b. Have the patient sit up and lean forward so the blood does not enter the airway or stomach.

80. a. The combination of direct pressure, elevation, pressure dressing, and pressure point pressure is almost always successful in stopping bleeding in the extremities. Tourniquets are seldom needed. PASG use is performed cautiously under direct medical control, and it is never the first line of treatment.

81. d. Lifting the jaw is necessary to dislodge the tongue from the back of the throat and provide a patent airway.

82. b. The head-tilt/chin-lift may jeopardize the patient's cervical spine. The other two procedures will not adequately open the airway.

83. d. A pneumatic splint, which conforms and molds to the shape of an injury, is the splint of choice for an angulated, or deforming, injury.

84. d. Assess pulse, motor function, and sensation distal to a splint both before and after applying the splint to ensure that the splint is not adversely affecting circulation to the limb.

85. c. Tilting the head may compromise the stabilization of the cervical spine when using the modified jaw thrust.

86. a. The position of function, or the most natural position for the hand, is achieved by placing a roll of gauze in the patient's palm. You should always support the hand when you splint the arm because any movement of the hand is controlled with muscles all along the arm.

87. c. The most common statistical risk factors for suicide include being over 40, with a history of a recent divorce or widowhood, alcoholism, depression, and previous history of self-destructive behavior.

88. a. Blood is too fluid to be cleared adequately by a finger sweep. The other two answers are not appropriate unless the airway was cleared first by suction.

89. d. Before transporting a patient without consent, it is best to always seek medical direction.

90. c. While the other answers may be true, they may occur regardless of the time interval.

91. c. The one-way valve minimizes potential cross-exposure of the patient's secretions and exhaled breath to the rescuer.

92. b. Doing this will allow you to maintain the cervical spine while keeping the tongue from blocking the back of the pharynx.

93. a. Administer oral glucose on medical direction (through protocol or standing order) only to patients with altered mental status and history of diabetes. Patient **b** should be first treated as a trauma patient, and because research shows poor outcomes following brain injuries and glucose administration, it is best to withhold its use until blood sugar can be checked (which is an ALS provider skill in many areas). Patient **c** is not appropriate because of an inability to swallow properly; ALS should be called to provide IV dextrose to this patient. Glucose should be withheld until you can better determine if patient **d** is actually diabetic or not. (A blood glucose reading would be helpful with this patient as well.)

94. c. Common causes of altered mental status include trauma, diabetes, seizures, and infectious disease. Asking about fever helps determine if there is a history of recent infection.

95. d. The use of a reservoir ensures that the patient receives the highest concentration of oxygen available.

96. d. Signs of allergic reactions include increased heart rate, as the heart attempts to compensate for hypoperfusion. The two primary life-threatening events that occur during an allergic reaction are profound vasoconstriction (resulting in shock) and compromised airway due to swelling, constriction, or mucous production.

97. c. EMTs can administer epinephrine under medical direction only if the medication was previously prescribed for this patient. The patient will be prescribed the correct dosage by the physician and you are only allowed to administer the patient's own medication.

98. a. Activated charcoal is given to absorb ingested (oral route) poisons, but it does not work for strongly acid or alkaline substances, such as lye.

99. b. Care for a hypothermic patient with a diminished level of responsiveness should include passive rewarming (blankets and heated room) only; active rewarming should take place only in the hospital environment, and hypothermic patients should not be allowed to exercise or to take stimulants, such as coffee or tea. However, your protocols may allow you to give warmed liquids that are not alcoholic or caffeinated to slightly hypothermic patients with a normal mental status.

100. b. Cold environments, immersion in water, age, alcohol, and shock are the most important factors that predispose patients to hypothermia.

101. d. Cool skin on the abdomen is a reliable sign of hypothermia in a patient because the abdomen is in the central core of the body and is generally covered under layers of clothing.

102. c. The goal of care in cases of localized cold damage is to prevent further damage by removing the patient from the cold environment and protecting the damaged tissues from further injury. Rewarming is best accomplished in the hospital setting where pain medication can be administered and the danger of reinjury due to recooling is diminished.

103. a. A hyperthermic patient with hot skin must be treated aggressively before permanent organ damage sets in. When the skin is hot and dry, the normal sweating mechanisms have stopped functioning and the patient is in danger of brain damage due to excessive high body temperature.

104. d. Because of the risk of aspiration, do not attempt to relieve gastric distention unless it interferes with artificial ventilation.

105. c. Grabbing a stinger with tweezers or your fingers can squeeze more venom into the wound (also, there is personal risk of accidental exposure to the venom if you use your hands). Instead, scrape the stinger out of the skin with a piece of cardboard or rigid plastic (a credit card is ideal). Cutting around the stinger causes more tissue damage.

106. b. The other three signs are indications that ventilations are NOT adequate.

107. c. A parent can often calm a frightened child and therefore should be enlisted to hold the blow-by device in place. You should never withhold the administration of oxygen from any patient that you feel genuinely needs it.

108. b. Choice **b** describes early respiratory distress. Choice **a** describes the signs of impending respiratory arrest from insufficiency, choice **c** describes respiratory failure, and choice **d** describes airway obstruction.

109. d. For patients who have routine seizures and whose condition returns to normal quickly after a seizure, you should request medical direction about whether to transport.

110. b. Multiple injuries, conflicting stories of the cause, and repeated calls to the same address are characteristic of child abuse.

111. a. Suctioning the baby's mouth and nose will help to open the airway while the baby has not yet begun breathing. You should not force any part of the delivery process.

112. b. Care for a responsive child consists of standing behind the child and attempting to relieve the obstruction with a series of sub-diaphragmatic thrusts.

113. a. Signs of respiratory failure include altered mental status and a slow or fast breathing rate with fatigue. There is not enough information to determine if patients **b** and **c** are in respiratory insufficiency, respiratory failure, or impending respiratory arrest. Patient **d** is in impending respiratory arrest.

114. b. Profuse vaginal bleeding may indicate a true obstetrical emergency such as uterine rupture or torn placenta.

115. b. Select the correct-size oral airway for an infant or child by measuring from the corner of the patient's mouth to the angle of the jaw.

116. d. Because of her developmental level, a 9-year-old will be best comforted by clear explanations and reassurance.

117. c. If the cord is wrapped around the infant's neck and you cannot easily loosen and remove it, you should clamp it in two places and cut the cord.

118. a. This newborn has a high Apgar score; there is no need for respiratory support unless the condition changes. You should always follow the steps in the inverted pyramid for neonatal resuscitation by drying and warming, positioning head down for drainage, suctioning the airway and nose as needed, and providing tactile stimulation to stimulate breathing.

119. d. As delivery becomes imminent, the woman will feel increasing pressure in her vaginal area and will feel the urge to bear down and push. Asking about the due date, prenatal care, and number of previous children helps determine if delivery is imminent as well. Oral intake has no bearing on delivery.

120. c. Toxins related to eclampsia usually build up to high enough levels in late pregnancy to cause seizures.

121. c. The presence of a bloody show (which is the expulsion of the mucous plug from the mouth of the cervix) occurs during the first stage of labor. It is normal and indicates that the cervix is beginning to open or dilate and may occur several hours prior to delivery. The second stage of labor begins after the baby is born.

122. d. There can be large blood loss suffered by the mother during a miscarriage. The EMT-Basic should treat the patient for possible shock as well as provide emotional care.

123. a. More than 500 ml of blood loss after delivery is excessive; massage the mother's abdomen by rubbing firmly in one direction from the symphasis pubis bone towards the umbilicus. This will help the uterus contract and stop the bleeding. Oxygen administration, shock treatment, and rapid transport will follow uterine massage.

124. d. If meconium is present in the amniotic fluid, suction the infant before stimulating it to cry; then notify the hospital of the presence of meconium. An ALS crew may be able to perform tracheal suctioning and intubate the infant. If the lungs are stiff and noncompliant, it may indicate that aspiration of the meconium has occurred. Aspiration pneumonia due to meconium is often fatal.

125. d. In addition to providing routine emergency care, care for a rape victim should focus on preserving evidence and providing comfort and reassurance. Although you want to provide comfort to the patient, you should not allow him or her to shower or change clothes as this will destroy evidence. Any clothing or personal effects that are removed from the patient should be placed in paper bags to prevent the growth of bacteria that might occur if stored in plastic bags. You should not need to examine the genital or rectal area unless you note significant bleeding.

126. a. This condition, called supine hypotension syndrome, is the result of compression that the enlarged uterus causes on the vena cava of the maternal circulatory system. This corrective position, called the left lateral recumbent position, is accomplished by placing the mother on her left side with her legs bent slightly or kept straight. Maternal positional changes have no effect on the speed of labor or the position of the infant in the birth canal. By assisting in venous blood return in the mother, you will get the secondary effect of increasing blood flow to the uterus, but this is a secondary effect seen in correcting supine hypotension syndrome.

127. b. The patient is likely to deliver imminently, so prepare for a normal delivery.

128. c. The average length of labor for a first baby is 12 to 18 hours, but duration of labor varies greatly from one woman to another.

129. c. When the top of the baby's head is seen at the vaginal opening, birth is imminent.

130. c. Never enter a scene where hazardous materials are present until you have verified that the scene is safe. Use binoculars to survey the scene from a distance in order to identify hazardous materials placards. Consider victims and bystanders contaminated and take appropriate precautions.

131. d. Bleeding control with spurting blood carries maximum danger of contamination, and maximum protection is therefore required. Airway suctioning or intubation does not generally require the use of a cover gown, and cleaning contaminated instruments does not generally require eye/facial protection unless there is danger of splashing.

132. a. Abandonment occurs when you relinquish care without a patient's consent or without insuring that care is continued by someone of the same or higher level, such as a paramedic, ALS unit, or physician.

133. c. EMTs should not enter a crime scene until it has been secured by police. As you travel to the scene, you should determine where it is most appropriate to park your vehicle. Generally, you want cover (protection from attack) and concealment (out of direct visual range) in your staging area.

134. a. If the patient states that the contractions are very lose to each other and that each contraction lasts for a long time, imminent birth is probable; you should prepare for delivery.

135. b. To avoid misunderstanding, always repeat medical orders exactly as you heard them. Once you have done that, you can question any order you do not understand or about which you are unclear. When you complete your written patient care report, you should include the order in your report.

136. c. Speak respectfully to all patients regardless of intoxication or mental impairment; when talking to a child, consider his or her developmental level.

137. b. The sensation of needing to move one's bowels during labor is the result of the head pressing down on the anal sphincter as the baby passes through the birth canal. The head is very close to the opening of the birth canal, and delivery is imminent.

138. b. An adult of sound mind can refuse treatment, but the EMT should first make an effort to clearly explain the consequences; refusal of treatment should be documented in writing.

139. a. An emergency move is required in a situation where a patient is in immediate life-threatening danger. Emergency moves require only cervical spine stabilization (if it is a trauma situation) and should be performed quickly. Once the patient is in a safer location, you should begin with your initial assessment as you do in all patient situations.

140. a. The common procedure is to safely dispose of used airways.

141. b. The uterus is most easily felt just above the navel.

142. c. An incident management system is a coordinated system of procedures that allows for smooth operations at the scene of an emergency.

143. b. Placing napkins in the birth canal will not stop the source of bleeding. Placing bulky dressings or sanitary napkins at the vaginal opening will help prevent the blood from spreading.

144. d. Patients with breathing difficulties and serious bleeding receive the highest priority in a multiple-casualty situation.

145. c. Patients who have already died are assigned to the lowest priority when there are still living patients who require care.

146. c. Do not assume that an elderly patient is incompetent, deaf, or confused. Address all patients respectfully.

147. d. Patient information can be released only if the patient has signed a specific consent form.

148. d. This position best allows the EMT-Basic to receive the newborn baby.

149. a. If you are informed of a Do Not Resuscitate order but do not actually see it, you must still provide all necessary care.

150. c. You are responsible for helping make your patient feel at ease, but you are also responsible for operating your ambulance in the safest possible way.

EMT-Basic Practice Exam 2

CHAPTER SUMMARY

This is the second of four practice exams in this book based on the National Registry EMT-Basic written exam. Having taken one test before, you should feel more confident of your ability to pick the correct answers. Use this test to continue your study and practice. Notice how knowing what to expect makes you feel better prepared!

L ike the first exam in this book, this test is based on the National Registry exam. It should not, however, look exactly like the first test you took, because you know more now about how the test is put together. You have seen how different types of questions are presented and are perhaps beginning to notice patterns in the order of questions. You see that questions on each area are grouped together. This pattern will help you develop your own test-taking strategy.

If you're following the advice of this book, you've done some studying between this exam and the first. This second exam will give you a chance to see how much you've improved.

The answer sheet, the test, and the answer key appear next (in that order). Read the answer explanations carefully, especially the explanations for the questions you missed.

1.	(a)	(b)	(c)	(d)
2.	(a)	(b)	(c)	(d)
3.	(a)	(b)	(c)	(d)
4.	(a)	(b)	(c)	(d)
5.	(a)	(b)	(c)	(d)
6.	(a)	(b)	(c)	(d)
7.	(a)	(b)	(c)	(d)
8.	(a)	(b)	(c)	(d)
9.	(a)	(b)	(c)	(d)
10.	(a)	(b)	(c)	(d)
11.	(a)	(b)	(c)	(d)
12.	(a)	(b)	(c)	(d)
13.	(a)	(b)	(c)	(d)
14.	(a)	(b)	(c)	(d)
15.	(a)	(b)	(c)	(d)
16.	(a)	(b)	(c)	(d)
17.	(a)	(b)	(c)	(d)
18.	(a)	(b)	(c)	(d)
19.	(a)	(b)	(c)	(d)
20.	(a)	(b)	(c)	(d)
21.	(a)	(b)	(c)	(d)
22.	(a)	(b)	(c)	(d)
23.	(a)	(b)	(c)	(d)
24.	(a)	(b)	(c)	(d)
25.	(a)	(b)	(c)	(d)
26.	(a)	(b)	(c)	(d)
27.	(a)	(b)	(c)	(d)
28.	(a)	(b)	(c)	(d)
29.	(a)	(b)	(c)	(d)
30.	(a)	(b)	(c)	(d)
31.	(a)	(b)	(c)	(d)
32.	(a)	(b)	(c)	(d)
33.	(a)	(b)	(c)	(d)
34.	(a)	(b)	(c)	(d)
35.	(a)	(b)	(c)	(d)
36.	(a)	(b)	(c)	(d)
37.	(a)	(b)	(c)	(d)
38.	(a)	(b)	(c)	(d)
39.	(a)	(b)	(c)	(d)
40.	(a)	(b)	(c)	(d)
41.	(a)	(b)	(c)	(d)
42.	(a)	(b)	(c)	(d)
43.	(a)	(b)	(c)	(d)
44.	(a)	(b)	(c)	(d)
45.	(a)	(b)	(c)	(d)
46.	(a)	(b)	(c)	(d)
47.	(a)	(b)	(c)	(d)
48.	(a)	(b)	(c)	(d)
49.	(a)	(b)	(c)	(d)
50.	(a)	(b)	(c)	(d)

51.	(a)	(b)	(c)	(d)
52.	(a)	(b)	(c)	(d)
53.	(a)	(b)	(c)	(d)
54.	(a)	(b)	(c)	(d)
55.	(a)	(b)	(c)	(d)
56.	(a)	(b)	(c)	(d)
57.	(a)	(b)	(c)	(d)
58.	(a)	(b)	(c)	(d)
59.	(a)	(b)	(c)	(d)
60.	(a)	(b)	(c)	(d)
61.	(a)	(b)	(c)	(d)
62.	(a)	(b)	(c)	(d)
63.	(a)	(b)	(c)	(d)
64.	(a)	(b)	(c)	(d)
65.	(a)	(b)	(c)	(d)
66.	(a)	(b)	(c)	(d)
67.	(a)	(b)	(c)	(d)
68.	(a)	(b)	(c)	(d)
69.	(a)	(b)	(c)	(d)
70.	(a)	(b)	(c)	(d)
71.	(a)	(b)	(c)	(d)
72.	(a)	(b)	(c)	(d)
73.	(a)	(b)	(c)	(d)
74.	(a)	(b)	(c)	(d)
75.	(a)	(b)	(c)	(d)
76.	(a)	(b)	(c)	(d)
77.	(a)	(b)	(c)	(d)
78.	(a)	(b)	(c)	(d)
79.	(a)	(b)	(c)	(d)
80.	(a)	(b)	(c)	(d)
81.	(a)	(b)	(c)	(d)
82.	(a)	(b)	(c)	(d)
83.	(a)	(b)	(c)	(d)
84.	(a)	(b)	(c)	(d)
85.	(a)	(b)	(c)	(d)
86.	(a)	(b)	(c)	(d)
87.	(a)	(b)	(c)	(d)
88.	(a)	(b)	(c)	(d)
89.	(a)	(b)	(c)	(d)
90.	(a)	(b)	(c)	(d)
91.	(a)	(b)	(c)	(d)
92.	(a)	(b)	(c)	(d)
93.	(a)	(b)	(c)	(d)
94.	(a)	(b)	(c)	(d)
95.	(a)	(b)	(c)	(d)
96.	(a)	(b)	(c)	(d)
97.	(a)	(b)	(c)	(d)
98.	(a)	(b)	(c)	(d)
99.	(a)	(b)	(c)	(d)
100.	(a)	(b)	(c)	(d)

101.	(a)	(b)	(c)	(d)
102.	(a)	(b)	(c)	(d)
103.	(a)	(b)	(c)	(d)
104.	(a)	(b)	(c)	(d)
105.	(a)	(b)	(c)	(d)
106.	(a)	(b)	(c)	(d)
107.	(a)	(b)	(c)	(d)
108.	(a)	(b)	(c)	(d)
109.	(a)	(b)	(c)	(d)
110.	(a)	(b)	(c)	(d)
111.	(a)	(b)	(c)	(d)
112.	(a)	(b)	(c)	(d)
113.	(a)	(b)	(c)	(d)
114.	(a)	(b)	(c)	(d)
115.	(a)	(b)	(c)	(d)
116.	(a)	(b)	(c)	(d)
117.	(a)	(b)	(c)	(d)
118.	(a)	(b)	(c)	(d)
119.	(a)	(b)	(c)	(d)
120.	(a)	(b)	(c)	(d)
121.	(a)	(b)	(c)	(d)
122.	(a)	(b)	(c)	(d)
123.	(a)	(b)	(c)	(d)
124.	(a)	(b)	(c)	(d)
125.	(a)	(b)	(c)	(d)
126.	(a)	(b)	(c)	(d)
127.	(a)	(b)	(c)	(d)
128.	(a)	(b)	(c)	(d)
129.	(a)	(b)	(c)	(d)
130.	(a)	(b)	(c)	(d)
131.	(a)	(b)	(c)	(d)
132.	(a)	(b)	(c)	(d)
133.	(a)	(b)	(c)	(d)
134.	(a)	(b)	(c)	(d)
135.	(a)	(b)	(c)	(d)
136.	(a)	(b)	(c)	(d)
137.	(a)	(b)	(c)	(d)
138.	(a)	(b)	(c)	(d)
139.	(a)	(b)	(c)	(d)
140.	(a)	(b)	(c)	(d)
141.	(a)	(b)	(c)	(d)
142.	(a)	(b)	(c)	(d)
143.	(a)	(b)	(c)	(d)
144.	(a)	(b)	(c)	(d)
145.	(a)	(b)	(c)	(d)
146.	(a)	(b)	(c)	(d)
147.	(a)	(b)	(c)	(d)
148.	(a)	(b)	(c)	(d)
149.	(a)	(b)	(c)	(d)
150.	(a)	(b)	(c)	(d)

▶ EMT-Basic Practice Exam 2

1. Which patient's vital signs are NOT within normal limits?
   a. newborn: pulse, 100; respirations, 30; blood pressure, 70/30
   b. 3-year-old child: pulse, 90; respirations, 28; blood pressure, 86/50
   c. 10-year-old child: pulse, 88; respirations, 18; blood pressure, 100/60
   d. adult: pulse, 76; respirations, 17; blood pressure, 116/86

2. To determine a patient's pulse rate, you would count the number of beats in
   a. 15 seconds and multiply by three.
   b. 30 seconds and multiply by two.
   c. 45 seconds and divide by three.
   d. 60 seconds and divide by two.

3. A 45-year-old patient is breathing at a rate of 32 times per minute, with shallow respirations. He is altered, and his skin signs are cool, cyanotic, and diaphoretic. You should
   a. provide oxygen at six liters per minute using a nasal cannula.
   b. provide oxygen at 12 liters per minute using a nonrebreather mask.
   c. provide artificial ventilation with a BVM and high-flow oxygen.
   d. place the patient into the left lateral "recovery" position.

4. You should assess skin color by examining an adult patient's
   a. extremities.
   b. face.
   c. nailbeds.
   d. palms.

5. Which of the following patients would be described as alert and oriented?
   a. 40-year-old woman who appears to be asleep but answers you appropriately when questioned
   b. 4-year-old who refuses to tell you his name and cries to be returned to his mother's arms
   c. 65-year-old man who grimaces when you pinch his shoulder but does not answer you
   d. 59-year-old woman who tells you her name but can't remember why you are there

6. A 45-year-old patient is breathing at a rate of 22 times per minute, with adequate tidal volume. She is alert, but her skin signs are cool, pale, and diaphoretic. You should
   a. provide oxygen at six liters per minute using a nasal cannula.
   b. provide oxygen at 12 liters per minute using a nonrebreather mask.
   c. provide artificial ventilation with a BVM and high-flow oxygen.
   d. place the patient into the left lateral "recovery" position.

7. The quality of a patient's pulse consists of its strength and its
   a. rate.
   b. regularity.
   c. pressure.
   d. perfusion.

8. You would locate a patient's carotid pulse by first finding the Adam's apple and then
   a. pressing hard on only one side of the patient's neck.
   b. placing one hand gently on each side of the neck.
   c. pressing with your thumb on one side of the neck.
   d. sliding two fingers toward one side of the neck.

9. Your patient's pupils react unequally to light. You should suspect the presence of
   a. head injury.
   b. shock.
   c. airway obstruction.
   d. cardiac arrest.

10. A 70-year-old patient is complaining of shortness of breath. She has a history of emphysema. You should
   a. withhold oxygen, since these patients do not respond to oxygen.
   b. withhold oxygen, because you could eliminate the hypoxic drive.
   c. administer oxygen, because in most cases, the hypoxic drive will not be a problem.
   d. withhold oxygen, because these patients become apneic if they receive high-flow oxygen.

11. A *contusion* refers to a
   a. cut.
   b. deformity.
   c. scrape.
   d. bruise.

12. *Ecchymosis* refers to
   a. an unreactive left pupil.
   b. bruising or discoloration.
   c. motion sickness.
   d. a bad taste in the mouth.

13. Which of the following is an example of a symptom?
   a. Your patient's blood pressure is 90/65 and falling.
   b. Your patient's skin color is slightly jaundiced.
   c. Your patient is complaining of pain and nausea.
   d. Your patient has a 102-degree fever.

14. In which situation should you determine the patient's blood pressure through palpation?
   a. Your patient is under one year old.
   b. The setting is unusually quiet, such as a private home.
   c. Your patient's pulse is very weak and difficult to hear.
   d. Your patient cannot tolerate pressure to the cartoid artery.

15. The correct way to select the proper size oropharyngeal airway is to measure the distance from the
   a. corner of the mouth to the tip of the earlobe.
   b. nose to the tip of the earlobe.
   c. corner of the mouth to the nose.
   d. nose to the tip of the chin.

16. Which patient should receive only a focused physical exam and SAMPLE history?
   a. a 46-year-old man, unresponsive after falling from a 10-meter scaffold
   b. an 80-year-old man, responsive to painful stimuli after being hit by a car
   c. a 5-year-old child, responsive and in pain who fell from a standing position
   d. a 16-year-old girl, responsive to verbal stimuli after a gunshot wound

17. Your patient is a 19-year-old man who has been in a motorcycle accident and shows deformity and bleeding to the left leg. You would NOT perform a detailed physical exam if the patient
   a. said that he was feeling fine except for his leg.
   b. began to spurt blood from an open wound.
   c. was in a great deal of pain and discomfort.
   d. showed a weak pulse or other signs of shock.

18. Continuous monitoring of a patient's mental status is best accomplished by
   a. repeatedly asking the patient's name and address.
   b. continuously monitoring the patient's vital signs.
   c. continuously interacting with the patient.
   d. repeatedly assessing the peripheral circulation.

19. The reason for asking a patient her normal blood pressure reading is to determine
   a. if she is alert and oriented.
   b. if her general state of health is poor.
   c. whether you should perform a detailed exam.
   d. if a current reading is cause for concern.

20. You should assess the brachial pulse in patients who
   a. have a weak peripheral pulse.
   b. are younger than one year old.
   c. have a history of cardiac problems.
   d. have a pulse rate less than 60/min.

21. Which patient is showing early signs of shock (decreased tissue perfusion)?
   a. 23-year-old woman: pulse, 104; respiration, 25/min; BP, 118/78; cool, clammy skin
   b. 45-year-old woman: pulse, 68; respiration, 20/min; BP, 110/72; warm, moist skin
   c. 5-year-old boy: pulse, 110; respiration, 22/min; BP, 88/52; cool, dry skin
   d. 60-year-old man: pulse, 76; respiration, 10/min; BP, 96/60; hot, dry skin

22. Which of the following is the most important sign of a diabetic emergency?
   a. altered mental status
   b. warm, dry skin
   c. decreased heart rate
   d. nausea and vomiting

23. Signs and symptoms of breathing difficulty in an adult include all of the following EXCEPT
   a. distended jugular veins.
   b. accessory muscle use.
   c. decreased pulse rate.
   d. coughing.

24. Your patient, a 12-year-old girl, complains of tightness in her chest and itchy, red skin. You observe rapid, labored breathing. You should suspect the presence of
   a. a cardiac emergency.
   b. an allergic reaction.
   c. head trauma.
   d. a post-seizure state.

25. Your patient is a 45-year-old homeless man who is suspected of hypothermia. The most important question to ask him is
   a. do you know who you are and where you are?
   b. are you having any trouble breathing?
   c. are you currently taking any prescription medications?
   d. what makes the pain feel better or worse?

26. Your patient is a 68-year-old obese man who lives in an attic room. It is a summer day, and the patient is complaining of weakness, muscle and abdominal cramps, and rapid heartbeat. You should suspect
   a. cardiac emergency.
   b. respiratory emergency.
   c. hyperthermia.
   d. hypoglycemia.

27. You should suspect the possibility of shock in an adult patient who
   a. has lost 800 mL of blood.
   b. has diabetes and heart disease.
   c. takes prescription nitroglycerin.
   d. has a blood pressure of 166/120.

28. What is the most common cause of airway obstruction in an unconscious patient?
   a. vomitus
   b. mucous
   c. the tongue
   d. blood

29. All of the following are reasons that infants and children are prone to respiratory difficulties EXCEPT that they
   a. breathe faster than adults.
   b. have smaller air passages.
   c. use their diaphragm rather than their inter-costal muscles.
   d. are prone to respiratory infections.

30. Your patient is a newborn. You should consider the possibility of breathing difficulty if the respiratory rate is
   a. 40/min.
   b. 50/min.
   c. 60/min.
   d. 70/min.

31. When assessing your patient's airway, you hear snoring sounds. You should suspect that
   a. there is fluid in the airway.
   b. the tongue is blocking the airway.
   c. the bronchioles are constricted.
   d. the patient is forcefully exhaling.

32. What sign indicates that your patient's tidal volume might be inadequate?
   a. noisy, labored breathing
   b. rapid breathing
   c. inadequate chest movement
   d. slow breathing

33. As you insert an oropharyngeal airway into your patient, he begins to gag. You should
   a. attempt to reinsert the airway.
   b. remove the airway.
   c. restrain your patient and hold the airway in.
   d. contact medical control for direction.

34. You hear gurgling in your patient's airway. You should immediately
   a. administer high-flow oxygen.
   b. open and suction the airway.
   c. insert a nasopharyngeal airway.
   d. insert an oropharyngeal airway.

35. Your patient, a 49-year-old woman with a history of heart disease, has collapsed in her home. What should you do first?
   a. Administer supplemental high-flow oxygen.
   b. Find out if the patient has taken nitroglycerin.
   c. Insert an oropharyngeal airway adjunct.
   d. Open the airway and assess breathing.

36. During suctioning, you ensure that your patient does not become deprived of oxygen by
   a. suctioning for no longer than 15 seconds at a time.
   b. administering oxygen at the rate of four to six L/min.
   c. administering mouth-to-mouth respiration while suctioning.
   d. suctioning only during insertion of the catheter.

37. The correct way to select the size of a nasopharyngeal airway is to measure
- **a.** from the corner of the mouth to the angle of the jaw.
- **b.** from the earlobe to the corner of the jaw.
- **c.** the diameter of the patient's little finger.
- **d.** from the chin to the Adam's apple.

38. In what position should you place a child's head for ventilation?
- **a.** in the neutral position
- **b.** slightly hyperextended
- **c.** slightly flexed foward
- **d.** in the recovery position

39. Your patient has a foreign-body airway obstruction. Three attempts to clear the airway have been unsuccessful. You should
- **a.** transport and attempt to clear the airway en route.
- **b.** call for an Advanced Life Support unit as backup.
- **c.** request medical direction for further instructions.
- **d.** carry out three additional cycles before requesting help.

40. Your patient's chest rise during bag-valve-mask ventilation is inadequate, even after you reposition the jaw. Your next step should be to
- **a.** suction the patient.
- **b.** check for cyanosis.
- **c.** check the heart rate.
- **d.** check the mask seal.

41. After obtaining medical direction, you are helping your patient use a prescribed inhaler. You should tell the patient to
- **a.** take three quick, shallow breaths.
- **b.** inhale deeply and hold his or her breath.
- **c.** exhale as slowly as he or she can.
- **d.** lie down to prevent dizziness.

42. Your patient, a 78-year-old man, has no pulse and agonal respirations. You should
- **a.** begin CPR immediately.
- **b.** administer high-flow oxygen via bag-valve mask.
- **c.** transport immediately to the closest medical facility.
- **d.** request the patient's permission to administer nitroglycerin.

43. Most inhalers work by
- **a.** providing moisture to the lungs.
- **b.** dilating the bronchioles.
- **c.** increasing alveolar blood flow.
- **d.** increasing the respiratory rate.

44. You have assisted a patient in administering a prescribed inhaler. After one dose of the medication, the patient's pulse rate increases, and he reports feeling nauseated. You should
- **a.** administer another dose of the medication.
- **b.** assess respiratory rate, rhythm, and quality.
- **c.** document and report the signs and symptoms.
- **d.** begin cardiopulmonary resuscitation.

45. You should remove your patient's dentures in order to provide ventilation when
- **a.** head trauma has occurred.
- **b.** it is necessary to insert an oral airway.
- **c.** they become dislodged.
- **d.** they make the patient uncomfortable.

46. During the management of a cardiac arrest, the automated external defibrillator gives a "no shock indicated" message. Which of the following statements will most likely prompt this condition?
   a. The patient's rhythm is asystole.
   b. The patient has a pulse.
   c. The patient is in ventricular tachycardia.
   d. The patient is in ventricular fibrillation.

47. You should use a nasal cannula for a patient who
   a. cannot tolerate a mask.
   b. cannot hold the mask in place.
   c. is elderly.
   d. has a blocked airway.

48. The purpose of quickly opening and closing the valve on an oxygen tank before attaching the regulator is to
   a. ensure the valve is facing away from you and the patient.
   b. blow dirt or contamination out of the opening.
   c. ensure the tank is filled.
   d. check the pressure inside the tank.

49. All of the following are signs of difficult breathing EXCEPT
   a. abdominal pain.
   b. restlessness.
   c. retractions.
   d. unequal breath sounds.

50. A set of "stacked" shocks means that
   a. six shocks have been delivered with no pause for a pulse check.
   b. one shock, followed by CPR, and then three more shocks are delivered.
   c. three shocks have been delivered with no pause for a pulse check.
   d. three shocks have been delivered with pulse checks after each shock.

51. You have delivered three shocks with the semiautomatic defibrillator. Your cardiac arrest patient has shallow, agonal respirations with a pulse. What should you do next?
   a. Deliver second shock to assure patient does not arrest again.
   b. Provide artificial ventilation with high-concentration oxygen.
   c. Give high-concentration oxygen by nonrebreather mask.
   d. Check pulse and deliver two more shocks.

52. For an adult patient, you would deliver artificial ventilations at the rate of one breath every
   a. two seconds.
   b. five seconds.
   c. eight seconds.
   d. ten seconds.

53. It is permissible to use the head-tilt/chin-lift on a trauma patient only if
   a. there is no other way to open the airway.
   b. a third EMT is available to stabilize the spine.
   c. you have already performed CPR for 15 minutes.
   d. no medical backup is available.

54. The nasopharyngeal airway is preferred over the oropharyngeal airway for responsive patients because it
   a. is shorter and easier to insert.
   b. can move the tongue out of the airway.
   c. is unlikely to stimulate the gag reflex.
   d. comes in a wide variety of sizes.

55. The function of the white blood cells is to
   a. form clots.
   b. fight infection.
   c. carry oxygen.
   d. carry nutrients.

56. Angina differs from a heart attack because in an attack of angina, the
   a. patient feels severe chest pain.
   b. pain radiates outward from the heart.
   c. administration of nitroglycerin provides no relief.
   d. heart muscle is not permanently damaged.

57. The following patients all have signs and symptoms of cardiac chest pain and have their own prescriptions for nitroglycerin. Which patient should you NOT assist with taking nitroglycerin?
   a. 67-year-old man: BP, 98/72; pulse, 90; respirations, 26/min
   b. 72-year-old woman: BP, 140/96; pulse, 88; respirations, 23/min
   c. 78-year-old man: BP, 160/112; pulse, 98; respirations, 26/min
   d. 51-year-old woman: BP, 130/80; pulse, 72; respirations, 14/min

58. When deciding whether to assist a patient in administering nitroglycerin, you should check the medicine for the patient's name, the route of administration, the dose, and the
   a. doctor who prescribed it.
   b. quantity still available.
   c. pharmacy.
   d. expiration date.

59. Your patient, a 67-year-old man with a history of cardiac disease, is unresponsive. After checking ABCs and finding no pulse, you begin CPR. The next thing you should do is
   a. administer oxygen.
   b. call for ALS backup.
   c. attach the AED.
   d. request medical direction.

60. Your patient is showing signs and symptoms of shock and has a tender abdomen. She reports vomiting material that "looked like coffee grounds." You should suspect
   a. ruptured appendix.
   b. internal bleeding.
   c. fractured pelvis.
   d. inhaled poisoning.

61. Which patient is showing signs and symptoms of cardiac compromise?
   a. 85-year-old man: difficulty breathing, high fever, rapid pulse
   b. 72-year-old woman: wheezing, labored breathing, tightness in throat
   c. 53-year-old woman: dull chest pain, sudden sweating, difficulty breathing
   d. 51-year-old man: headache, dizziness, gagging, chest pain

62. Which blood vessel carries oxygen-poor blood to the heart?
   a. vena cava
   b. aorta
   c. pulmonary artery
   d. pulmonary vein

63. Which chamber of the heart pumps oxygen-rich blood out to the body tissues?
   a. right atrium
   b. right ventricle
   c. left atrium
   d. left ventricle

64. Central pulses may be palpated at the
   a. carotid and radial arteries.
   b. radial and brachial arteries.
   c. carotid and femoral arteries.
   d. brachial and femoral arteries.

65. The diastolic blood pressure represents the pressure in the brachial artery when the
   a. ventricles contract.
   b. ventricles are at rest.
   c. cardiac artery is stressed.
   d. aorta is distended.

66. If the AED provides a "no shock indicated" message after delivering four shocks, what should you do next?
   a. Check pulse and deliver a shock if the pulse is absent.
   b. Check patient's pulse and breathing.
   c. Contact medical control for further direction.
   d. Deliver oxygen by nonrebreather mask.

67. Your patient is complaining of chest pain. Which question would you ask to assess the O part of the OPQRST algorithm?
   a. What were you doing when the pain started?
   b. What does the pain feel like?
   c. How long ago did the pain begin?
   d. How bad is the pain now?

68. All of the following are contraindictions for the administration of nitroglycerin EXCEPT when the patient
   a. has a systolic blood pressure of less than 100 mm Hg.
   b. has taken a previous dose of nitroglycerin two minutes ago.
   c. has a heart rate less than 60 beats per minute.
   d. is an infant or child.

69. Which of the following is a side effect of nitroglycerin?
   a. hypertension
   b. drowsiness
   c. nausea
   d. headache

70. A patient is in greater danger of severe internal bleeding from fracturing which bone?
   a. pelvis
   b. rib
   c. femur
   d. tibia

71. Your patient suffered head trauma in a fall from a ladder. There is slight bleeding, mixed with clear fluid, from the ears. After stabilizing the spine and managing the airway and breathing, you should care for this bleeding by
   a. applying concentrated direct pressure.
   b. covering lightly with a sterile dressing.
   c. applying the PASG/MAST garment.
   d. requesting permission to use a tourniquet.

72. Your patient, the victim of a stabbing, is bleeding profusely from a wound on his upper arm. Your first action should be to
   a. apply concentrated direct pressure.
   b. apply diffuse direct pressure.
   c. manage the airway and breathing.
   d. elevate the limb and apply pressure points.

73. A 64-year-old female has just collapsed in cardiac arrest. You are alone. After your initial assessment, you should give two ventilations, then
   a. analyze the rhythm, and deliver a shock if indicated.
   b. begin chest compressions for one minute.
   c. analyze the rhythm, and begin chest compressions.
   d. call medical control, and begin chest compressions.

74. You have received medical control permission to apply the PASG/MAST to your patient who has severe bleeding, caused by soft-tissue damage, below the knee on both legs. Which compartments of the PASGs should you inflate?
   a. all three compartments
   b. the abdominal compartment
   c. both leg compartments
   d. None, PASG is not indicated.

75. A patient who has been resuscitated from a cardiac arrest is
   a. at a high risk of going back into arrest.
   b. not likely to go into arrest again.
   c. less likely to arrest if shocked at least six times.
   d. less likely to arrest after three shocks.

76. Your patient is bleeding heavily from a puncture wound on her right leg. Your attempt to stop the bleeding with a gloved fingertip placed over the wound is unsuccessful. Your next step should be to
   a. remove the gauze to ensure you have it over the right location.
   b. elevate the limb and apply more diffuse pressure on the leg.
   c. use pressure point pressure on the femoral artery.
   d. apply and inflate the right leg of the PASG/MAST garment.

77. You should elevate a patient's leg to control bleeding only if
   a. medical direction has refused permission to apply PASGs.
   b. no other method successfully stops the bleeding.
   c. there are no signs or symptoms of skeletal injury.
   d. arterial bleeding is present.

78. One of the most common problems with automated external defibrillators is
   a. battery failure.
   b. arcing.
   c. misinterpretation of shockable rhythms.
   d. battery explosions.

79. After assisting a patient to administer nitroglycerin, you should
   a. transport the patient immediately.
   b. place the patient in Trendelenburg position.
   c. give a second dose two minutes later.
   d. reassess vital signs and chest pain.

80. The automated external defibrillator is used to detect
   a. the patient's pulse rate and rhythm.
   b. electrical activity of the heart.
   c. the contraction force of the heart.
   d. degree of cardiac compromise.

81. Your patient, the victim of a car accident, has an obvious injury to her right leg. You should splint the injury before moving her UNLESS
   a. transport time is less than 15 minutes.
   b. the patient is in severe pain.
   c. bones are protruding through the skin.
   d. life-threatening injuries are present.

82. External bleeding that is profuse and spurting with each heartbeat, is from
   a. an artery.
   b. a vein.
   c. a capillary.
   d. all of the above.

83. To help control profuse bleeding from the wrist, you should apply pressure at the
   a. brachial artery.
   b. femoral artery.
   c. temporal artery.
   d. carotid artery.

84. Which mechanism of injury suggests the likelihood of a spinal injury?
a. restrained patient in a motor vehicle crash
b. stabbing penetration to the upper torso
c. arm injured while playing tennis
d. gunshot wound to the upper thigh

85. Your patient is a 17-year-old who has just fallen off a tall ladder. What is the first thing you should do after you have immobilized the cervical spine?
a. Transport the patient immediately.
b. Ask the patient to try to turn his or her head.
c. Reassess the airway.
d. Provide oxygen.

86. Your patient is a 33-year-old woman with a suspected spinal cord injury. After you have immobilized her to a long board, she vomits. What should you do?
a. Reassess her vital signs.
b. Ask her what she last ate.
c. Remove the board and suction the airway.
d. Tilt the board to clear the airway.

87. Your patient is a 28-year-old man who appears intoxicated. Bystanders report that the man seemed fine but suddenly began "acting strange." You should first suspect
a. alcohol abuse.
b. poisoning.
c. diabetic emergency.
d. allergic reaction.

88. Which of the following signs may indicate shock?
a. a blood pressure of 120/80
b. a pulse rate of 78
c. a respiration rate of 18
d. cool, pale skin

89. Your patient is a 23-year-old woman who calmly tells you that her thoughts are controlling the weather. Her body language and speech are nonthreatening and gentle. You should
a. request immediate police backup for protection.
b. talk quietly to this patient and keep her calm.
c. request permission to restrain the patient.
d. take a detailed medical history.

90. A 17-year-old patient is experiencing difficulty breathing and abdominal pain after being struck with a bat in his left lower quadrant. He is alert, cool, and diaphoretic, with a tachycardic heart rate. You should provide oxygen using a
a. nonrebreather mask at 15 liters per minute.
b. nasal cannula at six liters per minute.
c. nasal cannula at two liters per minute.
d. nonrebreather mask at eight liters per minute.

91. Which patient should receive oral glucose?
a. 25-year-old man: collapsed after exercise, unresponsive, history of diabetes
b. 31-year-old woman: altered mental status, history of epileptic seizures
c. 33-year-old man: altered mental status, sudden onset, no medical history
d. 38-year-old woman: altered mental status, sudden onset, history of diabetes

92. The last vital sign to change in a patient going into shock is
a. an increased pulse rate.
b. a decreased blood pressure.
c. an increased respiration rate.
d. cool, clammy, pale skin.

93. The central nervous system consists of the brain and the
a. spinal cord.
b. spinal nerves.
c. cranial nerves.
d. spinal vertebrae.

94. Your patient has climbed out of his car unassisted after a car crash, but he is now complaining of back pain. You should
a. transport him in whatever position is the most comfortable.
b. immobilize him to a long spine board with a standing take-down.
c. immobilize him to a short spine board in the sitting position.
d. immobilize him with a Kendrick Extrication Device.

95. Which of the following sign or symptom is NOT associated with hypoperfusion?
a. nausea
b. increased pulse rate
c. decreased blood pressure
d. diarrhea

96. Your first priority when dealing with a patient in shock is to
a. maintain an open airway.
b. control external hemorrhage.
c. assess the carotid pulse.
d. administer high-concentration oxygen.

97. Which of the following signs or symptoms might you expect to see in a patient suffering from hypothermia?
a. confused behavior
b. excessive mucous production
c. blood tinged sputum
d. burning or itching in the underarms

98. With medical direction, you may administer epinephrine from a patient's own autoinjector if the patient displays signs and symptoms of respiratory distress or
a. cardiac arrest.
b. diabetic emergency.
c. hypoperfusion.
d. poisoning.

99. Emergency care for the early local cold injury includes
a. gently massaging the affected area.
b. preventing the affected area from any further cold exposure.
c. covering the affected area with cold, moist dressings.
d. forcing the patient to drink hot fluids.

100. Which patient is most likely suffering from hypothermia?
a. 79-year-old woman: living in unheated house, outside temperature 40 degrees Fahrenheit
b. 65-year-old man: dressed appropriately, walking briskly, outside temperature 26 degrees Fahrenheit
c. 43-year-old woman: swimming actively, outside temperature 85 degrees Fahrenheit
d. 10-year-old child: swimming actively, outside temperature 78 degrees Fahrenheit

101. Which set of vital signs suggests early hypothermia?
a. pulse, 56 and faint; respirations, 9/min, shallow; BP, 96/60; cyanotic; sluggish pupils
b. pulse, 74; respirations, 16/min, strong; BP, 124/80; cool, dry skin; reactive pupils
c. pulse, 92; respirations, 26/min; BP, 118/76, flushed (red) skin, reactive pupils
d. pulse, 68; respirations, 13/min, irregular; BP, 110/70; hot, moist skin; reactive pupils

102. As a result of the mental status changes that accompany hypothermia, a patient may
a. speak rapidly and fluently.
b. behave inappropriately.
c. become extremely thirsty.
d. complain of headache.

103. What is the goal of emergency care for a hypothermic patient with a reduced level of consciousness?
  a. to actively warm the patient
  b. to keep the patient active
  c. to provide fluids and oxygen
  d. to prevent further heat loss

104. Your patient, a 76-year-old male, lives in a trailer without air conditioning. He complains of weakness and cramps in his legs and abdomen. Emergency care includes all of the following EXCEPT
  a. giving the patient oxygen by a non-rebreather mask.
  b. placing the patient in a bathtub with cool water.
  c. applying moist towels over cramped muscles.
  d. putting the patient in supine position with his legs elevated.

105. You should suspect a heat-related emergency if the patient
  a. has constricted pupils.
  b. complains of leg cramps after running several miles.
  c. has breath that smells like nail polish remover after strenuous exercise.
  d. complains of itchy skin on a warm summer day.

106. A child's tongue is more likely to cause an airway obstruction than an adult's because it
  a. is relatively large compared to the size of the mouth.
  b. is more flexible than an adult's tongue.
  c. is softer than an adult's tongue.
  d. has weaker muscles than an adult's tongue.

107. While providing artificial ventilation to a 14-year-old near-drowning patient, you feel resistance in the airway. The possible cause of the resistance is that
  a. the trachea is too short.
  b. there is water in the stomach.
  c. the patient has chronic obstructive pulmonary disease.
  d. the epiglottis is swollen, causing an obstruction.

108. The correct rate for providing artificial ventilations to infants and children is
  a. 8 breaths per minute.
  b. 12 breaths per minute.
  c. 20 breaths per minute.
  d. 24 breaths per minute.

109. All of the following conditions are common causes of behavioral emergencies EXCEPT
  a. low blood sugar.
  b. lack of oxygen.
  c. head trauma.
  d. an allergic reaction.

110. Care for an unresponsive infant with a complete airway obstruction includes
  a. giving sub-diaphragmatic thrusts and ventilation.
  b. performing back blows and ventilation attempts.
  c. performing continuous chest thrusts until clear.
  d. giving back blows, chest thrusts, and ventilation.

111. It is important to recognize signs of early respiratory distress in a child. A sign of early respiratory distress includes
  a. audible wheezing.
  b. decreased heart rate.
  c. breathing rate of 22.
  d. altered mental status.

112. A common side effect of high fever in infants and small children is
  a. shock.
  b. seizures.
  c. hives.
  d. cardiac arrest.

113. Your patient is an 8-month-old infant with a recent history of vomiting and diarrhea. Which signs should alert you to the possibility of shock?
  a. dry diaper and the absence of tears while crying
  b. capillary refill time of two seconds or less
  c. strong peripheral pulses; heart rate of 100
  d. skin that is flushed and hot to the touch

114. An 11-month-old crying female has swallowed a piece of a hot dog. She is coughing, and you can hear high-pitched sounds coming from the throat. You should
  a. administer back blows and chest thrusts.
  b. perform a blind finger sweep to attempt removal of the object.
  c. provide high concentration oxygen by blow-by mask.
  d. provide ventilations by bag-valve mask and oxygen.

115. Your patient is a 3-year-old girl. What is the best way to calm her before examining her?
  a. Have her parents leave the room.
  b. Talk to her in a soft baby-talk voice.
  c. Pretend to examine her doll or teddy bear.
  d. Perform painful procedures last.

116. The "sniffing position" refers to the
  a. way children position themselves when feeling respiratory distress.
  b. recovery position used for children in respiratory distress.
  c. position used to insert the oropharyngeal or nasopharyngeal airway.
  d. placement of a child's head for the head-lift/chin-tilt maneuver.

117. Your patient is a 29-year-old woman pregnant with her third child. She tells you, "My water broke fifteen minutes ago, and the contractions are two minutes apart, lasting one minute each." The nearest hospital is 30 minutes away. You should
  a. call for ALS assistance.
  b. transport the patient.
  c. prepare for delivery.
  d. provide oxygen.

118. A 5-year-old male is experiencing severe respiratory distress. He is altered with poor skin signs. You should
  a. assist ventilations with a pediatric bag-valve mask and supplemental oxygen.
  b. perform blind finger sweeps to attempt to remove an obstruction.
  c. provide oxygen by pediatric nonrebreather mask.
  d. provide oxygen by the blow-by method.

119. You are assisting in a delivery in the field. When the baby's head appears during crowning, the first thing you should do is
   a. exert gentle pressure on the mother's perineum and the baby's head to prevent too-rapid delivery and tearing the perineum.
   b. pull gently downward to deliver the baby's upper shoulder, then tilt the child downward to deliver the other shoulder.
   c. break the amniotic sac, push it away from the baby's face, and check for the location of the umbilical cord.
   d. suction the baby's mouth and then the nose, and monitor the ventilatory efforts providing supplemental oxygen via blow-by.

120. Fontanelles are the
   a. strong contractions that signal the end of labor.
   b. soft spots located on the infant's head.
   c. blood vessels in the umbilical cord.
   d. special forceps doctors use to assist the delivery.

121. After an infant is born, wrap him in a blanket and position him on his side with his
   a. arms and legs tightly wrapped.
   b. head lower than his trunk.
   c. head on his mother's shoulder.
   d. back resting on his mother's breast.

122. The third stage of labor consists of the
   a. delivery of the placenta.
   b. full dilation of the cervix.
   c. birth of the baby.
   d. onset uterine contractions.

123. You have just assisted in the delivery of a newborn who has good color, a strong pulse, and is not yet breathing. You should
   a. suction the infant again.
   b. slap the baby's back vigorously.
   c. massage the baby's back gently.
   d. provide artificial ventilation.

124. Amniotic fluid with a yellow or brownish color means a high likelihood of
   a. miscarriage.
   b. infectious disease.
   c. excessive bleeding.
   d. fetal distress.

125. Your patient is a 19-year-old woman who is experiencing profuse vaginal bleeding. Which question is most appropriate to ask the patient during the SAMPLE history?
   a. What is causing the bleeding?
   b. When was the last sexual contact?
   c. Could you be pregnant?
   d. Are you scared?

126. You are assessing a newborn. To give an APGAR score of "1" for appearance, you would need to see
   a. blue extremities and trunk.
   b. blue extremities and pink trunk.
   c. pink trunk and head.
   d. red trunk and head.

127. Your patient is a 24-year-old woman who tells you that she is three months pregnant. She is experiencing profuse vaginal bleeding and severe cramping. After administering oxygen, you should
- **a.** be alert for signs and symptoms of shock, and transport quickly.
- **b.** prepare for an emergency on-scene delivery of a premature infant.
- **c.** attempt to stop the bleeding before transporting the patient.
- **d.** place the patient on her left side and call for an ALS unit.

128. Your patient is a 28-year-old pregnant woman who has just been in a minor car accident. Which set of vital signs would be normal for this patient?
- **a.** pulse, 80; respirations, 14; BP, 108/72
- **b.** pulse, 58; respirations, 24; BP, 118/78
- **c.** pulse, 96; respirations, 8; BP, 124/86
- **d.** pulse, 82; respirations, 22; BP, 140/96

129. Which of the following signs and symptoms may indicate shock in children?
- **a.** an alert mental state
- **b.** increased urine output
- **c.** excessive tear production
- **d.** cool, clammy skin

130. As an EMT-Basic, you are acting as a patient advocate when you
- **a.** document the care you provide.
- **b.** treat patients with dignity and respect.
- **c.** continue your education and training.
- **d.** consult with medical direction in the field.

131. The first stage of the grieving process is likely to consist of which of the following?
- **a.** denial
- **b.** anger
- **c.** bargaining
- **d.** depression

132. The following are all effective techniques for stress reduction EXCEPT
- **a.** getting more exercise.
- **b.** seeking professional help.
- **c.** working extra hours.
- **d.** eating a healthy diet.

133. To be effective, hand washing should continue for at least
- **a.** 1–2 minutes.
- **b.** 45–50 seconds.
- **c.** 25–30 seconds.
- **d.** 10–15 seconds.

134. It is necessary to wear a mask and eye protection when
- **a.** transporting a patient.
- **b.** suctioning a patient.
- **c.** splinting a closed injury.
- **d.** administering oxygen.

135. Which statement about disposable gloves is correct?
- **a.** You should remove gloves by grasping the ends of the fingers and pulling them off right side out.
- **b.** It is not necessary to wear gloves when suctioning or ventilating a patient with a bag-valve-mask device.
- **c.** Gloves protect both you and the patient from the transmission of infectious diseases.
- **d.** One pair of gloves is sufficient for any call, no matter how many patients there are.

136. Which of the following situations illustrates implied consent?
  a. You splint the broken arm and leg of a 6-year-old girl with her mother's permission.
  b. You care for a cardiac patient who asks you to help him take a dose of nitroglycerin.
  c. You arrive at the scene of a car crash, and the injured driver says, "Please help my child first."
  d. You provide life support to a man who was found unconscious by bystanders who called EMS.

137. Placing a patient in the recovery position allows
  a. the patient to breathe more deeply.
  b. secretions to drain more easily.
  c. the EMT to position the airway.
  d. the EMT to provide basic life support.

138. During the scene size-up, you should determine whether the scene is safe to enter and whether
  a. you need any additional help.
  b. the patient's ABCs are normal.
  c. you need to contact dispatch.
  d. the patient is sick or a trauma victim.

139. Because EMS communications channels are considered to be public channels, you should transmit confidential information
  a. without naming the patient.
  b. in confidential codes.
  c. by spelling the name.
  d. only if a tape is being made.

140. Which of the following is NOT part of the standard medical report you give to the receiving facility?
  a. mental status
  b. history of present illness
  c. medical diagnosis
  d. vital signs

141. You are splinting the injured leg of a 5-year-old. What should you say?
  a. "It is necessary to immobilize the extremity to prevent further injury."
  b. "After I strap your leg to this board, it won't hurt so much."
  c. "Stop crying! I can't work when you're making loud noises."
  d. "Mom, if your child stops crying, I'll explain what I'm doing."

142. When your patient does not speak English, it is best to
  a. avoid speaking to the patient, so you are not misunderstood.
  b. write down everything you do, and have the patient sign it.
  c. try to find a relative or bystander who can interpret.
  d. refuse the call and request a bilingual EMT.

143. Which of the following is an example of a subjective statement that could be included in a prehospital care report?
  a. Bystander stated, "He was drunk as a skunk."
  b. Patient vomited two times during transport.
  c. Bystanders assisted EMTs in moving patient.
  d. Patient is unsure of the reason for the call.

144. While caring for a distraught child, you are too busy to take a required set of vital signs. When filling out the patient record, you should
  a. repeat the values for the last set of vital signs you took.
  b. omit any mention of vital signs.
  c. file an error report.
  d. document only the care you actually gave.

145. As an EMT-Basic, your first responsibility when called to a potentially hazardous scene is to
a. protect your own safety.
b. extricate patients.
c. triage patients.
d. protect the safety of bystanders and patients.

146. Which of the following is an example of care that would be provided by the EMT performing triage at a mass-casualty incident?
a. covering the patient to prevent shock
b. opening the airway
c. starting CPR
d. applying PASGs

147. Which patient would be given the lowest priority during triage?
a. an 80-year-old man: multiple fractures on extremities without severe bleeding
b. a 56-year-old woman: compromised airway
c. a 34-year-old man: signs of internal bleeding from pelvic injury
d. a 28-year-old woman: second degree burns, intact airway

148. Which of the following describes an emergency patient move?
a. The patient cannot be cared for adequately in the present location.
b. Because of danger, there is no time to immobilize the spine.
c. The patient is being moved to a more comfortable location.
d. The patient is being moved against his or her will.

149. You are called to the scene of a shooting. While caring for the victim, you see a gun and some empty cartridges. You should
a. ignore them while you continue to provide treatment to the patient.
b. pick them up and give them to the nearest law enforcement officer.
c. collect them as evidence, but include their locations in your report.
d. inform a law enforcement officer immediately of your discovery.

150. In which situation should you wear protective eyewear, in addition to gloves and a gown?
a. when handling contaminated instruments
b. when taking vital signs
c. when controlling arterial bleeding
d. when splinting a closed wound

► Answers

1. a. Normal values for a newborn are: pulse, 120–160; respirations, 40–60; blood pressure, 80/40.

2. b. Pulse rate is the number of beats per minute, determined by counting the number of beats in 30 seconds and multiplying by two. Some providers take a shortcut by counting the pulse for 15 seconds and multiplying by four, but this practice is not encouraged, as you could miss a patient with an abnormal pulse rate.

3. c. Based on the information provided, the patient is breathing too quickly to provide his own adequate ventilations. This patient cannot be managed with a nonrebreather alone; artificial ventilations are needed to oxygenate the patient adequately.

4. c. Assess skin color in an adult patient by examining the nailbeds, oral mucosa, and conjunctiva.

5. b. An alert child of any age will prefer his or her parent to a stranger and may refuse to answer your questions.

6. b. Based on the information provided, the patient is ventilating adequately but has poor skin signs, indicating inadequate perfusion. High-flow oxygen via a nonrebreather mask should ensure that the patient is fully oxygenated.

7. b. The *quality* of a patient's pulse refers to strength and regularity, or rhythm. When you assess pulse, you should assess rate and quality.

8. d. When assessing the carotid pulse, first locate the Adam's apple and then slide two fingers toward one side of the neck; never exert strong pressure or assess the carotid pulse on both sides of the neck at the same time.

9. a. Head injury, eye injury, or drug use may cause the pupils to be nonreactive or unequally reactive. Shock, airway obstruction, and cardiac arrest will cause both pupils to dilate equally.

10. c. While it may be true that providing high levels of oxygen over prolonged time periods may cause the hypoxic drive to fail, it is a rare occurrence in the prehospital field. With the complaint of shortness of breath, it is better to ensure that the patient is fully oxygenated rather than taking a chance that she is hypoxic. The EMT-Basic is prepared to ventilate the patient if she goes into respiratory arrest due to the high levels of oxygen.

11. d. A contusion is a bruise, or damage to the underlying tissues without a break in the skin. A scrape is called a contusion. A cut is a laceration, and a deformity is an oddly shaped body structure.

12. b. Blood under the skin, appearing on the surface as a bruise, is also known as ecchymosis.

13. c. A symptom is subjective information, something your patient described to you, such as pain or nausea; the other options are objective signs, or conditions you note, such as vital signs.

14. c. Use palpation only when it is difficult to hear the pulse, either because the setting is extremely noisy or because the patient's pulse is very weak.

15. a. The other methods will provide an either too large or too small measurement of an OPA.

16. c. You can omit the detailed physical exam if your patient shows no alterations in consciousness and if the mechanism of injury does not suggest high risk of trauma.

17. b. Do not perform a detailed physical exam if, as in the case of suspected arterial bleeding, your time should be devoted to caring for the airway, breathing, or circulation.

18. c. The best way to monitor the patient's mental status is to interact with the patient so that you are immediately aware of any changes.

19. d. Always ask the patient her normal pulse or blood-pressure reading, since it will help you determine if the current reading is abnormal or normal for the particular patient.

20. b. Assess the brachial pulse instead of the radial or carotid in patients less than one year old.

21. a. Patient **a**, with elevated pulse and respiratory rate and cool, clammy skin, is showing early signs of shock. Patients **b** and **c** have normal vital signs. Patient **d** has a normal pulse, low blood pressure, and slow respiratory rate but hot and dry skin, so shock is not clearly evident in this patient.

22. a. The most important sign of a diabetic emergency is altered mental status; patients may appear intoxicated or act anxious or combative. Patients who present an altered level of consciousness should have an evaluation for diabetic emergency.

23. c. Decreased pulse rate may mean breathing difficulty in a child, but not in an adult. Distended neck veins indicate a chest wall injury or fluid overload. Coughing may indicate an asthma attack in a child, but not an adult.

24. b. Rash and breathing difficulty are the two most common signs of an allergic reaction.

25. a. Assessing the patient's level of consciousness will help you find out the stage of hypothermia and what treatment the patient needs.

26. c. Because of the patient's age, the signs and symptoms, and his living conditions, you should suspect hyperthermia.

27. a. You should suspect that a patient with this amount of blood loss will have decreased tissue perfusion, and be prepared to treat accordingly.

28. c. Although all the choices can cause airway obstruction, the tongue is the most common cause, especially in unconscious patients.

29. a. Infants and children are prone to breathing difficulties because they have small air passages that are easily occluded; they also rely heavily on their diaphragms and suffer frequent respiratory infections.

30. d. The normal respiratory rate for an infant is 40–60 per minute.

31. b. Snoring indicates that the tongue has relaxed into the upper airway, partially obstructing it.

32. c. Inadequate chest movement with breathing indicates that the tidal volume (the amount of air moved with each breath) may be inadequate.

33. b. Attempting to reinsert the airway, or forcibly keeping it in, will very likely cause the patient to vomit and compromise his airway.

34. b. Gurgling is a sign that fluid is present in the airway; the correct procedure is to immediately open and suction the airway. An airway adjunct may be used to assist in maintaining airway patency once it is cleared.

35. d. The first step in treating a nonresponsive patient is to open the airway.

36. a. To ensure that the patient does not become deprived of oxygen while suctioning, suction for no longer than 15 seconds at a time. Provide high-flow oxygen via the device most appropriate for that patient.

37. c. An alternative method is to measure from the tip of the nose to the tip of the ear. The other choices will produce too small or too large of a measurement.

38. b. A child's head should be slightly hyperextended for ventilation in a position called the "sniffing position." For infants, the correct position is the neutral position with padding placed below the shoulders and upper back. You should never flex the airway forward as this will close off the airway. The recovery position is used for spontaneously breathing patients to protect their airway.

39. a. If you are unsuccessful at clearing the airway after three attempts, transport immediately, continuing your attempts en route.

40. d. After repositioning the jaw to make sure the airway remains open, you should make sure that the mask seal is adequate by listening for air leaking through the sides of the mask.

41. b. The patient should inhale deeply and hold his or her breath to absorb the medicine.

42. a. Agonal respirations are a sign that the patient is nearing death. Because he is also pulseless, begin CPR immediately.

43. b. Inhalers, also called bronchodilators, work by dilating the bronchioles and thus decreasing resistance inside the airways and increasing airflow.

44. c. Document all side effects of medication administration and report them to the receiving facility; besides increased pulse rate and nausea, other common side effects are tremors and nervousness.

45. c. Because dentures can make it easier to obtain a good mask seal, you should remove them only if they become dislodged.

46. a. While **b** may seem correct, an AED cannot detect a pulse. It can only detect an organized rhythm that may produce a pulse.

47. a. While a nasal cannula is a low-flow oxygen device, it is also used for supplemental oxygen when a mask will not be tolerated. The liter flow of the nasal cannula shold not be set above six liters per minute.

48. b. Before attaching a regulator to an oxygen tank, always open and close the valve quickly to remove dirt or contamination from the opening so it does not clog the regulator.

49. a. Abdominal breathing, not abdominal pain, may be a sign of a breathing difficulty.

50. c. During the initial defibrillation attempts, up to three shocks are delivered immediately after each other without delaying for a pulse check in between each shock.

51. b. A nonrebreather mask will not be adequate to provide ventilations. Additional electrical shocks may actually send the patient back into a pulseless rhythm.

52. b. Deliver artificial ventilations to an adult patient at the rate of one breath every five seconds, or 12 per minute.

53. a. Use the head-tilt/chin-lift on a suspected trauma patient only if you cannot open the airway by any other means.

54. c. The nasopharyngeal airway is preferable for responsive patients because it is less likely to stimulate the gag reflex than an oropharyngeal airway.

55. b. The white blood cells, which make up a part of the body's immune system, fight infections.

56. d. In angina, unlike a heart attack, the reduced blood flow to the heart does not result in permanent damage.

57. a. Do not administer nitroglycerin if the patient's systolic blood pressure is below 100 mm Hg.

58. d. Before assisting a patient to administer nitroglycerin, check for the right patient, the right route of administration, the right dose, and the expiration date.

59. c. After verifying that there is no pulse and opening the airway, your first priority is to attach the AED and determine if defibrillation is required.

60. b. "Coffee-grounds" vomit is digested blood and indicates the presence of internal bleeding, as do abdominal tenderness and signs and symptoms of shock. A ruptured appendix and fractured pelvis will not cause bleeding into the GI tract. Ingested poisoning may or may not result in GI bleeding, but inhaled poisoning will result in respiratory problems.

61. c. This woman shows classic signs of cardiac compromise: dull chest pain, sudden onset of sweating, and difficulty breathing.

62. a. The vena cava carries oxygen-poor blood from the body to the right atrium, so it can be transported to the right ventricle and from there, to the lungs.

63. d. Oxygen-rich blood reaches the left atrium from the lungs via the pulmonary veins; then, the left ventricle pumps it out to the rest of the body.

64. c. Central pulses may be palpated at the carotid artery in the neck and at the femoral artery in the groin. The brachial and radial pulses are peripheral pulses.

65. b. The diastolic blood pressure represents the pressure in the brachial artery when the ventricles are at rest (diastole).

66. b. The AED cannot determine if the patient has regained a pulse, only the operator can.

67. c. Assess onset by asking when the pain began and how long it took to reach its greatest severity.

68. b. A patient may take up to three doses of nitroglycerin, each dose three to five minutes apart. The blood pressure should be greater than 100, and the pulse rate should be greater than 60 BPM. Nitroglycerine use is contraindicated in children.

69. d. Headache is a possible side effect of nitroglycerin, as are decreased blood pressure and pulse rate and a burning sensation on or under the tongue. Some patients experience reflex tachycardia following the administration of nitroglycerine due to the rapid drop in blood pressure.

70. a. Pelvic fractures carry danger of severe internal bleeding.

71. b. A light covering with sterile dressing materials will decrease the risk of infection; the slight bleeding is not itself your major concern in this case, although it indicates that the head injury is severe.

72. c. Always manage the airway and breathing before controlling bleeding.

73. a. While there is limited information that people in extended periods of cardiac arrest may benefit from CPR before defibrillation, overwhelming information indicates that defibrillating very early in a "fresh" arrest situation will provide the best opportunity for correcting the most common cause of cardiac arrest—ventricular fibrillation.

74. c. To stop bleeding caused by massive soft-tissue injury, inflate only the compartments that cover the damaged areas.

75. a. This fact requires EMT-Basics to remain vigilant and reassess cardiac arrest patients frequently.

76. a. Before taking further action in this case, be sure you are applying concentrated direct pressure at the right location. Your next steps are **b** and **c**, in that order.

77. c. Elevate the extremity to control bleeding only after checking for signs and symptoms of skeletal injury.

78. a. With AEDs as reliable as they are, it is most likely that battery failure may be a likely cause of equipment malfunction.

79. d. After helping a patient take prescribed nitroglycerin, reassess vital signs and chest pains; a second dose may be given three to five minutes later.

80. b. The AED can detect only the electrical activity within the patient's heart. It does not assess rate, mechanical activity (pumping action), or the degree of cardiac compromise.

81. d. If life-threatening conditions are present, you will focus on those injuries or begin to package the patient for rapid transport if you cannot manage her life-threatening problems.

82. a. The pulsating pressure found in an artery can cause it to bleed quite profusely, especially in the larger vessels.

83. a. The brachial artery provides blood flow to the distal arm. Therefore, if direct pressure to the wound does not stop the bleeding, pressure applied to the medial arm at the pressure point can slow bleeding long enough for clotting to occur.

84. a. A patient who sustains injuries in a motor vehicle crash should be suspected of spinal injury.

85. c. Reassess the airway immediately after providing any intervention to a patient with a suspected spinal cord injury. Do not allow the patient to turn his or her head. Oxygen should be applied after you assess respiratory rate, rhythm, and effort when you know what intervention is appropriate.

86. d. If a patient is immobilized to a long board, you can tilt the entire board to clear the airway.

87. c. Sudden onset of altered mental status strongly suggests diabetic emergency. Alcohol intoxication will have a slower onset. Poisoning may also cause altered mental status, but you should first rule out the possibility of a diabetic emergency as it is a more common occurrence. An allergic reaction will not cause the sudden onset of altered mental status.

88. d. By themselves, the other signs do not indicate possible or actual shock.

89. b. Talk quietly with the patient to help her remain calm and persuade her to seek medical help. Be on guard for a violent outburst. Restraints and police backup are not necessary to manage this patient. Asking too many personal questions may agitate her.

90. a. This patient may be experiencing internal bleeding and possible signs of shock. High-flow oxygen is warranted.

91. d. A patient should receive oral glucose only if he or she has a history of diabetes and altered mental status; unresponsive patients should not receive oral glucose.

92. b. In shock, the body attempts to preserve perfusion by shunting blood away from the skin, increasing heart rate, and increasing respiratory rate.

93. a. The central nervous system consists of the brain and spinal cord.

94. b. Even if the patient has extricated himself from the car, immobilize him to a long spine board if the mechanisms of injury leads you to suspect spine damage. A standing take-down will allow you to immobilize the patient from the standing position.

95. d. It is not generally expected to see diarrhea as a primary sign or symptom of shock. On the other hand, the remaining choices can be easily seen in shock.

96. a. A patent airway must be maintained first before continuing the initial assessment of any patient.

97. a. The other choices do not make sense as potential signs or symptoms of hypothermia. As blood flow to the brain diminishes, altered mental status may occur, causing confusion and eventually, unconsciousness.

98. c. Indications for use of epinephrine are signs and symptoms of respiratory distress or hypoperfusion (shock). Glucose is indicated for diabetic patients. There are no medications (other than oxygen) indicated for use by EMTs in the treatment of cardiac arrest patients.

99. b. The other choices may either further injure the site or otherwise not be effective in managing a local cold injury like frostbite.

100. a. Elderly persons are especially prone to hypothermia, even when the temperature is not extremely cold.

101. c. Patients with early hypothermia have a rapid pulse and respiratory rate and red skin; option **a** lists the signs of late hypothermia. Patient **d** has hyperthermia. Patient **b** has normal vital signs.

102. b. Patients with hypothermia may behave inappropriately or exhibit poor coordination, mood changes, or speech difficulties.

103. d. The most important principle of care for patients with severe hypothermia is to prevent further heat loss by removing the patient from the cold environment; active rewarming should be done in the hospital.

104. b. Placing the patient in cool water may cause the patient to lose too much heat too quickly.

105. b. Leg cramps may result from an electrolyte imbalance from excessive sweating during exercise.

106. a. Because a child's tongue is large in relation to the size of the airway, it is likely to cause an obstruction.

107. b. Water or air in the stomach caused by involuntary swallowing during a drowning episode may cause the stomach to expand and press against the diaphragm, making it difficult to ventilate the lungs.

108. c. The correct rate of providing artificial ventilations to infants and children is 20 breaths per minute, or one breath every three seconds.

109. d. The other three choices are common medical reasons why patients can act in a bizarre manner. It is unlikely that an allergic reaction will produce a mental stuatus change without other noticeable signs.

110. d. Care for an unresponsive infant with a foreign-body airway obstruction includes a series of back blows, followed by chest thrusts, alternating with ventilation attempts.

111. a. Decreased heart rate and altered mental status are considered late signs of respiratory distress and most likely are really signs of respiratory failure. A breathing rate of 22 can be normal for a child.

112. b. Seizures, seen as body stiffness and/or shaking, are a common side effect of high fevers in infants and small children.

113. a. A dry diaper and absence of tears when the infant cries are signs of dehydration, a cause of hypovolemic shock.

114. c. The patient is not experiencing a foreign-body airway obstruction, and she appears to be ventilating adequately. Therefore, oxygen provided with a blow-by mask and reassurance will help ensure adequate oxygenation of the patient.

115. c. Children of this age group want to remain with their parents and are best calmed by simple demonstrations. Keep the parent in the room and speak softly to her, using simple terms, but do not use baby-talk. A good practice is to perform any painful procedures last, but this will not serve to calm her down before you begin the procedure.

116. d. The "sniffing position" refers to the placement of a child's head when you perform the head-tilt/chin-lift, with the face lying parallel to the surface he or she is lying on. It improves breathing by opening the airway further than hyperextending does.

117. c. This patient is likely to deliver her baby before you can reach the hospital; prepare for an emergency on-scene delivery.

118. a. With the patient being altered in his mental status, it appears that he is not ventilating adequately. A nonrebreather mask will not be able to ventilate the child appropriately. There is no information to indicate a foreign body obstruction.

119. a. To prevent the baby from being delivered too rapidly and to prevent the mother's perineum from tearing, exert gentle pressure on the baby's head and the mother's perineum.

120. b. The fontanelles are the soft spots on the baby's head where the bony parts of the skull have not yet grown together, allowing the head to contract somewhat during delivery.

121. b. Position a newborn on its side with its head lower than its trunk to facilitate drainage of amniotic fluid from the lungs. Generally, the infant is placed near the mother's breast to encourage suckling and bonding.

122. a. The third stage of labor consists of the delivery of the placenta after the baby is delivered.

123. c. To stimulate a healthy newborn to breathe, rub its back, or flick the soles of its feet.

124. d. Meconium, or fetal stool, appears as yellow, brown, or green material in the amniotic fluid. When present, it is associated with an increased risk of fetal distress.

125. c. In a case of vaginal bleeding, it is important to find out if the patient is pregnant, since she may be experiencing a miscarriage or complication of pregnancy.

126. b. A score of "1" for appearance denotes blue extremities but a pink trunk; this is normal for a newborn. The condition, called acrocyanosis, goes away once the circulation in the extremities improves.

127. a. The patient is likely to be experiencing a miscarriage; shock is possible. If she delivers, the child will be too small to survive. There is no method to stop the bleeding in the prehospital setting. There is no need to place her in the left lateral recumbent position.

128. a. It is normal for a pregnant woman to have a slightly increased pulse and decreased blood pressure. The respiratory rate of patient **b** is too fast. Patient **c** has a too-slow respiratory rate, and patient **d** is hypertensive and has a respiratory rate that is too high.

129. d. Blood is shunted away from the skin early in children with shock, causing it to pale, become cool, and sweat.

130. b. Acting as a patient advocate means treating all patients as you would like to be treated yourself.

131. a. The five stages of the grieving process are denial, anger, bargaining, depression, and acceptance. Most people progress through the grief stages in this order.

132. c. Effective stress-reduction techniques include balancing work and recreation, getting enough rest, eating a healthy diet, getting regular exercise, and seeking help if necessary.

133. d. Rub your hands together vigorously with soap for at least 10 to 15 seconds, then rinse in running water.

134. b. Wear a mask and eye protection when there is a high probability of splattering, such as when suctioning a patient.

135. c. Because gloves protect both you and your patients, most protocols now call for EMTs to wear gloves for any patient contact. Remove gloves by pulling them off inside out, so you do not touch the soiled outer surface; change gloves for each new patient contact.

136. d. Implied consent means that, because your adult patient cannot give consent to treatment, you act without it.

137. b. The recovery position, with the patient on the left side with the left arm under the head, allow secretions to drain more easily from the airway.

138. a. During scene size-up, determine whether the scene is safe for you to enter, the number of patients, if you have the appropriate BSI equipment and precautions, and whether you will need back-up from additional EMS units or other services.

139. a. EMS channels are considered to be public by the FCC and are frequently scanned by the general public. Therefore, do not use a patient's name on the radio.

140. c. The EMT's report should not include a diagnosis, but rather a complete description of the patient's condition.

141. b. Always speak directly to the patient, and explain what you are doing in words he or she can understand. If the parent is present, explain your treatment to them as well.

142. c. When your patient does not speak English, try to find an interpreter, and be especially careful to avoid misunderstandings. Try using sign language and gestures until an interpreter can be found.

143. d. This is a subjective statement. Statement **a** is inappropriate and unnecessary. Statements **b** and **c** are objective statements.

144. d. Never falsify a patient record; document only the care you actually gave, but you may write that you omitted to take the vital signs at a particular time.

145. a. Your first responsibility is to protect your own safety by calling for backup when needed and not entering the scene until it is secure; your next responsibility is to protect patients and bystanders.

146. b. Only the most critical care, such as opening the airway to assess respirations, is provided during triage. Unfortunately, CPR cannot be started by the individuals performing triage.

147. a. From the choices offered, the patient with multiple fractures, unless severe bleeding occurred, would be given lowest priority. Patient **b** would have the highest priority followed by patient **c** then **d**.

148. b. An emergency move is one required to remove the patient from imminent danger, such as a fire, or when you much move a patient to gain access to other critically wounded patients. You should stabilize the head and neck with your hands, and if possible, apply a cervical collar before moving the patient.

149. d. If you discover any important evidence while caring for patients at a crime scene, tell a police officer, but do not touch or move the evidence yourself.

150. c. Wear protective eyewear in all situations when you are likely to be exposed to splashing or spurting of bodily fluids, such as when controlling arterial bleeding or assisting at childbirth.

EMT-Basic
Practice Exam 3

CHAPTER SUMMARY

This is the third of four practice exams in this book based on the National Registry EMT-Basic written exam. Use this test to identify which types of questions continue to give you problems.

You should now be familiar with the format of the National Registry EMT-Basic exam. Your practice test-taking experience will help you most, however, if you have created a situation as close as possible to the real one.

For this third exam, simulate a real test. Find a quiet place where you will not be disturbed. Have two sharpened pencils and a good eraser. Complete the test in one sitting, setting a timer or a stopwatch. You should have plenty of time to answer all of the questions when you take the real exam, but be sure to practice maintaining your concentration and maintaining a steady pace.

As before, the answer sheet you should use is on the next page. Following the exam is an answer key, with all the answers explained. These explanations will help you see where you need to concentrate further study. When you've finished the exam and scored it, note your weaknesses so that you'll know which parts of your textbook to concentrate on before you take the fourth exam.

1.	ⓐ	ⓑ	ⓒ	ⓓ	51.	ⓐ	ⓑ	ⓒ	ⓓ	101.	ⓐ	ⓑ	ⓒ	ⓓ
2.	ⓐ	ⓑ	ⓒ	ⓓ	52.	ⓐ	ⓑ	ⓒ	ⓓ	102.	ⓐ	ⓑ	ⓒ	ⓓ
3.	ⓐ	ⓑ	ⓒ	ⓓ	53.	ⓐ	ⓑ	ⓒ	ⓓ	103.	ⓐ	ⓑ	ⓒ	ⓓ
4.	ⓐ	ⓑ	ⓒ	ⓓ	54.	ⓐ	ⓑ	ⓒ	ⓓ	104.	ⓐ	ⓑ	ⓒ	ⓓ
5.	ⓐ	ⓑ	ⓒ	ⓓ	55.	ⓐ	ⓑ	ⓒ	ⓓ	105.	ⓐ	ⓑ	ⓒ	ⓓ
6.	ⓐ	ⓑ	ⓒ	ⓓ	56.	ⓐ	ⓑ	ⓒ	ⓓ	106.	ⓐ	ⓑ	ⓒ	ⓓ
7.	ⓐ	ⓑ	ⓒ	ⓓ	57.	ⓐ	ⓑ	ⓒ	ⓓ	107.	ⓐ	ⓑ	ⓒ	ⓓ
8.	ⓐ	ⓑ	ⓒ	ⓓ	58.	ⓐ	ⓑ	ⓒ	ⓓ	108.	ⓐ	ⓑ	ⓒ	ⓓ
9.	ⓐ	ⓑ	ⓒ	ⓓ	59.	ⓐ	ⓑ	ⓒ	ⓓ	109.	ⓐ	ⓑ	ⓒ	ⓓ
10.	ⓐ	ⓑ	ⓒ	ⓓ	60.	ⓐ	ⓑ	ⓒ	ⓓ	110.	ⓐ	ⓑ	ⓒ	ⓓ
11.	ⓐ	ⓑ	ⓒ	ⓓ	61.	ⓐ	ⓑ	ⓒ	ⓓ	111.	ⓐ	ⓑ	ⓒ	ⓓ
12.	ⓐ	ⓑ	ⓒ	ⓓ	62.	ⓐ	ⓑ	ⓒ	ⓓ	112.	ⓐ	ⓑ	ⓒ	ⓓ
13.	ⓐ	ⓑ	ⓒ	ⓓ	63.	ⓐ	ⓑ	ⓒ	ⓓ	113.	ⓐ	ⓑ	ⓒ	ⓓ
14.	ⓐ	ⓑ	ⓒ	ⓓ	64.	ⓐ	ⓑ	ⓒ	ⓓ	114.	ⓐ	ⓑ	ⓒ	ⓓ
15.	ⓐ	ⓑ	ⓒ	ⓓ	65.	ⓐ	ⓑ	ⓒ	ⓓ	115.	ⓐ	ⓑ	ⓒ	ⓓ
16.	ⓐ	ⓑ	ⓒ	ⓓ	66.	ⓐ	ⓑ	ⓒ	ⓓ	116.	ⓐ	ⓑ	ⓒ	ⓓ
17.	ⓐ	ⓑ	ⓒ	ⓓ	67.	ⓐ	ⓑ	ⓒ	ⓓ	117.	ⓐ	ⓑ	ⓒ	ⓓ
18.	ⓐ	ⓑ	ⓒ	ⓓ	68.	ⓐ	ⓑ	ⓒ	ⓓ	118.	ⓐ	ⓑ	ⓒ	ⓓ
19.	ⓐ	ⓑ	ⓒ	ⓓ	69.	ⓐ	ⓑ	ⓒ	ⓓ	119.	ⓐ	ⓑ	ⓒ	ⓓ
20.	ⓐ	ⓑ	ⓒ	ⓓ	70.	ⓐ	ⓑ	ⓒ	ⓓ	120.	ⓐ	ⓑ	ⓒ	ⓓ
21.	ⓐ	ⓑ	ⓒ	ⓓ	71.	ⓐ	ⓑ	ⓒ	ⓓ	121.	ⓐ	ⓑ	ⓒ	ⓓ
22.	ⓐ	ⓑ	ⓒ	ⓓ	72.	ⓐ	ⓑ	ⓒ	ⓓ	122.	ⓐ	ⓑ	ⓒ	ⓓ
23.	ⓐ	ⓑ	ⓒ	ⓓ	73.	ⓐ	ⓑ	ⓒ	ⓓ	123.	ⓐ	ⓑ	ⓒ	ⓓ
24.	ⓐ	ⓑ	ⓒ	ⓓ	74.	ⓐ	ⓑ	ⓒ	ⓓ	124.	ⓐ	ⓑ	ⓒ	ⓓ
25.	ⓐ	ⓑ	ⓒ	ⓓ	75.	ⓐ	ⓑ	ⓒ	ⓓ	125.	ⓐ	ⓑ	ⓒ	ⓓ
26.	ⓐ	ⓑ	ⓒ	ⓓ	76.	ⓐ	ⓑ	ⓒ	ⓓ	126.	ⓐ	ⓑ	ⓒ	ⓓ
27.	ⓐ	ⓑ	ⓒ	ⓓ	77.	ⓐ	ⓑ	ⓒ	ⓓ	127.	ⓐ	ⓑ	ⓒ	ⓓ
28.	ⓐ	ⓑ	ⓒ	ⓓ	78.	ⓐ	ⓑ	ⓒ	ⓓ	128.	ⓐ	ⓑ	ⓒ	ⓓ
29.	ⓐ	ⓑ	ⓒ	ⓓ	79.	ⓐ	ⓑ	ⓒ	ⓓ	129.	ⓐ	ⓑ	ⓒ	ⓓ
30.	ⓐ	ⓑ	ⓒ	ⓓ	80.	ⓐ	ⓑ	ⓒ	ⓓ	130.	ⓐ	ⓑ	ⓒ	ⓓ
31.	ⓐ	ⓑ	ⓒ	ⓓ	81.	ⓐ	ⓑ	ⓒ	ⓓ	131.	ⓐ	ⓑ	ⓒ	ⓓ
32.	ⓐ	ⓑ	ⓒ	ⓓ	82.	ⓐ	ⓑ	ⓒ	ⓓ	132.	ⓐ	ⓑ	ⓒ	ⓓ
33.	ⓐ	ⓑ	ⓒ	ⓓ	83.	ⓐ	ⓑ	ⓒ	ⓓ	133.	ⓐ	ⓑ	ⓒ	ⓓ
34.	ⓐ	ⓑ	ⓒ	ⓓ	84.	ⓐ	ⓑ	ⓒ	ⓓ	134.	ⓐ	ⓑ	ⓒ	ⓓ
35.	ⓐ	ⓑ	ⓒ	ⓓ	85.	ⓐ	ⓑ	ⓒ	ⓓ	135.	ⓐ	ⓑ	ⓒ	ⓓ
36.	ⓐ	ⓑ	ⓒ	ⓓ	86.	ⓐ	ⓑ	ⓒ	ⓓ	136.	ⓐ	ⓑ	ⓒ	ⓓ
37.	ⓐ	ⓑ	ⓒ	ⓓ	87.	ⓐ	ⓑ	ⓒ	ⓓ	137.	ⓐ	ⓑ	ⓒ	ⓓ
38.	ⓐ	ⓑ	ⓒ	ⓓ	88.	ⓐ	ⓑ	ⓒ	ⓓ	138.	ⓐ	ⓑ	ⓒ	ⓓ
39.	ⓐ	ⓑ	ⓒ	ⓓ	89.	ⓐ	ⓑ	ⓒ	ⓓ	139.	ⓐ	ⓑ	ⓒ	ⓓ
40.	ⓐ	ⓑ	ⓒ	ⓓ	90.	ⓐ	ⓑ	ⓒ	ⓓ	140.	ⓐ	ⓑ	ⓒ	ⓓ
41.	ⓐ	ⓑ	ⓒ	ⓓ	91.	ⓐ	ⓑ	ⓒ	ⓓ	141.	ⓐ	ⓑ	ⓒ	ⓓ
42.	ⓐ	ⓑ	ⓒ	ⓓ	92.	ⓐ	ⓑ	ⓒ	ⓓ	142.	ⓐ	ⓑ	ⓒ	ⓓ
43.	ⓐ	ⓑ	ⓒ	ⓓ	93.	ⓐ	ⓑ	ⓒ	ⓓ	143.	ⓐ	ⓑ	ⓒ	ⓓ
44.	ⓐ	ⓑ	ⓒ	ⓓ	94.	ⓐ	ⓑ	ⓒ	ⓓ	144.	ⓐ	ⓑ	ⓒ	ⓓ
45.	ⓐ	ⓑ	ⓒ	ⓓ	95.	ⓐ	ⓑ	ⓒ	ⓓ	145.	ⓐ	ⓑ	ⓒ	ⓓ
46.	ⓐ	ⓑ	ⓒ	ⓓ	96.	ⓐ	ⓑ	ⓒ	ⓓ	146.	ⓐ	ⓑ	ⓒ	ⓓ
47.	ⓐ	ⓑ	ⓒ	ⓓ	97.	ⓐ	ⓑ	ⓒ	ⓓ	147.	ⓐ	ⓑ	ⓒ	ⓓ
48.	ⓐ	ⓑ	ⓒ	ⓓ	98.	ⓐ	ⓑ	ⓒ	ⓓ	148.	ⓐ	ⓑ	ⓒ	ⓓ
49.	ⓐ	ⓑ	ⓒ	ⓓ	99.	ⓐ	ⓑ	ⓒ	ⓓ	149.	ⓐ	ⓑ	ⓒ	ⓓ
50.	ⓐ	ⓑ	ⓒ	ⓓ	100.	ⓐ	ⓑ	ⓒ	ⓓ	150.	ⓐ	ⓑ	ⓒ	ⓓ

▶ EMT-Basic Practice Exam 3

1. If a preschool child suffers an injury, you should keep in mind that she
   a. is not frightened of you as a rescuer.
   b. does not mind being undressed for a physical exam.
   c. does not mind being separated from her parents.
   d. thinks that she is being punished for being bad.

2. Adolescent patients have all of the following characteristics EXCEPT
   a. they want their parents to be present during examination.
   b. they are modest and embarrassed about having clothing removed.
   c. they prize their dignity and want to be talked to as if they are adults.
   d. they are especially fearful of permanent injury and disfigurement.

3. Which patient is breathing adequately?
   a. male, age 3 months: respiratory rate, 62/min, using diaphragm and muscles in chest and neck
   b. female, age 7: respiratory rate, 12/min, irregular rhythm, using diaphragm primarily
   c. male, age 18: respiratory rate, 28/min, shallow chest motions
   d. female, age 43: respiratory rate, 15/min, regular chest motions

4. One anatomical difference between infants and adults is that
   a. infants have a slower respiratory rate.
   b. infants have a smaller surface area relative to body mass.
   c. infants' brain tissues are thinner and softer.
   d. infants' spleen and liver are more protected.

5. A patient should receive oxygen via a nonrebreather mask if he or she is having difficulty breathing or is
   a. frightened.
   b. in pain.
   c. cyanotic.
   d. mentally unstable.

6. When should you use the jaw thrust to open the airway of your patient?
   a. if he or she is under one year of age
   b. if you suspect spinal trauma
   c. if he or she is unconscious
   d. if he or she has a curvature of the spine

7. A danger of using a rigid suction catheter with infants and young children is that stimulating the back of the throat can
   a. cause changes in the heart rhythm.
   b. be ineffective in suctioning.
   c. lead to immediate vomiting.
   d. cause the tongue to fall into the airway.

8. When an EMT-B suctions a patient, he or she should only insert the catheter to what point?
   a. only to the front of the mouth
   b. never past the last molar
   c. only to the top of the epiglottis
   d. never past the base of the tongue

9. The flow-restricted, oxygen-powered ventilation device should not be used on
   a. hypoxic elderly patients.
   b. infants or very young children.
   c. patients with diabetes mellitus.
   d. patients without airway control.

10. You are ventilating an adult patient with the two-person bag-valve-mask procedure. Which sign would indicate that the patient is being adequately ventilated?
  a. The patient's heart rate remains below 60/min.
  b. The patient is receiving 12 ventilations per minute.
  c. The chest rises and falls with each ventilation.
  d. The patient is able to speak in complete sentences.

11. Your patient is a 35-year-old trauma victim who is not breathing. You are unable to open the airway by means of the jaw thrust and suctioning. You should
  a. attempt a mouth-to-mask ventilation.
  b. use the head-tilt/chin-lift technique.
  c. ventilate with a bag-valve-mask unit.
  d. insert an airway through a tracheostomy.

12. Which statement about inadequate breathing is correct?
  a. A breathing rate that is either too fast or too slow may indicate inadequate breathing.
  b. Inadequate breathing is much less common in small children than in older adults.
  c. Increased effort of breathing is often a normal sign and is not associated with inadequate breathing.
  d. A patient breathing very deeply or very shallowly is compensating for an abnormal respiratory rate.

13. Stridor is a sign of
  a. mucus in the lower airway.
  b. accessory muscle use.
  c. upper airway obstruction.
  d. altered mental status.

14. Why is an infant more likely to suffer an airway obstruction than an adult?
  a. An infant's ribs are less flexible than an adult.
  b. The shape of the infant's head will cause the neck to flex when child is supine.
  c. The adult has a relatively larger tongue compared to an infant.
  d. The adult has a relatively smaller airway compared to the infant.

15. Which patient would be most likely to have a barrel chest?
  a. male, age 10 months: premature birth and history of respiratory problems
  b. female, age 6 years: history of asthma and frequent respiratory infections
  c. male, age 58 years: history of emphysema and years of smoking
  d. female, age 70 years: recent history of pneumonia and bronchitis

16. The primary reason you auscultate both sides of the chest is to determine whether breath sounds are
  a. strong and regular.
  b. fast or slow.
  c. noisy or quiet.
  d. present and equal.

17. When performing a painful procedure to a child, you should
  a. tell the child it won't hurt.
  b. tell the child to look away.
  c. tell the child it will hurt, but be reassuring.
  d. tell the child that he or she should act like a "big boy" or "girl".

18. Your patient is a 24-year-old woman with a history of asthma. She is wheezing and gasping for air and has a pulse rate of 88/min. You may assist her in using an inhaler if
   a. she has not yet taken more than three doses of medication.
   b. she has her own inhaler and you obtain medical direction.
   c. her respiratory rate is greater than 24/min.
   d. her blood pressure is greater than 100/70.

19. Your 18-month-old patient is experiencing respiratory distress. Which of the following conditions is NOT a likely cause of the difficulty in breathing?
   a. a partial foreign body obstruction
   b. the flu
   c. epiglottitis
   d. COPD

20. A seesaw (chest/abdomen move in opposite directions) pattern of breathing is a sign of
   a. breathing difficulty in infants.
   b. normal respirations in elderly patients.
   c. adequate artificial respiration.
   d. diseases such as COPD.

21. Your patient is unresponsive and has no gag reflex. After opening the airway, you should
   a. insert a nasopharyngeal airway.
   b. insert an oropharyneal airway.
   c. clear the airway with a finger sweep.
   d. begin mouth-to-mouth ventilation.

22. The flow-restricted, oxygen-powered ventilation device is preferable to the bag-valve-mask technique when
   a. the patient is a trauma victim.
   b. the patient is an infant or small child.
   c. only one EMT is available to ventilate the patient.
   d. the EMT is unable to maintain an open airway.

23. Your patient has incurred facial trauma. Because of severe bleeding, blood is re-entering the airway as fast as you can suction it away. In this situation, you would
   a. suction for as long as two minutes at a time, then ventilate for one minute.
   b. suction for up to 30 seconds at a time, using the largest catheter.
   c. logroll the patient onto his or her side before attempting to suction.
   d. alternate suctioning for 15 seconds and ventilating for two minutes.

24. Your patient is complaining of shortness of breath but cannot tolerate a mask. You should
   a. provide artificial ventilation.
   b. insert a nasopharyngeal airway.
   c. use a nasal cannula.
   d. avoid providing oxygen.

25. All of the following are early signs of inadequate breathing EXCEPT
   a. reduced effort of breathing.
   b. breathing rate that is too fast.
   c. unequal chest expansion.
   d. cyanosis around the lips.

26. A sign of early respiratory distress in the pediatric patient is
   a. an increased blood pressure.
   b. an increased heart rate.
   c. flush warm skin.
   d. a decreased breathing rate.

27. During the normal respiratory cycle, when does inhalation begin?
   a. when the supraclavicular muscles contract
   b. when the size of the thoracic cavity decreases
   c. when the diaphragm and intercostal muscles contract
   d. when the accessory muscles of the chest relax

28. Which patient's vital signs are within normal ranges?

   a. newborn: pulse, 96; respirations, 32/min; BP, 70/30

   b. 5-year-old girl: pulse, 90; respirations, 24/min; BP, 90/50

   c. 15-year-old boy: pulse, 102; respirations, 28/min; BP, 124/80

   d. 28-year-old woman: pulse, 52; respirations, 9/min; BP, 80/40

29. To determine if the pupils of a patient's eyes are normal, you would check to see whether they are equal and

   a. reactive.

   b. constricted.

   c. dilated.

   d. dark.

30. *Perfusion* refers to the

   a. color and temperature of the skin.

   b. pulse rate and blood pressure.

   c. amount of oxygen reaching the cells.

   d. severity of a patient's symptoms.

31. All of the following are signs of labored respiration EXCEPT

   a. grunting.

   b. snoring.

   c. stridor.

   d. use of accessory muscles.

32. A weak pulse may be an early sign of

   a. diabetes.

   b. cardiac compromise.

   c. shock.

   d. head injury.

33. Your patient is a 37-year-old woman who has been in a minor accident. The patient is alert and oriented, and baseline vital signs are pulse, 76 and regular; respirations, 16/min and unlabored; and BP, 118/78. When you check her vital signs 15 minutes later, you find that her pulse rate is now 92 and her respirations are 24/min and shallow. You should

   a. continue to reassess her every 15 minutes.

   b. call for medical direction to treat her dyspnea.

   c. administer oxygen by nonrebreather mask.

   d. treat for shock and reassess every five minutes.

34. For which patients should you palpate the pulse in the brachial artery?

   a. infants only

   b. infants and children

   c. infants, small children, and elderly people

   d. all patients with no palpable radial pulse

35. A 1-year-old patient is crying after swallowing a piece of a hot dog. You can hear stridor when she breathes. Your treatment should include:

   a. blind finger sweep to attempt removal of the object.

   b. artificial ventilations by bag-valve mask and oxygen.

   c. high-concentration oxygen by blow-by mask.

   d. back blows followed by chest thrusts, repeat until airway is clear.

36. Your 4-year-old male patient has swallowed a marble. He is conscious, but you cannot hear air exchange or feel air coming from the mouth. You should

   a. begin CPR.

   b. provide oxygen by pediatric nonrebreather.

   c. deliver back blows and chest thrusts.

   d. administer abdominal thrusts.

37. A 2-year-old patient is in severe respiratory distress. Her skin is mottled, and she does not respond to verbal or physical stimulus. You should
   a. administer oxygen by the blow-by method.
   b. assist her ventilations with a bag-valve mask and supplemental oxygen.
   c. administer blind finger sweeps to attempt removal of an obstruction.
   d. provide oxygen by pediatric nonrebreather mask.

38. When you use the DCAP-BTLS acronym to assess patients for injuries, the P refers to
   a. perfusion.
   b. pulse.
   c. punctures.
   d. pressure.

39. What does the term *crepitation* refer to?
   a. the sound of broken bones moving against each other
   b. the use of accessory muscles during respirations
   c. the presence of jugular vein distention in the neck
   d. the absence of a pedal pulse in one or both extremities

40. Which question would you ask to evaluate the Q component of the OPQRST acronym?
   a. What makes the pain feel worse?
   b. How bad is the pain right now?
   c. Can you describe the pain to me?
   d. What time did the pain start today?

41. A medical patient should receive a rapid trauma assessment if he or she
   a. shows signs and symptoms of shock.
   b. is unresponsive to verbal or painful stimuli.
   c. has difficulty taking a deep breath.
   d. is in cardiac or respiratory arrest.

42. You and two other rescuers have just arrived at the side of an apneic and pulseless patient. After assessing the patient, what should you do next?
   a. Perform CPR for one minute, then apply the AED.
   b. Apply the AED pads to the patient's chest, push to analyze the rhythm, then perform CPR.
   c. Begin CPR and apply the AED pads to the patient's chest, then stop all activity while the AED analyzes the patient's rhythm.
   d. Ventilate the patient for 30 seconds, apply the AED pads, then begin chest compressions.

43. Your fully automated defibrillator has delivered three shocks. Your patient has no pulse and is not breathing. You should
   a. transport and deliver no further shocks.
   b. reposition patient and deliver three more shocks.
   c. resume CPR.
   d. contact medical control.

44. To ensure that your patient does not consciously change the rate of breathing while you are assessing respirations, you should assess respirations
   a. while the patient is engaged in a conversation with another EMT.
   b. after checking the pulse, while your hand is still on the patient's wrist.
   c. only in unresponsive patients because it is in inaccurate in others.
   d. immediately after entering the scene, before introducing yourself.

45. In a normal environment, how does normal skin feel to the touch?
   a. cool and moist
   b. cool and dry
   c. warm and dry
   d. warm and moist

46. What is a good way to assess the skin color of infants and children?
   a. Check the area around the mouth.
   b. Check the oral mucosa.
   c. Check inside the inner eyelid.
   d. Check the soles of the feet.

47. When assessing a patient's pupils in bright sunlight, you should
   a. have the patient look directly at the sun for a few seconds.
   b. cover each eye for a few seconds and then assess the reaction.
   c. pass your penlight across the eyes and note the reaction of each pupil.
   d. take the patient into a darkened room and then use your penlight.

48. Your patient, a 26-year-old male, has a suspected broken ankle sustained while playing tennis. His vital signs are pulse, 58; respirations, 12; BP, 108/70; pupils normal and reactive; skin warm and dry. After recording these vital signs, you should
   a. ask the patient what his normal pulse and BP are.
   b. treat for signs and symptoms of shock.
   c. administer oxygen and prepare to transport immediately.
   d. recheck pulse, respiration, and BP every five minutes.

49. What does the presence of abdominal breathing signify in infants and small children?
   a. labored breathing
   b. noisy breathing
   c. shallow breathing
   d. normal breathing

50. Nonreactive pupils may be a sign of
   a. diabetic emergency.
   b. respiratory emergency.
   c. head injury.
   d. internal bleeding.

51. When applying defibrillation pads, what should you do for the patient with a hairy chest?
   a. Press the pads lightly on the chest.
   b. Quickly shave some of the hair away.
   c. Apply pads to right and left shoulders.
   d. Apply pads to patient's back.

52. Your patient is a 26-year-old male who has been in a motor vehicle accident. The patient's radial pulse is weak, while the carotid pulse is strong. You should
   a. treat for signs and symptoms of shock.
   b. recheck by taking the brachial pulse.
   c. wait 15 minutes, then recheck vital signs.
   d. check for low blood pressure on the other arm.

53. Diastolic pressure is a measure of the
   a. force exerted against the walls of the blood vessels when the heart contracts.
   b. force exerted against the walls of the blood vessels when the heart relaxes.
   c. rhythm and strength of the heart's contractions during arterial circulation.
   d. time it takes the capillary beds in the extremities to refill after being blanched.

54. You are called to the home of an elderly woman who is obviously in respiratory distress. Gasping for breath, she tries to tell you the history of her lung problems, beginning in her youth. You should
   a. ignore her and proceed with the assessment.
   b. record the information in detail.
   c. ask her to describe her present illness.
   d. tell her to try not to speak too much.

55. Where does blood travel when it leaves the right ventricle of the heart?
   a. to the pulmonary veins, then to the lungs
   b. to the aorta, then out to the body
   c. to the vena cava then to the left atrium
   d. to the pulmonary arteries then to the lungs

56. What artery can be palpated on the thumb side of the wrist?
   a. brachial artery
   b. radial artery
   c. ulnar artery
   d. pulmonary artery

57. What is the function of platelets?
   a. form blood clots
   b. carry oxygen
   c. fight infections
   d. carry blood cells

58. Your patient is a 68-year-old man who is complaining of chest pain. Your focused assessment findings include a pulse rate of 92, a BP of 140/90, and some difficulty breathing. After administering oxygen, you should focus your questioning to determine if the patient has a history of
   a. asthma.
   b. diabetes mellitus.
   c. cardiac problems.
   d. strokes.

59. You are the driver of a two-person crew that is transporting a 62-year-old cardiac patient to the hospital. The patient goes into cardiac arrest during transport. You should
   a. notify the receiving hospital and request medical direction.
   b. call for ALS backup to rendezvous at a predetermined location.
   c. reroute your ambulance to the closest medical facility.
   d. stop the ambulance, request backup, and assist your partner.

60. When using an AED, after delivering the third shock, you should
   a. perform CPR for one minute.
   b. check the patient's pulse.
   c. analyze the rhythm again.
   d. assess ABCs and transport.

61. What are the earliest signs of shock?
   a. fatigue and depression
   b. weak pulse and low blood pressure
   c. anxiety and tachycardia
   d. cyanosis and shallow respirations

62. Why is it important to maintain body heat in a patient with shock?
   a. Shivering wastes vital oxygen and energy.
   b. Patients in shock often have fever as well.
   c. Blood congeals more easily when the body is cold.
   d. Hypothermia may increase the severity of shock.

63. Your patient has a wound on her anterior left lower leg that is spurting large amounts of blood. Direct pressure alone is ineffective. Where should you apply indirect pressure?
   a. on the left side of the groin
   b. medially to the left knee
   c. in the medial mid-thigh area
   d. both above and below the wound

64. Which of the following mechanisms of injury is NOT generally associated with severe internal bleeding?
   a. motorcycle accidents
   b. car collisions
   c. penetrating injuries
   d. sports injuries

65. How should you treat a sucking chest injury?

a. Apply a moist sterile dressing covered by an occlusive dressing.

b. Cover it with an occlusive dressing taped on three sides.

c. Leave it uncovered as long as bleeding is not severe.

d. Cover it lightly with gauze dressings soaked with sterile saline.

66. Your patient is an 84-year-old woman who is complaining of severe abdominal pain. The abdomen is rigid and tender. What should you suspect?

a. cardiac disease

b. internal bleeding

c. pregnancy

d. thoracic aneurysm

67. Your patient is a 6-year-old boy who is having a severe nosebleed. No trauma is suspected. How should you treat this child?

a. Pinch his nostrils together and transport him sitting upright, leaning forward.

b. Pack the nostrils with gauze, then place the patient in the recovery position.

c. Apply indirect pressure to the upper lip and have the patient lie supine.

d. Apply an occlusive dressing and place the patient in the recovery position.

68. How does cardiac pain differ from respiratory pain?

a. Cardiac pain increases when the patient breathes.

b. Cardiac pain is localized around the heart and arms.

c. Cardiac pain does not change with movement or palpation.

d. Cardiac pain generally occurs on the left side of the chest.

69. Which of the following is a contraindication for the administration of nitroglycerin?

a. The patient presents with an altered mental status.

b. The patient complains of chest pain with exertion.

c. The systolic blood pressure is above 100 mm Hg.

d. Nitroglycerin has been taken within the previous 24 hours.

70. Research shows that most of the cases of inappropriately delivered shocks from an AED have been caused by

a. mechanical interference.

b. improperly charged batteries.

c. malfunctioning electrodes.

d. human error.

71. Your patient is a 67-year-old woman whom you found in cardiac arrest. You have resuscitated her by using an AED and are now transporting her. If she again becomes pulseless, you should

a. request online medical direction.

b. stop the ambulance and use the AED.

c. begin CPR and continue en route.

d. defibrillate quickly while en route.

72. While transporting a 65-year-old female who is experiencing chest pain, she becomes unconscious, pulseless, and apneic. You and your partner should immediately

a. contact medical control for direction.

b. drive faster to the hospital.

c. administer CPR for one minute, then apply AED pads to the patient's chest.

d. apply the AED pads to the patient's chest while administering CPR.

73. All of the following are indications for the use of nitroglycerin EXCEPT
   a. the patient has a history of cardiac problems.
   b. the patient complains of chest pain.
   c. the systolic blood pressure is less than 90.
   d. the patient's physician has prescribed nitroglycerin.

74. Your patient is a 24-year-old man with a chest wound and signs and symptoms of shock. In what position should you place him?
   a. Trendelenburg's position
   b. on his back with legs elevated
   c. recovery position
   d. flat on his back

75. You are treating a 39-year-old woman who has been in a motor vehicle accident. She has a suspected broken arm and leg, moderate bleeding from the leg wound, and signs and symptoms of early shock. Vital signs are pulse, 96 and thready; respirations, 28 and shallow; BP, 110/78. Your treatment should focus on
   a. stabilizing the patient and transporting her to the hospital.
   b. carefully splinting and bandaging all the patient's injuries.
   c. performing a detailed trauma assessment in the field.
   d. opening the airway and monitoring vital signs every 15 minutes.

76. Your patient is bleeding from a leg wound. The blood is dark red and oozing steadily. This describes which type of bleeding?
   a. internal
   b. arterial
   c. venous
   d. capillary

77. The purpose of using the PASG for a pelvic injury is to immobilize the pelvis and
   a. reduce pain.
   b. reduce internal bleeding.
   c. help clot external bleeding.
   d. lower the patient's blood pressure.

78. All of the following are signs of internal bleeding into the gastrointestinal tract EXCEPT
   a. dark, tarry stools.
   b. coffee-ground vomit.
   c. bloody urine.
   d. distended abdomen.

79. Your trauma patient has an amputated foot. How should you care for an amputated foot?
   a. Wrap it in a sterile dressing, then in plastic, and keep it cool.
   b. Immerse it in a tub of ice water and transport it with the patient.
   c. Put it inside the PASG and inflate the other leg of the garment.
   d. Put the foot back on the leg and then splint it in place.

80. Which statement about the assessment of a patient with cardiac compromise is correct?
   a. You cannot determine the degree of cardiac damage in the field.
   b. You should not ask patients about nitroglycerin or other drug use.
   c. The purpose of the focused history is to determine whether to use the AED.
   d. Patients usually describe cardiac pain as localized and moderately severe.

81. The three types of muscle tissue in the body are skeletal muscle, smooth muscle, and
   a. voluntary muscle.
   b. involuntary muscle.
   c. cardiac muscle.
   d. gastrointestinal.

82. All of the following are signs of bone and joint injury EXCEPT
  a. deformity.
  b. crepitus.
  c. bleeding.
  d. false movement.

83. Your patient is a 19-year-old male who has been in a motorcycle crash. Vital signs are pulse, 92 and weak; respirations, 24 and shallow; BP 116/80. He has a suspected spinal injury, as well as a painful, deformed, swollen right foot. Blood loss is not significant. What should your treatment plan focus on?
  a. immobilizing the injured foot in position of function
  b. immobilizing the patient and transporting him rapidly
  c. opening the airway and ventilating the patient
  d. applying the PASG and inflating all compartments

84. Which statement about the assessment of a splinted extremity is correct?
  a. Move the limb to assess for crepitation before splinting.
  b. Assess the patient's vital signs before and after splinting.
  c. Assess the injured extremity before and after splinting.
  d. Assess the degree of nerve damage before splinting.

85. The sling and swathe is used to protect an injury to the
  a. hip.
  b. shoulder.
  c. neck.
  d. wrist.

86. For which kind of injury should you use a pneumatic splint?
  a. angulated
  b. open
  c. crush
  d. indirect

87. The use of reasonable force when dealing with a patient with a behavioral disorder refers to
  a. the force necessary to incapacitate the patient.
  b. calling in police backup in a reasonable way.
  c. using soft restraints rather than handcuffs.
  d. the force necessary to restrain the patient.

88. Which of the following statements would be considered a contraindication for the use of nitroglycerin?
  a. "I am having chest pain."
  b. "I have a history of heart problems."
  c. "I get a headache when I take nitroglycerin."
  d. "My face gets swollen and I have trouble breathing when I receive nitroglycerin."

89. Risk factors for behavioral changes include diabetic emergency, drugs or alcohol, exposure to excessively hot or cold environments, and
  a. trauma.
  b. pregnancy.
  c. race.
  d. gender.

90. When should you check the readiness of an automated external defibrillator?
  a. each shift
  b. every 90 days
  c. once a week
  d. every other week

91. Your patient is a 61-year-old man who tells you that his wife died recently. He is depressed and speaks of wanting to join his wife in heaven. As you speak to him, you notice a large number of various pills in a bowl on his kitchen table. You should suspect that the
   a. patient's wife took a great deal of medication.
   b. patient has a serious medical condition.
   c. patient has a lot of medical conditions.
   d. patient may try to commit suicide.

92. What does the term *hypoglycemia* refer to?
   a. high blood pressure
   b. hemorrhagic shock
   c. elevated blood sugar
   d. low blood sugar

93. Rapid onset of altered mental status in a diabetic patient often results when the patient
   a. decreases their insulin dose.
   b. gets too little exercise.
   c. skips a meal.
   d. drinks alcohol.

94. Your patient is a 20-year-old man who has been in a motorcycle accident. Because of clues from the mechanism of injury on the scene, spinal and head injury are suspected. After your initial assessment, how often should you reassess vital signs?
   a. after every intervention
   b. every 15 minutes
   c. continuously during transport
   d. every 30 seconds

95. Your patient is a 23-year-old man who has suffered possible spinal trauma while playing football. He is still wearing his sports helmet as you begin your initial assessment. When should you remove his helmet?
   a. when it is time to apply a cervical collar
   b. if it prevents you from assessing the airway
   c. before you position him on the long board
   d. when you assess his level of consciousness

96. You should NOT attempt to stop bleeding from a cut on the head by applying direct pressure if you suspect
   a. skull fracture.
   b. spinal injury.
   c. internal bleeding.
   d. altered mental status.

97. Your patient, a 45-year-old woman, is still seated in her car after a crash. She does not appear to be in a life-threatening situation. What technique should you use to immobilize her spine?
   a. Logroll her directly onto the ground; then apply a long spine board.
   b. Have her get out of the car; then immobilize her while standing.
   c. Apply a cervical collar before assisting her out of the car.
   d. Apply a short spine board and then transfer her to a long spine board.

98. A blood clot that is attached to the inner wall of an artery, obstructing some or all blood flow through the artery is called a
   a. coronary impasse.
   b. hemobolus.
   c. thrombus.
   d. hemocoagulant.

99. Which patient should probably receive epinephrine via autoinjector in the field?
   a. male, age 23: extreme difficulty breathing, history of asthma
   b. female, age six: rapid, labored respirations, history of acute bronchial infection
   c. female, age 38: difficulty breathing, history of allergic reactions to stings
   d. male, age 64: difficulty breathing and chest pain, history of respiratory disease

100. Your patient is showing signs of possible carbon monoxide poisoning. What should be your first concern on this call?
   a. Secure the safety of yourself, other people, and the patient.
   b. Open the airway and administer supplemental oxygen.
   c. Transport the patient rapidly to the closest facility.
   d. Obtain medical direction to administer activated charcoal.

101. If a clinical problem is identified in the EMS service, a plan is developed and implemented to reduce further occurrences of the same problem. This is called
   a. quality improvement.
   b. call-sheet review.
   c. ongoing system redesign.
   d. quality assurance.

102. For any patient found unresponsive in the water, you should also suspect
   a. cardiac arrest.
   b. spinal injury.
   c. diabetic emergency.
   d. hyperthermia.

103. You can help improve the quality of care in your service by
   a. maintaining your equipment.
   b. continuing your education.
   c. getting feedback from patients.
   d. all of the above.

104. An essential component of any EMS system is
   a. medical oversight by a physician.
   b. plans for every type of disaster.
   c. means of communicating by cellular phone.
   d. tiered response of medical providers.

105. You would evaluate the severity of a patient's hyperthermia by assessing the
   a. temperature of the skin.
   b. color of the skin.
   c. blood pressure and heart rate.
   d. presence of muscle cramps.

106. The major differences between the airway of a child and that of an adult are that the child's airway is
   a. straighter and moister.
   b. longer and more extended.
   c. smaller and more flexible.
   d. weaker and wider.

107. In the case of children, airway adjuncts are used when the
   a. child is in respiratory distress and needs supplemental oxygen.
   b. usual means of opening and maintaining the airway are ineffective.
   c. child is frightened of the oxygen mask and nasal cannula.
   d. respiratory rate is less than 20/min or greater than 60/min.

108. You should select the correct size oropharyngeal airway for a child by measuring from the
   a. angle of the jaw to the corner of the mouth.
   b. central incisor to the angle of the jaw.
   c. central incisor to the tragus of the ear.
   d. corner of the mouth to the cricoid cartilage.

109. You can expand your knowledge that you received in your original EMT-Basic training by
   a. having dinner with your crew nightly.
   b. attending EMS continuing education opportunities.
   c. taking a recertification test.
   d. drilling on a skill already learned in class.

110. When providing artificial ventilation to infants and small children, the correct rate is to provide one breath every ___ seconds.
   a. two
   b. three
   c. four
   d. five

111. Which symptoms are signs of a partial upper airway obstruction due to the presence of a foreign body?
   a. increased work of breathing during expiration with a wheezy cough
   b. gasping respiratory efforts and the patient is unable to cough or speak
   c. no effort of breathing, absent chest wall movement, unable to cough or speak
   d. stridor during inspiration, inability to speak, and dyspnea

112. What is the main priority of care for a child who is having a seizure?
   a. Determine the cause of the seizure.
   b. Hold the patient's mouth open.
   c. Maintain a patent airway.
   d. Protect the patient's privacy.

113. Which of the following patients is showing signs and symptoms of imminent respiratory arrest?
   a. male, age two: respirations, 60/min; severe retractions; cyanosis
   b. female, age three: respirations, 50/min; nasal flaring; wheezing
   c. male, age four; respirations, 8/min; unresponsive; limp muscle tone
   d. female, age three: respirations, 10/min; cyanosis; decreased muscle tone

114. The role of the emergency medical dispatcher is to
   a. discourage the public from making unnecessary calls to 911.
   b. provide prearrival medical instructions for emergency care.
   c. determine exactly what is happening with the patient.
   d. ascertain medical insurance information before dispatch.

115. Which of the following describes a possible victim of child neglect?
   a. a child who appears malnourished and unsupervised
   b. a child who has many bruises in various stages of healing
   c. a child who has been burned repeatedly with cigarettes
   d. a child who is afraid to tell you what has happened

116. Your patient is a 9-month-old infant who has been scalded over 40% of her body. Her mother explains that the baby climbed into the bathtub and turned on the hot water by mistake. You should
   a. accuse the mother of child abuse and call social service workers.
   b. accept the mother's story and care for the child as a regular burn victim.
   c. refuse to enter the house without first getting police backup.
   d. care for the child and file a report of suspected child abuse.

117. Your partner has been involved with a number of serious trauma calls. She has become irritable both at home and work and is unable to sleep. She may be suffering from
   a. mononucleosis.
   b. a cumulative stress reaction.
   c. hypertension syndrome.
   d. physical exhaustion.

118. When caring for a patient whose baby is delivering in a breech presentation, you should do all of the following EXCEPT
   a. position the mother with her knees flexed, drawn up, and widely separated.
   b. administer high-flow oxygen to the mother and begin transport quickly.
   c. pull gently on the infant's trunk or legs if delivery of the head is delayed.
   d. allow the delivery to occur spontaneously until the trunk is delivered.

119. The correct way to stimulate a newborn to breathe is to
   a. rub its back or flick the soles of its feet.
   b. position it with the head higher than its body.
   c. suction its nose and then its mouth.
   d. smack it gently on the buttocks.

120. An infant who has a pink body and blue extremities, a pulse rate of 110/min, moderate muscle tone, good respirations, and who cries when you suction the nose has an APGAR score of
   a. two.
   b. four.
   c. six.
   d. eight.

121. You are assisting with childbirth in the field. As the infant's head is delivered, you should immediately check to see if the
   a. infant is spontaneously breathing.
   b. cord is wrapped around its neck.
   c. mouth and nose need suctioning.
   d. amniotic sac has broken open.

122. You are caring for a victim of a motor-vehicle accident who is approximately seven months pregnant. The mechanism of injury strongly suggests spinal trauma. How should you position the patient during transport?
   a. immobilized on a long back board that is then tilted to the left
   b. immobilized and transported supine on a long back board
   c. immobilized in whatever position he or she is most comfortable
   d. seated upright with his or her torso immobilized in a short spine device

123. The left atrium
   a. receives blood from the veins of the body.
   b. receives blood from the pulmonary veins.
   c. pumps blood to the lungs.
   d. pumps blood to the body.

124. Which patient is most likely to deliver her baby on the scene?
  a. 27-year-old, weak urge to push, contractions are three minutes apart and lasting 30 seconds
  b. 29-year-old, crowning visible, contractions two minutes apart and lasting 60 seconds
  c. 22-year-old, recent bloody show, contractions five minutes apart and lasting 30 seconds
  d. 30-year-old, water broke, contractions four minutes apart and lasting 45 seconds

125. The major blood vessel in the thigh that carries oxygen rich blood to the leg is called the
  a. femoral vein.
  b. femoral artery.
  c. brachial vein.
  d. brachial artery.

126. When caring for a rape victim, it is important to discourage the patient from
  a. bathing or douching.
  b. reporting the crime.
  c. talking about her feelings.
  d. naming her assailant.

127. When assisting at a delivery in the field, you should clamp, tie, and cut the umbilical cord
  a. right after the head is delivered.
  b. after the pulsations have stopped.
  c. after the placenta has delivered.
  d. before suctioning the newborn's mouth and nose.

128. If a newborn infant's respiratory effort is inadequate, your first intervention should be to
  a. provide artificial ventilations at a rate of 120/min.
  b. provide positive pressure ventilations at a rate of 60/min.
  c. administer high-flow oxygen via the blow-by method.
  d. transport immediately to a hospital with a newborn intensive care unit.

129. As an EMT-Basic, you can demonstrate positive professional attributes by maintaining a professional appearance and
  a. carrying out the functions of a paramedic in the field whenever possible.
  b. training bystanders to serve as EMTs in the field.
  c. continually updating your knowledge and skills.
  d. carrying out biomedical research to upgrade the profession.

130. You should wear a high-efficiency particulate air (HEPA) respirator when you transport a patient with
  a. AIDS.
  b. severe bleeding.
  c. shock.
  d. tuberculosis.

131. The blood vessel that carries oxygen-poor blood to the right atrium is the
  a. posterior tibia.
  b. internal jugular vein.
  c. vena cava.
  d. aorta.

132. What protective equipment is recommended when you are suctioning a patient's airway?
   a. gloves, gown, mask, and goggles
   b. gloves only, but wear a mask and goggles if splashing is likely
   c. gloves only
   d. No protective equipment is recommended for this procedure.

133. In order for expressed consent to treatment to be valid, the patient must be of legal age and able to make a rational decision, and you must
   a. obtain consent from a parent or guardian.
   b. obtain the patient's written authorization.
   c. explain all procedures before you do them.
   d. determine the patient's name and address.

134. In which situation would you be treating a patient under an assumption of implied consent?
   a. male, age 4, with broken leg, parent gives permission for treatment
   b. female, age 19, with seizure, who refuses treatment or transport
   c. male, age 47, with chest pain, requests transport to the hospital
   d. female, age 80, unconscious, no friends or family members present

135. In which of the following situations might you be found to have committed assault against your patient?
   a. You leave your patient at the scene of an accident before additional help arrives.
   b. You tell the patient, "If you don't let me splint your leg, I'll have to tie you up."
   c. You tell the patient, "You're over 18 and you have the right to refuse treatment."
   d. You transfer care of your patient to a first responder who has just arrived on the scene.

136. In some circumstances, you may legally provide confidential patient information to the receiving hospital, law enforcement agencies, or the patient's
   a. insurer.
   b. relatives.
   c. employer.
   d. spouse.

137. You are called to a bank where a hold-up has just occurred. Police are on scene, and through the large front window, you can see several injured people. You should enter this scene
   a. as soon as you can gather your equipment.
   b. when dispatch tells you it is safe to do so.
   c. when the patients request your help.
   d. when police tell you it is safe to enter.

138. When you lift a patient, you should
   a. twist your torso to spread the weight evenly.
   b. bend over and lift from the shoulders.
   c. bend your knees and keep your back straight.
   d. sit down on the ground and lift as high as you can.

139. The proper technique for carrying a patient with possible spinal injury down a flight of stairs is to
   a. immobilize the patient to a long spine board.
   b. strap the patient tightly to a stair chair.
   c. place the patient on a regular stretcher.
   d. immobilize the patient to a short spine device.

140. All of the following are correct principles for lifting and moving patients EXCEPT
   a. it is always preferable to push rather than to pull.
   b. always keep your back in a "locked in" position.
   c. keep the patient's weight far away from your body.
   d. when pulling, keep the line of pull straight.

141. The purpose of encoders and decoders in a radio system is to
   a. avoid transmitting over other users on the same frequency.
   b. reduce unnecessary radio traffic on a frequency.
   c. extend the range of communication.
   d. communicate only with the base station.

142. The increased pressure on arterial walls produced when the left ventricle contracts is the
   a. systolic pressure.
   b. arterial pressure.
   c. diastolic pressure.
   d. residual pressure.

143. Which of the following is NOT part of the standard medical reporting format information?
   a. chief complaint
   b. patient's age and gender
   c. assessment findings
   d. detailed medical history

144. Which of the following is an example of subjective information that should NOT appear on a patient record?
   a. Patient may be a victim of child abuse.
   b. Patient stated that she did not want treatment.
   c. Patient had multiple lacerations and contusions on her trunk and legs.
   d. Patient stated that the pain was "very bad."

145. You discover an error in a patient report after you have submitted it. You should
   a. file a report with your supervisor.
   b. submit an addendum.
   c. do nothing.
   d. retrieve and change the original report.

146. You should file a special situations report for which of the following situations?
   a. You witness a crime while off duty.
   b. You persuade a reluctant patient to accept treatment.
   c. You are exposed to hazardous materials.
   d. You are in the field with a new partner.

147. When the environment is dark, the pupil will
   a. dilate to allow more light in.
   b. dilate to allow less light in.
   c. constrict to allow more light in.
   d. constrict to allow less light in.

148. When approaching an air transport helicopter, you should
   a. approach from under the helicopter rotor.
   b. approach from the rear of the helicopter.
   c. stand up straight so you are clearly visible.
   d. stay within the pilot's field of vision.

149. You are called to the scene of a car crash. The rescue crew tells you that the patient, who is still trapped inside the car, is not breathing. An emergency move is not possible at this time, as the patient is pinned. After determining that the scene is safe to enter, you should
   a. assist the rescue crew in extricating the patient.
   b. open the airway while extrication is going on.
   c. call for further backup to the scene.
   d. perform a complete physical exam immediately.

150. The bladder of a blood pressure cuff should be centered over the
   a. carotid artery.
   b. radial artery.
   c. brachial artery.
   d. femoral artery.

► Answers

1. d. Preschool children often imagine that their injury is a result of a "bad" behavior of some sort. It is important for the rescuer to make efforts to calm the child and reassure her that what happened was not her fault.

2. a. Although adolescent patients are physiologically more alike to adults than children, when under stress, they may revert to a younger emotional age. Teenagers in particular can be focused on their outward appearance, and any injury may be perceived as a significant issue.

3. d. The normal respiratory rate for an adult is 12–20 breaths per minute, and chest wall motion should be regular and neither shallow nor very deep. Patient **a** is breathing too quickly for a three-month-old (it should be around 40 at this age), and the use of accessory muscles in the neck shows some level of distress is present. Patient **b** has a slower than normal rate (it should be around 20), and the irregularity and diaphragmatic nature suggest a spinal cord injury may be present. Patient **c** is breathing much too fast (rate 12–20 for adults), and the shallow chest motions suggests insufficiency or distress.

4. c. Infants breathe at a faster rate and adults in order to supply more oxygen to a higher metabolic rate. Their surface area is relatively larger, especially at the head, making infants more susceptible to heat loss. An infant's rib cage and abdominal muscles are much less developed than adults, which places internal organs such as the spleen and liver at greater risk for injury.

5. c. Any patient who is having difficulty breathing or who is cyanotic should receive oxygen through a nonrebreather mask.

6. b. Use the jaw thrust rather than the head-tilt/chin-lift to open the airway in any patient who has suspected spinal trauma. Use the sniffing position with a minimal amount of head-tilt for an infant. If a patient is unconscious but there is no suggestion of trauma you should use the head-tilt/chin-lift. Modify your techniques as needed to open the airway in the presence of a curved spine, however, begin with the basics— a head-tilt/chin-lift, unless you suspect trauma, then use the jaw thrust.

7. a. When using a rigid catheter to suction infants and small children, take care not to touch the back of the throat, since stimulation here can cause bradycardia due to stimulation of the vagus nerve. Touching the back of the throat or around the base of the tongue in any patient can trigger a gag, which could lead to vomiting, but the chance of this is not any greater in pediatric patients. The tongue cannot "fall into the airway"; however, in the absence of proper positioning, a flaccid tongue can relax into a position that could lead to obstruction of the airway.

8. d. Suctioning by the EMT-B is limited to the oro- and nasopharyngeal airways. You should never insert the catheter farther than the base of the tongue. Make sure you measure the catheter like you would measure an oropharyngeal airway, mark that measurement, and insert no deeper than that mark.

9. b. The flow-restricted, oxygen-powered ventilation device should not be used on infants and young children because it can damage lung tissue and allow air to enter the stomach.

10. c. The best sign that artificial ventilation is adequate is seeing the patient's chest rise and fall with each ventilation. A heart rate below 60 beats/min is too slow to indicate adequate ventilation. Just because you are providing 12 breaths per minute does not mean that rate is adequate for the patient, and you should continue to assess vital signs, level of consciousness, and monitor chest rise and fall. A patient who has the ability to speak in complete sentences most likely doesn't need BVM assistance in the first place.

11. b. Although the head-tilt/chin-lift is not ordinarily used on trauma patients because it interferes with spinal immobilization and alignment, opening the airway takes priority over all other considerations. Be sure to document your actions in the patient care report.

12. a. A respiratory rate that is either too fast or too slow may be a sign of inadequate breathing. Respiratory distress occurs with many medical and trauma problems and spans the age groups, making choice **b** inaccurate. An increased work (effort) of breathing frequently accompanies inadequate breathing as the patient attempts to compensate, but it should never be considered a "normal sign" as suggested by choice **c**. Patients may breathe shallowly or deeply for a number of reasons, only one of which is to compensate for an abnormal rate, making choice **d** inaccurate.

13. c. Stridor, a harsh sound usually heard during inspiration, is a sign of upper airway obstruction.

14. b. The back of an infant's head (occiput) is relatively larger compared to an adult. Placing the infant on his back, without should padding, may cause the head to tilt forward excessively, closing the airway.

15. c. A barrel chest is associated with a long history of respiratory disease, such as bronchitis, emphysema, or chronic obstructive pulmonary diseases. Because the alveoli are not functioning properly, air trapping occurs in the lungs. The increased effort it takes to move air in and out of the lungs results in an overdevelopment of the chest muscles and in time, leads to the barrel-shaped appearance.

16. d. You auscultate (listen with a stethoscope) through the chest wall to determine if breath sounds are present and equal on both sides of the chest. As you are listening, you may also note the relative rate and quality of breathing, but those are secondary reasons for listening to the chest wall. If you are having trouble determining the respiratory rate when you are performing vital signs, you can listen to one side of the chest wall to determine the respiratory rate.

17. c. You should always tell the truth to a young child, to maintain the trust needed to provide care. Provide comfort and words of encouragement to help the child through what is undoubtedly one of more difficult experiences in his or her young life.

18. b. An EMT-Basic may help a patient in respiratory difficulty to administer an inhaler if the inhaler was prescribed for that patient and medical direction is obtained. In some jurisdictions, you may have standing orders to assist the patient, which means medical direction is provided ahead of time in the standing order. It is important for you to determine how many doses she has already taken (choice **a**), but you must first determine if the medication she took was prescribed to her before you can assist her further. The standard dosing regimen for an EMT-B assisting with a prescribed inhaler is to provide a total of two doses, one every three minutes.

19. d. COPD is unlikely to occur in pediatric patients. The other three choices may cause some level of respiratory distress in the pediatric patient.

20. a. A seesaw pattern is a sign of breathing difficulty in infants.

21. b. For an unresponsive patient with no gag reflex, insert an oropharyngeal airway before beginning artificial ventilation. The airway will help maintain patency during artificial ventilation.

22. c. The best artificial ventilation technique to use is two-rescuer BVM. The flow-restricted, oxygen-powered ventilation device is preferred when only one EMT is available because it is an easier technique to perform than one-rescuer BVM. It is not used on infants or small children as it is more difficult to control the tidal volume being delivered to the patient, and gastric distention or barotrauma (lung tissue trauma from high pressures) may develop.

23. d. In this situation, you should suction for no more than 15 seconds before ventilating for two minutes. Suction every two minutes, and inform the receiving hospital immediately of your situation so they can offer their direction and be ready to take over airway management upon your arrival. Medical direction may recommend you position the immobilized patient on their side to facilitate drainage, but that is their decision to make as your standard of care is to transport the patient supine.

24. c. Use a nasal cannula for patients who, even after your reassurance and calming measures, cannot tolerate wearing a mask. If they persist in being unable to tolerate a cannula, try blow-by methods. Never withhold the administration of oxygen in a patient who needs it.

25. a. Signs of inadequate breathing include shortness of breath, a respiratory rate that is either too fast or two slow, irregular rhythm, cyanosis, and increased effort of breathing. Reduced work of breathing is a sign of impending respiratory failure and arrest and is noted in pediatric patients who have lost their ability to compensate for their inadequate breathing. It is considered an ominous sign of impending respiratory failure or arrest.

26. b. As the body tries to compensate for a decrease in oxygen levels in the blood stream, the heart will try to beat more quickly to circulate blood to the cells more quickly. The skin will also turn pale and cool as the body shifts blood flow back to the critical organs. The patient will also breathe more quickly to draw in more oxygen and expel more carbon dioxide.

27. c. Normal inhalation, which is considered the start of the respiratory cycle, is an active process that begins when the diaphragm and intercostal muscles start to contract. This causes the chest cavity to increase in size and decreases the interthoracic pressure so that air begins to flow into the lungs. At the completion of this active stretching, when interthoracic pressure is slightly above atmospheric pressure, the exhalation phase begins. The diaphragm and intercostal muscles begin to relax, and air is passively expelled from the lungs. Supraclavicular and accessory muscles are not used during the normal respiratory cycle. Their use is a sign of dyspnea.

28. b. The values for the 5-year-old are within normal ranges; those for the newborn and the adult are all abnormally low, while those for the 15-year-old are too high.

29. a. Normal pupils are equal in size and react to light; if they remain either constricted or dilated, they are nonreactive and therefore abnormal, and the pupils are always dark-colored.

30. c. *Perfusion* refers to the amount of oxygen reaching the cells through the blood; assessing skin color is one way to evaluate perfusion.

31. b. Snoring is a sign of noisy respiration, which usually indicates the presence of an obstruction; signs of labored respirations are grunting, stridor, use of accessory muscles, and nasal flaring.

32. c. A weak pulse is a common early sign of shock; although shock may accompany other conditions, such as trauma, a weak pulse is specifically associated with decreased tissue perfusion.

33. d. The patient's condition has become unstable; you should treat her for shock and reassess every five minutes. She should already be on oxygen. Alert medical control of your findings, but permission is not needed to treat this patient for shock. Because she is unstable, 15 minutes is too long a time period to go between vital signs assessments.

34. a. Palpate the brachial pulse in infants only; for all other patients, palpate the carotid pulse if you do not feel a radial pulse.

35. c. The airway is only partially blocked. Attempts to dislodge it now may cause a full airway obstruction. It is best to monitor the patient closely and provide supplemental oxygen while transporting to a receiving facility.

36. d. The patient's airway appears obstructed. A 4-year-old is too heavy to hold onto during back blows and chest thrusts. Kneeling on one knee and administering abdominal thrusts with one hand will be necessary to dislodge the obstruction.

37. b. This patient is in late stages of respiratory distress. Simply providing oxygen without ventilation will be inadequate for this child's needs.

38. c. The P in the DCAP-BTLS acronym stands for penetrations or punctures.

39. a. *Crepitation* is the sound of broken bones moving against one another; you would evaluate the chest of a trauma victim for this sign.

40. c. The Q in the OPQRST acronym stands for the quality of the pain. Ask the patient to describe the pain in his or her own words.

41. b. Because an unresponsive patient cannot give you details of his or her history and present illness, you should perform a rapid trauma assessment to find out what is causing the illness.

42. c. With three rescuers, one can begin chest compressions while the second ventilates the patient with a bag-valve mask and supplemental oxygen. The third person can apply the pads while CPR is ongoing.

43. c. With no other information available, you should continue CPR for one minute, then stop all activity while the AED reanalyzes the patient's rhythm.

44. b. One way to avoid alerting the patient that you are assessing respirations is to do so immediately after assessing the pulse, without removing your hand from the patient's wrist.

45. c. Normal skin feels warm and dry to the touch in a normal environment. It will feel cooler in a cold environment and warmer when the environment is hot.

46. d. Assess skin color of infants and children by checking the soles of the feet or palms of the hands. You should look here because this assesses perfusion in the most distal area of the peripheral circulation.

47. b. When assessing the patient's pupils in bright light, cover each eye for a few seconds and then note the reaction. You can also ask the patient to close both eyes and shade them with your hand placed above the brows.

48. a. You should always ask a conscious patient his normal blood pressure and pulse rate because even though this patient's pulse rate and BP are low, they may be normal for him; also, no other signs or symptoms of shock are present.

49. d. In infants and children, who rely heavily on the diaphragm for breathing, abdominal breathing is normal in the absence of other signs of labored breathing, such as supraclavicular and intercostal retractions.

50. c. Nonreactive or unequal pupils may be a sign of head injury or neurological problems. Conditions that result in cerebral hypoxia result in dilated pupils that are slow (sluggish) to react to light. Drug use may result in constricted or dilated pupils, but they should remain reactive to light.

51. b. Removing some of the patient's excessive chest hair may improve the contact surface between the AED and the patient, allowing a more effective shock to be delivered if needed.

52. a. Suspect shock (decreased tissue perfusion) whenever the distal pulse is weaker than the central pulse. Low blood pressure is a late sign of shock; do not wait to treat the patient for shock until the blood pressure drops.

53. b. Diastolic pressure is a measure of the force exerted against the walls of the blood vessels when the heart muscle relaxes; it is thus the lower of the two numbers that make up a blood pressure reading. Choice **d** describes the capillary refill test. The force of arterial circulation is not assessed in the prehospital setting as it requires very invasive procedures.

54. c. Try to focus the patient's attention on the history of the present illness, not on the entire prior history.

55. d. Oxygen-poor blood arrives in the right atrium and is pumped out through the right ventricle via the pulmonary arteries, to the lungs.

56. b. The radial artery, which is used to assess the peripheral pulse, is located on the thumb side of the wrist. The ulnar artery is located on the little finger side of the wrist. The brachial artery is felt in the upper arm, under the biceps muscle. The pulmonary artery cannot be palpated as it lies deep inside the chest.

57. a. Platelets (thrombocytes) are fragments of blood cells that aid in the formation of clots. The red blood cell carries oxygen on hemoglobin protein. White blood cells (leukocytes) fight infection. Plasma is the fluid component of blood that carries around blood cells.

58. c. For a patient, such as this one, who is displaying signs and symptoms of cardiac compromise, use the SAMPLE survey to focus your questioning to determine if there is any past history of cardiac disease and if the patient has a prescription for nitroglycerin.

59. d. If an arrest occurs en route to the hospital, stop the ambulance so you both can work on the patient, request immediate backup, and perform two-person CPR and defibrillation with the AED. A single rescuer in the back of an ambulance cannot perform all the necessary procedures.

60. b. Check the patient's pulse at the end of each round of three shocks, and if the pulse is absent, continue with CPR. If the pulse is present, check ABCs and provide respiratory support as needed.

61. c. The earliest signs of shock are subtle changes in mental status, such as anxiety and restlessness, and tachycardia. Fatigue and depression are not common signs of shock. Cyanosis is not one of the earliest signs and shallow respirations can occur any time during the shock process. Low blood pressure is a late sign of shock.

62. a. Blood carries heat, and a loss of blood will result in a drop in body temperature. Shivering, the body's response to cold, increases metabolism by wasting oxygen and energy that would be better spent in fueling hypoxic cells.

63. a. Apply indirect pressure (pressure point pressure) on the femoral artery by pressing on the left side of the groin. By pressing on the femoral artery you will slow the flow of blood into the leg.

64. d. Mechanisms of injury associated with severe internal bleeding include falls, motorcycle and car crashes, explosions, and penetrating injuries.

65. b. A sucking chest wound, which allows air to enter the lung directly through the chest wall, should be covered with an occlusive dressing taped on only three sides so that air may escape from the chest cavity during exhalation, but self-seal to prevent air entry during inhalation.

66. b. Internal bleeding caused by the rupture of an abdominal artery is an occasional emergency among elderly patients; symptoms are abdominal pain, tenderness, and rigidity. This patient is too old to be pregnant. A thoracic aneurysm will not cause abdominal distension.

67. a. For a nosebleed, when no trauma is suspected, have the patient sit up and lean forward to prevent blood from entering the airway and gently pinch the nostrils together.

68. c. Cardiac pain, unlike respiratory pain, usually is not increased by movement or palpation; it is more diffuse than respiratory pain and may be felt in the shoulder, neck, and jaw, as well as in the chest.

69. a. Altered mental status is a contraindication to administration of nitroglycerin; otherwise, patients can take their prescribed dosage. With physician direction, nitroglycerine may be administered several times in a 24-hour period.

70. d. Almost all documented cases of inappropriate shocks have been attributed to human error, such as using the AED in a moving vehicle or operating it on a patient with a pulse.

71. b. For a pulseless patient, defibrillation takes precedence over either administering oxygen or performing CPR, but always stop the ambulance before using the AED. Do not analyze a heart rhythm in a moving vehicle.

72. d. It is critical to support life functions immediately and defibrillate a heart in ventricular fibrillation as soon as possible.

73. c. Nitroglycerin's action is to increase blood flow to the heart muscle by dilating the arteries. This can cause blood pressure to fall. A patient with blood pressure less than 90 systolic can go even lower, placing the patient at risk.

74. d. Do not elevate the legs of a shock patient if there is either chest injury or suspected spinal trauma; place the patient flat on his or her back. Generally, these patients are also immobilized to a long spine board.

75. a. Although you should quickly splint the patient's wounds and stop major bleeding, treatment of a patient in shock should focus on rapidly transporting her to the hospital. You can continue to stabilize and treat her injuries while you are transporting her. Perform any other examinations while en route to the hospital. Monitor and assess her vital signs every five minutes.

76. d. Capillary bleeding is dark red and oozes slowly from the wound. Internal bleeding, which can be arterial or venous, is found inside the body and generally has no visible evidence. Arterial bleeding is brighter red and spurts with each heartbeat, and venous bleeding is darker red and flows steadily.

77. b. The purpose of using the PASG for a patient with a pelvic injury and signs and symptoms of shock is to immobilize the injury and reduce internal bleeding. It reduces internal bleeding by preventing movement and by applying pressure and squeezing the vessels. This process is called *tamponade.*

78. c. Signs of internal bleeding into the gastrointestinal tract include bloody vomit or feces, coffee-ground vomit, tarry stools, and abdominal distention. Bloody urine indicates an injury or problem with the urinary tract, kidneys, or bladder.

79. a. Always transport an amputated part along with the patient, wrapped in sterile dressings and then in plastic. Keep the amputated part cool, but do not put the foot directly in contact with ice or ice water because the ice can cause further tissue damage, which may result in the inability to reimplant the amputated part.

80. a. It is impossible to determine the actual degree of tissue damage in the field, so the purpose of the focused assessment is to gather information for the receiving facility. You should always ask about medications; it is the M of SAMPLE. The focused history has nothing to do with AED use. Cardiac pain has all sorts of presentations, making it difficult to differentiate from other conditions.

81. c. The three types of muscle are skeletal (also called voluntary), smooth (also called involuntary), and cardiac muscle. The GI tract is made up of involuntary muscle tissue.

82. c. Bleeding is not a sign limited just to bone injury; any open wound will bleed. Signs of bone or joint injury include deformity, pain, crepitation, swelling, bruising, a joint that is locked into position, false movement, and exposed bone ends protruding through the skin.

83. b. For a patient who is showing signs of shock as well as possible spinal injury, care focuses on immobilization and rapid transport, rather than on caring for isolated extremity injuries. This patient already has an open airway and ventilation is not necessary, although oxygen should be administered by a nonrebreather mask and his respiratory status should be closely monitored as his respiratory rate is a little fast and his effort is shallow.

84. c. Always assess the pulse, motor function, and sensation distal to the injury before and after splinting, and record your findings.

85. b. The sling and swathe is used to immobilize both the arm and shoulder in patients with a shoulder or upper extremity injury.

86. a. Pneumatic splints, such as vacuum and air splints, are used for angulated injuries, or injuries that result in deformity of the limb because they can be conformed to the shape of the injury during their application.

87. d. *Reasonable force* refers to the amount of force necessary to prevent injury to the patient or anyone else, including the rescuers. It is sometimes necessary to use force to restrain a patient with a behavioral disorder. Reasonable force does not define the type of restraints needed.

88. d. These are signs of a severe allergic reaction. A headache is one side effect of nitroglycerin use, but by itself, is not a sign of an allergic reaction.

89. a. Trauma, either being injured oneself or seeing one's family member injured, often results in behavioral emergencies because of fear and stress. Hypoxia can also lead to an altered mental status that may mimic a behavioral emergency.

90. a. Checking at the beginning of every shift ensures that the batteries are charged and the pads are immediately available.

91. d. The patient has suffered a recent loss and may have a lethal dose of medication on hand, so you should suspect that he may try to commit suicide.

92. d. *Hypoglycemia* refers to decreased levels of blood glucose (sugar). Hypertension is elevated blood pressure. Hemorrhagic shock is also called hypoperfusion. Hyperglycemia is elevated blood sugar.

93. c. Rapid onset of altered mental status in diabetic patients is associated with hypoglycemia, or low blood sugar. This most commonly occurs when patients take their normal dose of insulin but skip a meal. Excessive exercise can also bring on a hypoglycemic state.

94. a. Because patients with spinal injuries are at risk of paralysis and breathing difficulties, reassess vital signs after every intervention, such as cervical immobilization or whole-body immobilizations. Once the patient is a little more stable, you would continue to reassess vital signs every five minutes because he would still be a critical patient.

95. b. Leave a helmet in place if it fits well, does not interfere with assessment or administration of oxygen, and the patient is not in cardiac arrest. Leave the shoulder pads in place along with the helmet. You do not need to apply a cervical collar to this patient, but you should immobilize his body and head to a long spine board. You can assess his level of consciousness without moving the helmet.

96. a. Do not apply direct pressure to the head to stop bleeding if there is any possibility of skull fracture because the pressure you exert may push bone fragments into the brain tissue.

97. d. Immobilize the patient to a short spine board like the Kendrick Extrication Device or other commercial device while she is still seated; then transfer her to a long spine board. If you suspected she was in shock or was unstable, you would perform a rapid extrication by applying a cervical collar and quickly removing her from the vehicle with the assistance of several rescuers while trying to maintain a neutral alignment to her spine.

98. c. Tissue "downstream" from the thrombus will experience a decrease in oxygen levels and waste build up, conditions that may injure the tissue as in a myocardial infarction.

99. c. When prescribed by a physician, epinephrine autoinjectors are used by patients with a history of severe allergic reaction in case of difficulty breathing or hypoperfusion. Epinephrine will not be given for bronchial infections. Epinephrine autoinjectors should not be given to patients with a cardiac history.

100. a. In cases of inhalation poisoning when the toxin may still be present, your first concern should be to ensure your own safety and that of other people in the area. Move the patient to your ambulance, then begin your assessment and treatment. Activated charcoal is administered in the case of ingested (swallowed) poisons, not inhaled poisons.

101. a. Quality assurance is the process that identifies the problem and focuses on the individual to make corrections. Quality improvement focuses on the system to identify an issue or process that is prone to failure and concentrates on making system corrections to solve the problem.

102. b. The incidence of spinal injury in near-drowning victims is extremely high; always suspect spinal injury when a patient is found unresponsive in the water. You should also treat for hypothermia, not hyperthermia.

103. d. All are excellent methods in improving your ability to provide competent care, which, in turn, improves the overall quality of the system's service.

104. a. A medical director is a crucial element of any EMS system, no matter how small. It is impossible to have a plan for every specific disaster that can happen in a community, although a system should have generalized operational procedures in place for disasters. Cellular phones may not provide the security or reach necessary to maintain communications, and not all systems have tiered responses of its medical providers.

105. a. Patients with hyperthermia with cool skin still retain their ability to eliminate heat; their condition is therefore not as serious as that of patients with hot skin, who have lost this ability. You should also closely monitor the patient's mental status.

106. c. In comparison to an adult's airway, a child's airway is smaller, narrower, and more flexible; therefore, there is danger of occluding the airway by hyperextending the neck.

107. b. Airway adjuncts, such as nasopharyngeal and oropharyngeal airways, are used only when the jaw thrust and head-tilt/chin-lift are ineffective in opening the airway.

108. a. Select the correct size oral airway for a child by measuring from the angle of the jaw to the corner of the mouth.

109. d. Continuing education is crucial for the ongoing development of any medical provider. While skill drilling and taking a test may be necessary to maintain ongoing certification, neither is designed to increase or expand your knowledge base.

110. b. The correct rate for providing artificial ventilation to an infant or small child is one breath every three seconds (20 breaths per minute) and the correct rate for an adult is one breath every five seconds.

111. d. Partial upper airway obstruction due to a foreign body is differentiated from complete obstruction by the patient's ability to breathe or speak. Stridor indicates upper airway obstruction. A wheezing sound (patient **a**) indicates a lower airway obstruction. Patients **b** and **c** have a total airway obstruction.

112. c. The main goal of care for a child who is having a seizure is to maintain a patent airway; do not place anything in the child's mouth, and make sure that suction is available. You should also protect the patient from any injuries while he or she is actively seizing and protect their privacy, but these are secondary concerns.

113. **c.** Signs of imminent respiratory arrest are a breathing rate of less than 10/min, limp muscle tone, slow or absent heart rate, and weak or absent distal pulses; the patient will also be unresponsive. These patients need artificial ventilation and chest compression. Patients **a**, **b**, and **d** are in respiratory insufficiency and the early stages of respiratory failure, which, if uncorrected, will lead to respiratory arrest.

114. **b.** The dispatcher can impact patient outcome by providing callers critical prearrival instructions such as CPR or clearing blocked airways.

115. **a.** Signs of neglect include malnourishment, lack of supervision, unsafe living conditions, or untreated chronic illness; options **b**, **c**, and **d** are examples of the signs of child abuse.

116. **d.** Because the mechanism of injury is not consistent with the baby's developmental age, you should provide emergency care and file a report of suspected child abuse.

117. **b.** Over time, exposure to many events that have poor or negative outcomes can impact the psychological well-being of even the most seasoned EMS professional.

118. **c.** Do not pull on the infant's trunk or legs to assist delivery. If the baby's head is not delivered spontaneously, place your hand inside the birth canal to hold the cord and walls of the vagina away from the baby's face, and transport immediately.

119. **a.** If necessary, stimulate a newborn to breathe by gently rubbing its back or flicking the soles of its feet. You should always suction the mouth first and then the nose because infants are obligate nasal breathers, and if you suction the nose first, it may stimulate them to take a breath, inhaling any amniotic fluid remaining in the oropharynx into the lungs.

120. **d.** The APGAR score would equal eight, or one point for Appearance (skin color), two points for Pulse rate, two points for Grimace, one point for Activity, and two points for Respirations.

121. **b.** As the head is delivered, make sure that the cord is not wrapped around the infant's neck. All newborns are suctioned at this point. You should check for spontaneous respirations after the infant is completely emerged from the birth canal, and if necessary, break the amniotic sac just as the head appears. You will note the presence of the amniotic sac during the time the infant is crowning.

122. **a.** The patient should be immobilized on a long backboard, but the entire board should be tilted to the left side with padding to reduce the pressure of the fetus on her circulatory systems. This condition is called supine hypotension syndrome.

123. **b.** Pulmonary veins return oxygen-rich blood from the lungs to the left atrium, where it is sent to the left ventricle and pumped to the rest of the body.

124. **b.** When crowning is visible, delivery is imminent; also, this patient's contractions are very close together and are lasting a full 60 seconds.

125. **b.** The femoral vein returns blood back to the heart. The brachial artery is located in the arm.

126. **a.** The rape victim should be discouraged from bathing, douching, urinating, or cleaning her wounds, since any of these activities may destroy evidence.

127. **b.** The EMT who is caring for the mother should clamp, tie, and cut the umbilical cord after its pulsations have stopped; a second EMT will simultaneously be caring for the infant.

128. **b.** If, on initial assessment, the newborn's respirations are slow, shallow, or absent, you should provide positive pressure ventilations with a bag-valve mask at the rate of 60/min. After about 30 seconds of this intervention, you should reassess the patient to determine if you need to continue with the BVM ventilation.

129. **c.** Positive professional attributes include maintaining a professional appearance and continually updating your knowledge and skills.

130. d. High-efficiency particulate air respirators are worn when in a confined area with patients whose diseases are spread through the air, such as tuberculosis.

131. c. The jugular vein also carries blood back to the heart, but it ends at the vena cava, which collects all of the blood from the body and channels it into the right atrium.

132. b. Wear gloves when suctioning, but wear a mask and protective goggles as well if splashing is likely.

133. c. Expressed consent depends on the patient being of age and able to understand, and you explaining all procedures clearly.

134. d. Implied consent is applicable in cases where the patient is unable to consent; you provide treatment under the assumption that any rational person would want to receive treatment under the circumstances.

135. b. Threatening the patient may be held to constitute assault; options **a** and **d** both constitute abandonment of a patient.

136. a. You may legally provide confidential information to the receiving facility, to law enforcement agencies or a court, and to the patient's insurance company.

137. d. Do not enter a crime scene until police tell you that it is safe to do so.

138. c. Bend your knees and keep your back straight when lifting to avoid straining your back.

139. a. The preferred technique for carrying a patient downstairs is to use a stair chair; however, for a patient with a possible spinal injury, use a long spine board instead.

140. c. Always keep the weight as close to your body as you can.

141. b. The purpose of encoders and decoders, which block out transmissions not intended for the specific unit, is to reduce unnecessary radio traffic on a frequency.

142. a. The diastolic pressure is the resting pressure in the artery when the left ventricle is relaxed.

143. d. Detailed medical history is not part of the EMT's standard reporting format, although pertinent recent history should be included.

144. a. This statement is an opinion, not an objective finding; in a case of suspected abuse, you should state the reasons for your suspicions. For example: "Patient had multiple burns on her legs and feet."

145. b. An addendum should clearly state the correct information; attach the addendum to the original report, and give a copy to the receiving facility.

146. c. Special situations reports are filed when you are exposed to hazardous materials or infectious agents, when you are involved in a crime scene or vehicle crash, or in cases of patient refusal of treatment or possible abuse or neglect.

147. a. When the pupil dilates, the opening through which light passes increases in size. In a low-light situation, this is beneficial in allowing the viewer to see more clearly in the dark.

148. d. When approaching a helicopter, stay low and approach from the front, within the pilot's field of vision. If you are using the clock method and the front of the helicopter is facing the twelve-o'clock position, you should approach between nine and three o'clock.

149. b. Always perform critical care, such as opening the patient's airway, while extrication is occurring.

150. c. The blood pressure cuff, when inflated, squeezes the brachial artery until it squeezes shut. As air is released from the bladder, at some point, the pressure in the artery exceeds the pressure in the cuff, causing blood to squirt past the cuff. In order for this to be accurate, the bladder should be as closely centered over the brachial artery as possible.

EMT-Basic Practice Exam 4

CHAPTER SUMMARY

This is the last of four practice exams in this book based on the National Registry EMT-Basic written exam. Using all the experience and strategies you gained from the other three, take this exam to see how far you have come since taking the first test.

This is the last of four practice exams in the book, but it is not designed to be any harder or any trickier than the other three. It is simply another representation of what you might expect for the real test. Just as when you go to take the real test, there shouldn't be anything here to surprise you. In fact, you probably already know what's in a lot of it! That's the idea for the real test, too—you will be prepared, so you will not be taken by surprise.

For this last test, pull together all the tips you've been practicing since the first test. Give yourself the time and the space to work, perhaps choosing an unfamiliar location such as a library, since you won't be taking the real test in your living room. In addition, draw on what you've learned from reading the answer explanations. Remember the types of questions that troubled you in the past, and when you are unsure, try to consider how those answers were explained.

Most of all, relax. You have worked hard and have every right to be confident.

1.	ⓐ	ⓑ	ⓒ	ⓓ	51.	ⓐ	ⓑ	ⓒ	ⓓ	101.	ⓐ	ⓑ	ⓒ	ⓓ
2.	ⓐ	ⓑ	ⓒ	ⓓ	52.	ⓐ	ⓑ	ⓒ	ⓓ	102.	ⓐ	ⓑ	ⓒ	ⓓ
3.	ⓐ	ⓑ	ⓒ	ⓓ	53.	ⓐ	ⓑ	ⓒ	ⓓ	103.	ⓐ	ⓑ	ⓒ	ⓓ
4.	ⓐ	ⓑ	ⓒ	ⓓ	54.	ⓐ	ⓑ	ⓒ	ⓓ	104.	ⓐ	ⓑ	ⓒ	ⓓ
5.	ⓐ	ⓑ	ⓒ	ⓓ	55.	ⓐ	ⓑ	ⓒ	ⓓ	105.	ⓐ	ⓑ	ⓒ	ⓓ
6.	ⓐ	ⓑ	ⓒ	ⓓ	56.	ⓐ	ⓑ	ⓒ	ⓓ	106.	ⓐ	ⓑ	ⓒ	ⓓ
7.	ⓐ	ⓑ	ⓒ	ⓓ	57.	ⓐ	ⓑ	ⓒ	ⓓ	107.	ⓐ	ⓑ	ⓒ	ⓓ
8.	ⓐ	ⓑ	ⓒ	ⓓ	58.	ⓐ	ⓑ	ⓒ	ⓓ	108.	ⓐ	ⓑ	ⓒ	ⓓ
9.	ⓐ	ⓑ	ⓒ	ⓓ	59.	ⓐ	ⓑ	ⓒ	ⓓ	109.	ⓐ	ⓑ	ⓒ	ⓓ
10.	ⓐ	ⓑ	ⓒ	ⓓ	60.	ⓐ	ⓑ	ⓒ	ⓓ	110.	ⓐ	ⓑ	ⓒ	ⓓ
11.	ⓐ	ⓑ	ⓒ	ⓓ	61.	ⓐ	ⓑ	ⓒ	ⓓ	111.	ⓐ	ⓑ	ⓒ	ⓓ
12.	ⓐ	ⓑ	ⓒ	ⓓ	62.	ⓐ	ⓑ	ⓒ	ⓓ	112.	ⓐ	ⓑ	ⓒ	ⓓ
13.	ⓐ	ⓑ	ⓒ	ⓓ	63.	ⓐ	ⓑ	ⓒ	ⓓ	113.	ⓐ	ⓑ	ⓒ	ⓓ
14.	ⓐ	ⓑ	ⓒ	ⓓ	64.	ⓐ	ⓑ	ⓒ	ⓓ	114.	ⓐ	ⓑ	ⓒ	ⓓ
15.	ⓐ	ⓑ	ⓒ	ⓓ	65.	ⓐ	ⓑ	ⓒ	ⓓ	115.	ⓐ	ⓑ	ⓒ	ⓓ
16.	ⓐ	ⓑ	ⓒ	ⓓ	66.	ⓐ	ⓑ	ⓒ	ⓓ	116.	ⓐ	ⓑ	ⓒ	ⓓ
17.	ⓐ	ⓑ	ⓒ	ⓓ	67.	ⓐ	ⓑ	ⓒ	ⓓ	117.	ⓐ	ⓑ	ⓒ	ⓓ
18.	ⓐ	ⓑ	ⓒ	ⓓ	68.	ⓐ	ⓑ	ⓒ	ⓓ	118.	ⓐ	ⓑ	ⓒ	ⓓ
19.	ⓐ	ⓑ	ⓒ	ⓓ	69.	ⓐ	ⓑ	ⓒ	ⓓ	119.	ⓐ	ⓑ	ⓒ	ⓓ
20.	ⓐ	ⓑ	ⓒ	ⓓ	70.	ⓐ	ⓑ	ⓒ	ⓓ	120.	ⓐ	ⓑ	ⓒ	ⓓ
21.	ⓐ	ⓑ	ⓒ	ⓓ	71.	ⓐ	ⓑ	ⓒ	ⓓ	121.	ⓐ	ⓑ	ⓒ	ⓓ
22.	ⓐ	ⓑ	ⓒ	ⓓ	72.	ⓐ	ⓑ	ⓒ	ⓓ	122.	ⓐ	ⓑ	ⓒ	ⓓ
23.	ⓐ	ⓑ	ⓒ	ⓓ	73.	ⓐ	ⓑ	ⓒ	ⓓ	123.	ⓐ	ⓑ	ⓒ	ⓓ
24.	ⓐ	ⓑ	ⓒ	ⓓ	74.	ⓐ	ⓑ	ⓒ	ⓓ	124.	ⓐ	ⓑ	ⓒ	ⓓ
25.	ⓐ	ⓑ	ⓒ	ⓓ	75.	ⓐ	ⓑ	ⓒ	ⓓ	125.	ⓐ	ⓑ	ⓒ	ⓓ
26.	ⓐ	ⓑ	ⓒ	ⓓ	76.	ⓐ	ⓑ	ⓒ	ⓓ	126.	ⓐ	ⓑ	ⓒ	ⓓ
27.	ⓐ	ⓑ	ⓒ	ⓓ	77.	ⓐ	ⓑ	ⓒ	ⓓ	127.	ⓐ	ⓑ	ⓒ	ⓓ
28.	ⓐ	ⓑ	ⓒ	ⓓ	78.	ⓐ	ⓑ	ⓒ	ⓓ	128.	ⓐ	ⓑ	ⓒ	ⓓ
29.	ⓐ	ⓑ	ⓒ	ⓓ	79.	ⓐ	ⓑ	ⓒ	ⓓ	129.	ⓐ	ⓑ	ⓒ	ⓓ
30.	ⓐ	ⓑ	ⓒ	ⓓ	80.	ⓐ	ⓑ	ⓒ	ⓓ	130.	ⓐ	ⓑ	ⓒ	ⓓ
31.	ⓐ	ⓑ	ⓒ	ⓓ	81.	ⓐ	ⓑ	ⓒ	ⓓ	131.	ⓐ	ⓑ	ⓒ	ⓓ
32.	ⓐ	ⓑ	ⓒ	ⓓ	82.	ⓐ	ⓑ	ⓒ	ⓓ	132.	ⓐ	ⓑ	ⓒ	ⓓ
33.	ⓐ	ⓑ	ⓒ	ⓓ	83.	ⓐ	ⓑ	ⓒ	ⓓ	133.	ⓐ	ⓑ	ⓒ	ⓓ
34.	ⓐ	ⓑ	ⓒ	ⓓ	84.	ⓐ	ⓑ	ⓒ	ⓓ	134.	ⓐ	ⓑ	ⓒ	ⓓ
35.	ⓐ	ⓑ	ⓒ	ⓓ	85.	ⓐ	ⓑ	ⓒ	ⓓ	135.	ⓐ	ⓑ	ⓒ	ⓓ
36.	ⓐ	ⓑ	ⓒ	ⓓ	86.	ⓐ	ⓑ	ⓒ	ⓓ	136.	ⓐ	ⓑ	ⓒ	ⓓ
37.	ⓐ	ⓑ	ⓒ	ⓓ	87.	ⓐ	ⓑ	ⓒ	ⓓ	137.	ⓐ	ⓑ	ⓒ	ⓓ
38.	ⓐ	ⓑ	ⓒ	ⓓ	88.	ⓐ	ⓑ	ⓒ	ⓓ	138.	ⓐ	ⓑ	ⓒ	ⓓ
39.	ⓐ	ⓑ	ⓒ	ⓓ	89.	ⓐ	ⓑ	ⓒ	ⓓ	139.	ⓐ	ⓑ	ⓒ	ⓓ
40.	ⓐ	ⓑ	ⓒ	ⓓ	90.	ⓐ	ⓑ	ⓒ	ⓓ	140.	ⓐ	ⓑ	ⓒ	ⓓ
41.	ⓐ	ⓑ	ⓒ	ⓓ	91.	ⓐ	ⓑ	ⓒ	ⓓ	141.	ⓐ	ⓑ	ⓒ	ⓓ
42.	ⓐ	ⓑ	ⓒ	ⓓ	92.	ⓐ	ⓑ	ⓒ	ⓓ	142.	ⓐ	ⓑ	ⓒ	ⓓ
43.	ⓐ	ⓑ	ⓒ	ⓓ	93.	ⓐ	ⓑ	ⓒ	ⓓ	143.	ⓐ	ⓑ	ⓒ	ⓓ
44.	ⓐ	ⓑ	ⓒ	ⓓ	94.	ⓐ	ⓑ	ⓒ	ⓓ	144.	ⓐ	ⓑ	ⓒ	ⓓ
45.	ⓐ	ⓑ	ⓒ	ⓓ	95.	ⓐ	ⓑ	ⓒ	ⓓ	145.	ⓐ	ⓑ	ⓒ	ⓓ
46.	ⓐ	ⓑ	ⓒ	ⓓ	96.	ⓐ	ⓑ	ⓒ	ⓓ	146.	ⓐ	ⓑ	ⓒ	ⓓ
47.	ⓐ	ⓑ	ⓒ	ⓓ	97.	ⓐ	ⓑ	ⓒ	ⓓ	147.	ⓐ	ⓑ	ⓒ	ⓓ
48.	ⓐ	ⓑ	ⓒ	ⓓ	98.	ⓐ	ⓑ	ⓒ	ⓓ	148.	ⓐ	ⓑ	ⓒ	ⓓ
49.	ⓐ	ⓑ	ⓒ	ⓓ	99.	ⓐ	ⓑ	ⓒ	ⓓ	149.	ⓐ	ⓑ	ⓒ	ⓓ
50.	ⓐ	ⓑ	ⓒ	ⓓ	100.	ⓐ	ⓑ	ⓒ	ⓓ	150.	ⓐ	ⓑ	ⓒ	ⓓ

► EMT-Basic Practice Exam 4

1. Which set of vital signs is within normal limits?
   a. newborn: pulse, 100; respirations, 36/min; BP, 60/30
   b. male, age 3: pulse, 98; respirations, 27/min; BP, 84/48
   c. female, age 9: pulse, 118; respirations, 24/min; BP, 120/80
   d. male, age 24: pulse, 92; respirations, 26/min; BP, 112/70

2. Use of accessory muscles, grunting, and stridor are all signs of
   a. labored respirations.
   b. noisy respirations.
   c. shallow respirations.
   d. agonal respirations.

3. Your patient is a 23-year-old male who has sprained his ankle. He tells you that he is a marathon runner. When taking baseline vital signs, you find that his resting pulse is 48. You should
   a. treat the patient for signs and symptoms of shock.
   b. consult online medical direction for advice.
   c. administer oxygen and nitroglycerin, and transport.
   d. ask the patient what his normal pulse rate is.

4. You assess the color, temperature, and condition of a patient's skin to gather information about his or her
   a. capillary refill.
   b. heart rate.
   c. perfusion.
   d. respiration.

5. The reason for assessing a patient's pupils is to look for signs of
   a. shock.
   b. trauma.
   c. cardiac compromise.
   d. head injury.

6. Which statement about assessing blood pressure is correct?
   a. If you obtain one normal reading, it is not necessary to reassess blood pressure.
   b. A single reading is not as useful as multiple readings used to look for a trend.
   c. Variation of more than 5 mm Hg from normal is considered very significant.
   d. Assess blood pressure by palpation only when the patient is in a quiet place.

7. While evaluating your 56-year-old patient with chest discomfort, he suddenly collapses and becomes unconscious. He is apneic and pulseless. Which of the following will most likely reverse this condition?
   a. Provide high-flow oxygen with a nonrebreather mask.
   b. Begin chest compressions at a rate of 80 beats per minute.
   c. Begin the process of defibrillating a patient with an AED.
   d. Ventilate the patient with a pocket mask and supplemental oxygen.

8. Your patient is unconscious as a result of a fall. In determining the mechanisms of injury, it is most important to find out
   a. what surface she fell from.
   b. if the fall was an accident.
   c. the distance she fell.
   d. the time she fell.

9. Which trauma patient is at greatest risk for serious injury?

  a. male, age 43, who fell seven feet from a step ladder

  b. female, age 24, involved in a moderate-speed vehicle collision

  c. male, age 17, who fell off a bicycle onto concrete

  d. female, age 5, involved in a moderate-speed vehicle collision

10. A bystander is doing CPR on a patient in cardiac arrest. You size up the scene, practice body substance isolation, and begin your initial assessment by having the bystander

  a. verify pulselessness.

  b. continue CPR.

  c. stop CPR.

  d. provide a history of cardiac arrest.

11. Your patient, a trauma victim, has flat jugular veins while he is lying down. What is this is a sign of?

  a. increased intracranial pressure

  b. respiratory distress

  c. spinal injury

  d. severe blood loss

12. Which of the following is an advantage of semiautomated defibrillation over a manual defibrillator?

  a. It is faster to deliver a shock to a cardiac arrest patient.

  b. You do not have to perform an initial assessment.

  c. You do not have to confirm cardiac arrest.

  d. It is easier for you to analyze the rhythms.

13. In addition to evaluating for DCAP-BTLS, you would evaluate a patient's lower extremities for which of the following?

  a. firmness, softness, or distention

  b. paradoxical motion and crepitation

  c. pulse, motor function, and sensation

  d. flexion, compression, and movement

14. For which patient can you safely perform only a focused assessment, after taking vital signs and a SAMPLE history?

  a. male, age 6, who fell off his bicycle in the road

  b. male, age 11, who had a diving accident

  c. female, age 25, with cuts and bruises after a car crash

  d. female, age 43, who cut her finger in the kitchen

15. Which question would you ask to evaluate the T part of the OPQRST acronym?

  a. How long have you felt this pain?

  b. How bad is this pain today?

  c. Does the pain spread anywhere else?

  d. What makes the pain feel better?

16. You should apply the AED pads to your patient when he

  a. complains of trouble breathing.

  b. appears confused and "out of it".

  c. is pulseless and apneic.

  d. is unconscious and vomiting.

17. You are en route to the receiving facility with a 71-year-old male patient with a history of heart disease. The patient's distress has been relieved with nitroglycerin, and his vital signs are stable. How often should you reassess the patient's vital signs?
   a. every 5 minutes or less
   b. every 15 minutes
   c. every 30 minutes
   d. There is no need to reassess a stable patient.

18. The major purpose of the EMT's interactions with a patient during transport is to continuously evaluate the patient's
   a. mental status and airway.
   b. pulse and respirations.
   c. anxiety and restlessness.
   d. skin color and pupils.

19. Your patient is a 62-year-old woman with chest pain. When assessing the P in the SAMPLE history, you might ask
   a. do you have any pain right now?
   b. are you allergic to any medications?
   c. have you ever had this pain before?
   d. what medications are you currently taking?

20. Your patient is in cardiac arrest. Your semiautomatic defibrillator does not deliver any shocks when you activate it. Your next action should be to
   a. turn off the AED and resume CPR.
   b. take off the AED pads and resume CPR.
   c. check for breathing and pulses.
   d. contact medical control.

21. If a patient's respiratory rate is irregular, you should count the respirations for how long?
   a. 15 seconds and multiply by four
   b. 30 seconds and multiply by two
   c. one full minute
   d. two full minutes

22. What should you assume when you hear wheezing during respiration?
   a. The small airways are constricted.
   b. The patient cannot keep the airway open.
   c. There is liquid in the airway.
   d. The patient is using accessory muscles.

23. Which patient's vital signs are abnormal?
   a. male, age 67: pulse, 68; respirations, 15; BP, 130/88
   b. female, age 44: pulse, 92; respirations, 22; BP, 120/80
   c. male, age 14: pulse, 88; respirations, 18; BP, 110/70
   d. female, age 7: pulse, 100; respirations, 23; BP, 96/50

24. You would check whether a patient was responsive to painful stimuli by
   a. jabbing the back of his or her hand with a needle.
   b. running a knife across the sole of the foot.
   c. eliciting a knee-jerk response with deep pain.
   d. pinching the skin on the shoulder muscle.

25. Which of the following is a priority patient who should be transported immediately?
   a. female, age 27: 40 weeks pregnant, crowning, no complications
   b. male, age 67: history of heart disease, pain leaves after taking nitroglycerin
   c. female, age 32: allergic reaction to bee sting, rapid pulse, difficulty breathing
   d. male, age 15: fell off bicycle, possible fractured wrist, cuts, and bruises

26. The main purpose of the detailed physical examination is to
   a. reveal hidden or less obvious injuries.
   b. detect changes in the patient's condition.
   c. obtain a complete medical history.
   d. check vital signs and breath sounds.

27. While performing a rapid trauma assessment of a patient who was injured in a motor vehicle accident, you note paradoxical motion. This indicates the presence of
   a. pelvic fracture.
   b. internal bleeding.
   c. chest injury.
   d. head injury.

28. The *glottis* is the
   a. soft tissue at the base of the tongue.
   b. nasopharynx and oropharynx.
   c. midaxillary intercostal muscles.
   d. opening between the pharynx and the trachea.

29. Which of the following is a sign of inadequate breathing?
   a. breathing through the mouth
   b. shallow breathing
   c. warm, dry skin
   d. bilateral breath sounds

30. An automated external defibrillator should deliver a shock to which of the following conditions?
   a. The patient's rhythm is flat line.
   b. The patient has a pulse.
   c. The heart has organized electrical activity.
   d. The patient's rhythm is ventricular fibrillation.

31. What is the general rule for administration of high-flow oxygen in the field?
   a. Administer high-flow oxygen only under specific online medical direction.
   b. Do not administer high-flow oxygen to children, elderly, or pregnant patients.
   c. Do not administer high-flow oxygen to patients with obvious signs of shock.
   d. Administer high-flow oxygen to all patients who are in respiratory distress.

32. Your patient is in cardiac arrest. An AED has been attached to the patient and activated. In the first round of defibrillation, the AED delivers two shocks and stops. What should you do next?
   a. Force the AED to deliver the third "stacked" shock.
   b. Turn off the AED because it only delivered two of the first three shocks.
   c. Set up the AED to deliver a second set of shocks.
   d. Check for a pulse and breathing.

33. What is the purpose of the jaw-thrust technique?
   a. to open the airway without moving the neck
   b. to reduce the possibility of a gag response
   c. to open the airway of infants and children
   d. to allow the insertion of an oropharyngeal airway

34. You have delivered one shock with the semiautomatic defibrillator. Your cardiac arrest patient is breathing adequately with a pulse. What should you do next?
   a. Deliver second shock to assure patient does not arrest again.
   b. Provide artificial ventilation with high-concentration oxygen and transport.
   c. Give high-concentration oxygen by nonrebreather mask and transport.
   d. Check pulse and deliver two more shocks.

35. When suctioning a patient, you would make sure that you did not insert the catheter too far by
   a. inserting it only until it reached the glottis or trachea.
   b. using the epiglottis as a landmark for inserting the catheter.
   c. measuring the catheter before inserting it in the mouth or nose.
   d. inserting it only until the point where it meets resistance.

36. While suctioning, if you cannot clear a patient's mouth in 15 seconds, you should
   a. immediately suction the airway again.
   b. suction the nose along with the mouth.
   c. suction for 15 more seconds and reassess.
   d. logroll the patient to clear the mouth.

37. A 65-year-old female is complaining of chest pressure, difficulty breathing, and is pale. She presents supine in bed. What should you do before sitting her up?
   a. Check her blood pressure to make sure it is adequate.
   b. Do nothing; sit her up right away.
   c. Help the patient administer her own nitro-glycerin tablets.
   d. Check her pupils to make sure they are reactive.

38. Which of the following describes the most correct technique for using mouth-to-mask ventilation?
   a. Ventilate the patient until the chest rises and begins to fall.
   b. Seal the mask to the patient's mouth and nose with one hand.
   c. Seal your mouth over the port and exhale for two seconds.
   d. Ventilate adult patients at least once every three to four seconds.

39. A 70-year-old male is complaining of chest pain and shortness of breath. He is alert, with pale, cool, sweaty skin. His pulse is 100, blood pressure, 136/64, and respirations, 24. Upon auscultation, you can hear crackles in the lung fields. Which of the following actions would be appropriate?
   a. Have the patient lie flat because he could be in shock.
   b. Provide oxygen at two liters per minute using a nasal cannula.
   c. Administer nitroglycerin that is prescribed to the patient's wife.
   d. Have the patient sit up to assist with his breathing effort.

40. The best indication that a patient is being ventilated adequately is
   a. skin color.
   b. heart rate.
   c. chest rise and fall.
   d. breathing rate.

41. The breathing process begins when the diaphragm contracts and
   a. the intercostal muscles relax.
   b. air is forced out of the mouth and nose.
   c. the size of the thoracic cavity increases.
   d. the lungs and bronchi contract.

42. You would assess a patient's breath sounds by placing your stethoscope over the midaxillary line and the
   a. midclavicular line.
   b. sternum.
   c. cricoid notch.
   d. xiphoid process.

43. Beta-agonist bronchodilators work by
   a. contracting the airway to create greater air pressure.
   b. dilating the bronchioles to decrease resistance.
   c. increasing the blood flow to the respiratory system.
   d. decreasing the body's total need for oxygen.

44. Your patient is a 68-year-old woman with chronic respiratory disease. She is experiencing difficulty breathing in spite of home oxygen delivery. You should
   a. increase the flow rate of her oxygen supply.
   b. replace her nasal cannula with a face mask.
   c. consult medical direction for instructions.
   d. treat the patient for the signs of shock.

45. In which situations should you assist a patient with using a prescribed inhaler?
   a. male, age 47: history of severe asthma; respirations 28/min, wheezing; unresponsive
   b. female, age 6; history of upper-respiratory infection; respiratory rate 24/min; coughing
   c. male, age 69; history of emphysema; difficulty breathing; inhaler was prescribed for his son
   d. female, age 14; history of asthma; respirations 24/min; alert, used the inhaler one time yesterday

46. Right before administering an inhaler to a patient, you should remove the patient's oxygen mask and
   a. substitute a nasal cannula.
   b. have the patient exhale deeply.
   c. check the patient's vital signs.
   d. make sure the medication has not expired.

47. If a toddler or small child is afraid to wear an oxygen mask, you should
   a. have the parent hold the mask in place.
   b. strap the child down; then, put the mask on.
   c. avoid administering oxygen to prevent distress.
   d. explain the body's need for oxygen.

48. Which patient's respiratory rate is normal?
   a. male, age 4: respirations, 38/min
   b. female, age 11: respirations, 12/min
   c. male, age 27: respirations, 14/min
   d. female, age 82: respirations 10/min

49. Which of the following is a sign of normal respiration in infants and children?
   a. reliance on the diaphragm instead of the intercostal muscles for movements
   b. use of accessory muscles in the chest and neck to expand the chest
   c. nasal flaring noted during respiratory efforts when the infant is sleeping
   d. seesaw breathing pattern noted when the child or infant is at rest

50. In order to control the flow rate of oxygen to the patient, you must
   a. select the right size tank.
   b. select the right size tubing.
   c. open the valve on the tank.
   d. adjust the regulator setting.

51. The airway of a child can become easily obstructed because, in comparison with an adult, a child has a
   a. shorter airway and more secretions.
   b. narrower airway and larger tongue.
   c. smaller nose and mouth.
   d. faster breathing rate.

52. The major hazard associated with using and transporting oxygen tanks is that they can
    a. fail to function properly if chilled.
    b. leak and emit poisonous fumes.
    c. explode if dropped or handled roughly.
    d. run out of battery power at any time.

53. The best way to minimize injuries to yourself when lifting a patient is to
    a. wear a back brace.
    b. keep the weight as far away from your body as possible.
    c. use your legs to do the lifting, not your back.
    d. never lift a patient over your own weight.

54. All of the following are signs of inadequate breathing EXCEPT
    a. slow rate of breathing.
    b. cool, clammy skin.
    c. respiratory rate of 12 to 20.
    d. shallow breathing.

55. Which of the following lists the correct order for cardiopulmonary circulation?
    a. vena cava, left atrium, left ventricle, pulmonary veins, lungs, pulmonary arteries, right atrium, right ventricle, aorta
    b. aorta, right ventricle, right atrium, pulmonary arteries, lungs, pulmonary veins, left ventricle, left atrium, vena cava
    c. aorta, right atrium, right ventricle, pulmonary veins, lungs, pulmonary arteries, left atrium, left ventricle, vena cava
    d. vena cava, right atrium, right ventricle, pulmonary arteries, lungs, pulmonary veins, left atrium, left ventricle, aorta

56. When lifting a patient, you should try to
    a. communicate clearly with your partner.
    b. twist your back.
    c. use your arms and back as much as possible.
    d. wait until your partner lifts first.

57. The artery that can be palpated on the anterior surface of the foot is the
    a. femoral artery.
    b. brachial artery.
    c. anterior tibial artery.
    d. dorsalis pedis artery.

58. Which component of the blood is part of the body's immune system?
    a. white blood cells
    b. red blood cells
    c. platelets
    d. plasma

59. Your patient is a 35-year-old woman who has been in an automobile accident. She has suspected injuries to the pelvis, right upper leg, and shoulder. Her vital signs are pulse, 96, weak; respirations, 28/min, shallow; BP, 120/80. After checking the airway and administering oxygen, the next thing you should do is
    a. splint the injured arm and leg injury the package for transport.
    b. perform a detailed physical assessment for internal bleeding.
    c. treat for signs and symptoms of shock and transport rapidly.
    d. determine the exact mechanism of injury to find all injuries.

60. A part of the heart that is ischemic is one that is
    a. bleeding profusely.
    b. receiving too little oxygen.
    c. shriveled up from injury.
    d. swollen with excessive fluid.

61. Your patient is a 79-year-old man who is experiencing chest pain. Which question would you ask to investigate the O part of the OPQRST acronym?
   a. Have you ever felt this kind of pain before?
   b. What were you doing when the pain started?
   c. How long ago did the pain begin?
   d. What does the pain feel like?

62. All of the following may be signs and symptoms of cardiac compromise EXCEPT
   a. shivering.
   b. anxiety.
   c. irregular pulse rate.
   d. nausea or vomiting.

63. Your patient is a 67-year-old woman with chest pains and a history of heart disease. After helping her take a dose of prescribed nitroglycerin, you find that her blood pressure is 96/68 and she is still in severe pain. Medical direction tells you to administer a second dose of nitroglycerin and transport. You should
   a. administer the medication and document the vital signs and the order.
   b. repeat the blood pressure reading and the order to medical direction.
   c. ask to speak to a senior physician.
   d. request ACLS backup immediately.

64. Before you can analyze a patient's heart rhythm with an automated external defibrillator, you must
   a. detect a pulse rate of 96 beats per minute or higher.
   b. verify that the patient is responsive.
   c. confirm a history of heart disease.
   d. stop performing cardiopulmonary resuscitation.

65. Your patient is a 72-year-old woman in cardiac arrest. You verify that she is pulseless and hook up the AED to the patient. The AED gives a "no shock advised" message. You reconfirm that there is no pulse. You should now
   a. perform CPR for one minute.
   b. shock the patient anyway.
   c. request medical direction.
   d. analyze the rhythm again.

66. While transporting a patient who has been resuscitated after cardiac arrest, you should check the pulse every
   a. 15 seconds.
   b. 30 seconds.
   c. one minute.
   d. five minutes.

67. The cool, clammy skin that is a sign of shock results from
   a. a rise in the patient's temperature.
   b. the body's attempt to increase the vascular space.
   c. decreased heart rate and blood pressure.
   d. diversion of blood flow to the vital organs.

68. Delayed capillary refill is a reliable test of peripheral circulation in
   a. elderly patients.
   b. infants and children.
   c. patients in early shock.
   d. pregnant women.

69. Your medical patient is experiencing clinical signs of shock. You should
   a. lay the patient flat on his or her stomach.
   b. lay the patient flat on his or her back.
   c. sit the patient up.
   d. lay the patient flat on his or her back with legs elevated.

70. The most important treatment intervention for shock is to maintain an open airway and to
   a. provide 100% oxygen.
   b. ventilate the patient with a bag-valve mask.
   c. provide 100 mL fluid every 15 minutes.
   d. splint and bandage all wounds.

71. Bleeding caused by a wound to one large artery or vein can usually be controlled by
   a. concentrated direct pressure.
   b. diffuse direct pressure.
   c. pressure points.
   d. extremity elevations.

72. The proper technique for applying the PASG to a patient with a suspected spinal injury is to
   a. immobilize the patient to a long spine board before applying the PASG.
   b. place the PASG on a long spine board, and logroll the patient on to it.
   c. apply both the PASG and the long spine board while the patient is standing.
   d. elevate the patient's legs while applying the PASG, but don't move the pelvis.

73. Performing a rapid trauma assessment identifies
   a. all sites of bleeding.
   b. life-threatening conditions.
   c. all fracture sites.
   d. any threat that will require surgical interventions.

74. Your patient is a 27-year-old man who has been in a motorcycle accident. He is also bleeding heavily from his nose. How should you position him?
   a. sitting up and leaning forward
   b. supine
   c. in shock position, with his feet elevated
   d. on a long spine board, tilted on one side

75. Your patient is a 43-year-old woman who was a pedestrian hit by a car. No spinal trauma is suspected, but the patient is showing signs of early shock and has a tender abdomen. You strongly suspect
   a. head injury.
   b. internal bleeding.
   c. evisceration.
   d. impaled objects.

76. A 14-year-old female is unconscious after a 15-foot fall off a ladder. When evaluating her chest during a rapid trauma assessment, you should assess for
   a. paradoxical motion.
   b. jugular vein distention.
   c. softness.
   d. distention.

77. Your patient is a 62-year-old man who has survived a serious car crash. He is unconscious, cyanotic, and bleeding profusely from a thigh wound. Breathing is rapid and shallow. Other injuries are suspected. In which order should you provide care?
   a. open the airway and provide oxygen, control bleeding, immobilize, transport
   b. immobilize, control bleeding, transport, open the airway and provide oxygen
   c. open the airway and provide oxygen, immobilize, control bleeding, transport
   d. control bleeding, open the airway and provide oxygen, immobilize, transport

78. For which type of wound should you use an occlusive dressing that is taped on only three sides?
   a. an impaled object
   b. a sucking chest wound
   c. an abdominal evisceration
   d. an amputation

79. Which patient has burns that would be considered critical?
   a. 30-year-old: partial-thickness burns covering 15% of the body
   b. 11-year-old: full-thickness burns covering 1% of the body
   c. 22-year-old: full-thickness burns covering 10% of the body
   d. 28-year-old: partial-thickness burns covering 35% of the body

80. When treating a patient who has suffered an electrical burn, you should be alert for the possibility of
   a. cardiac arrest.
   b. internal bleeding.
   c. heat shock.
   d. allergic reaction.

81. A 36-year-old male is a restrained passenger in a car crash. He complains of pain to his right leg. While assessing his leg, you palpate for
   a. distention.
   b. deformity.
   c. defasiculation.
   d. debridement.

82. Your patient has a painful deformity of the right lower leg. The pulse in the right posterior tibial artery is missing. Before splinting the injured leg, you should
   a. use gentle traction to attempt to align the limb.
   b. apply a tourniquet to stop internal bleeding.
   c. check the right brachial pulse as well.
   d. place the right foot in the position of function.

83. A 20-year-old female has been shot in the abdomen. You should inspect and palpate her posterior region for
   a. vein distention.
   b. paradoxical motion.
   c. muscular spasms.
   d. tenderness to the spine.

84. A 23-year-old male has suffered a penetrating head wound that is bleeding profusely and a cervical spine injury. During your rapid trauma assessment, you should
   a. treat the head wound and continue your rapid assessment.
   b. stop your exam and provide appropriate care for both injuries.
   c. manage the cervical spine injury and continue your rapid assessment.
   d. make a mental note of both injuries and continue the assessment.

85. What should you do if you do not have the right size cervical collar to fit a patient with a suspected spinal injury?
   a. Use the next larger or smaller sized collar.
   b. Use rolled towels secured with tape.
   c. Leave the neck unsecured and tape the head.
   d. Place the patient on a back board without a collar.

86. Whiplash injuries commonly occur when
   a. a pedestrian is hit by a moving vehicle and dragged along the ground.
   b. a patient's neck is not properly stabilized before the patient is transported.
   c. the neck of a passenger in a car is snapped back and forth by a rear impact.
   d. a person falls greater than ten meters and dislocates his or her neck during the fall.

87. Your patient is a 35-year-old woman who is conscious and alert after a serious car accident. She has multiple injuries that suggest spinal trauma. To help determine the extent of her spinal injury, you should ask her to
   a. move her fingers and toes.
   b. turn her head from side to side.
   c. lift both legs together.
   d. wiggle her hips.

88. A 12-year-old female fell while skating. She did not strike her head and is alert, complaining of pain to the left wrist. How should you assess this patient?
   a. Assess just the areas that the patient tells you are painful.
   b. Assess every body part from head to toe.
   c. Focus on just the patient's airway and cervical spine.
   d. Complete only the initial and ongoing assessment.

89. Which statement by a patient is most likely to suggest that the patient's thinking is psychotic?
   a. "I've never felt this bad before."
   b. "I know you can't help me."
   c. "Am I going to die now?"
   d. "They sent you to lock me up."

90. Your patient is agitated and confused and seems to be displaying symptoms of drug use. The best way to prevent the situation from becoming dangerous to the patient, yourself, or others is to
   a. restrain the patient as soon as possible.
   b. speak calmly and quietly to the patient.
   c. refuse to treat the patient until he or she calms down.
   d. inform the patient of your self-defense techniques.

91. A 20-year-old female patient complains of leg and hip pain after falling off a 20-foot ladder. You should conduct a
   a. focused physical exam.
   b. rapid trauma assessment.
   c. an OPQRST on the pain only.
   d. detailed physical exam.

92. Bystanders tend to think that patients who are in a diabetic emergency are
   a. drunk.
   b. high.
   c. dead.
   d. crazy.

93. A patient in a postictal state is one who has
   a. stopped breathing but not yet died.
   b. demonstrated the early signs of shock.
   c. had a seizure and is now unresponsive.
   d. just given birth but not yet delivered the placenta.

94. Oral glucose is administered to patients who have a known history of diabetes and
   a. a prescription for glucose.
   b. have ingested alcohol.
   c. recent seizures.
   d. altered mental status.

95. You are assessing an awake, alert patient complaining of abdominal pain. He denies any trauma. When conducting a focused history and physical exam, what should you do first?
   a. Conduct a rapid physical exam.
   b. Obtain baseline vital signs.
   c. Gather the history of the present illness.
   d. Question the patient about past medical problems.

96. The most serious complication of a severe allergic reaction is likely to be
a. cardiac arrest.
b. low blood pressure.
c. respiratory distress.
d. headache.

97. During your focused history and physical exam of an unresponsive patient, you should first
a. obtain vital signs then gather OPQRST from the patient.
b. conduct a rapid physical assessment then obtain vital signs.
c. gather a SAMPLE history then OPQRST from the family.
d. request ALS support and begin a detailed head to toe exam.

98. To help determine what poison a patient has ingested, you should be alert for chemical burns around the mouth as well as
a. burns on the hands.
b. red-colored vomitus.
c. moist or dry skin.
d. unusual breath odors.

99. Baseline vital signs in the unresponsive medical patient include the patient's
a. past medical history.
b. signs and symptoms.
c. blood pressure.
d. allergies.

100. Your patient has accidentally sprayed insecticide in his eye. What should immediate first aid involve?
a. placing an airtight dressing over the eye
b. administering activated charcoal to the patient
c. irrigating the eye with clean water for 20 minutes
d. placing 10 cc of sterile saline solution in the eye

101. You just completed a rapid physical exam on an unresponsive 65-year-old female patient. Your next action should be to
a. take a history of the present illness.
b. gather a SAMPLE history.
c. perform a focused physical exam.
d. obtain baseline vital signs.

102. Heat loss due to sweating is an example of which of the following?
a. evaporation
b. radiation
c. conduction
d. convection

103. Your patient is a 14-year-old male who struck his head on a diving board and nearly drowned. Your first reaction should be to
a. remove the patient from the water and warm him.
b. release gastric distention and provide artificial ventilation.
c. administer oxygen and provide artificial ventilation.
d. immobilize the patient while still in the water.

104. Your patient is a girl, age 2, who has injured her leg. The best way to calm her while you are examining her is to
  a. explain what you are doing in technical language.
  b. tell her that if she doesn't cooperate, she won't get better.
  c. examine her while she is sitting on her parent's lap.
  d. do any painful procedures first so she can calm down.

105. Which statement about suctioning infants and children is correct?
  a. Insert the suction catheter until it touches the back of the throat.
  b. Administer oxygen immediately before and after suctioning.
  c. Never suction for longer than 30 seconds at a time.
  d. The vacuum pump should be set no higher than 200 mm Hg.

106. When you provide oxygen via the blow-by method, you
  a. hold the mask close to the patient's face but do not attach it.
  b. administer large quantities of oxygen at high pressure.
  c. rely on the ambient (room) air to oxygenate the patient.
  d. ventilate the patient while delivering chest compressions.

107. In order to determine whether an infant is responsive to verbal stimuli, you would
  a. say the child's name.
  b. ask the child to say his or her name.
  c. make a sudden loud noise.
  d. have a parent speak to the child.

108. The correct procedure for inserting an oral airway in an infant or child is to
  a. use the tongue depressor to move the tongue forward, and insert the airway right side up.
  b. tip the head back and open the mouth wide, and then rotate the airway on insertion.
  c. lubricate the tip of the airway with sterile saline, and insert it until you feel resistance.
  d. insert the airway with the bevel toward the base of the throat, pushing gently if you feel resistance.

109. A child who has a complete upper airway obstruction would most likely be
  a. screaming.
  b. gasping.
  c. wheezing.
  d. coughing.

110. In order to care for a child who has a partial upper airway obstruction, you should
  a. use a combination of back blows and chest thrusts.
  b. open the airway and attempt to ventilate the child.
  c. provide oxygen, position the child, and transport rapidly.
  d. use back blows and finger sweeps to remove the obstruction.

111. The landmarks for abdominal thrusts in a child are the
  a. diaphragm and intercostal muscles.
  b. cricoid cartilage and diaphragm.
  c. carotid artery and umbilicus.
  d. umbilicus and xiphoid process.

112. In which of the following circumstances should you suspect the possibility of child abuse?
- **a.** A parent tells you the 4-month-old infant's injuries were caused by rolling off the bed.
- **b.** A distraught parent promptly reports and requests treatment for a seriously injured child.
- **c.** A parent tells you that the child walked into a door at school, but the teacher disagrees.
- **d.** The child and parent both give you an identical account of how an injury occurred.

113. You should suspect the possibility of shock in a child who has a recent history of
- **a.** vomiting and diarrhea.
- **b.** cardiac arrest.
- **c.** epileptic seizures.
- **d.** upper respiratory disease.

114. Your patient, a 27-year-old-woman who is pregnant with her second child, tells you, "My water broke an hour ago." This should alert you that the patient
- **a.** has signs and symptoms of shock.
- **b.** is pregnant with twins.
- **c.** will have her baby fairly soon.
- **d.** is having a miscarriage.

115. You should place your hand on a pregnant woman's abdomen during contractions to determine
- **a.** the strength of the contractions.
- **b.** the duration of the contractions.
- **c.** the size of the fetus.
- **d.** the fetal heart rate.

116. An average length of labor for a woman who is having her first baby is approximately
- **a.** one to two hours.
- **b.** five to six hours.
- **c.** eight to twelve hours.
- **d.** twelve to eighteen hours.

117. You are assisting with a delivery in the field. As the baby's head is born, you find that the cord is wrapped tightly around the infant's neck and cannot be dislodged. You should
- **a.** transport the mother immediately in the knee/chest position.
- **b.** clamp the cord in two places and cut it between the clamps.
- **c.** pull hard on the cord to force the placenta to deliver immediately.
- **d.** exert gentle pressure on the baby's head to slow the delivery.

118. Right after her baby is delivered, a mother tells you that she feels contractions starting up again. You should
- **a.** contact medical direction.
- **b.** prepare to deliver the placenta.
- **c.** expect the birth of a second infant.
- **d.** treat the mother for shock.

119. When is it normal for the baby's head to rotate from the face-down position to the side?
- **a.** during crowning
- **b.** right before the head delivers
- **c.** right after the head delivers
- **d.** as the body delivers

120. You are assessing a newborn that has a pink body but blue extremities, a pulse rate of 98/min, no response to suctioning, moderate flexion of the extremities, and a respiratory rate of 38/min. What is the APGAR score for this infant?

a. 2

b. 4

c. 6

d. 8

121. When should you expect an infant to start to breathe spontaneously?

a. one to five seconds after birth

b. 10–15 seconds after birth

c. 20–30 seconds after birth

d. one minute after birth

122. A prolapsed cord is an emergency situation in which the umbilical cord is

a. the first, or presenting, part of the delivery.

b. wrapped around the infant's neck.

c. collapsed and unable to deliver oxygen.

d. accidentally torn during the delivery.

123. Which of these situations is a true emergency that cannot be managed in the field?

a. breech presentation

b. meconium in the amniotic fluid

c. multiple births

d. limb presentation

124. Your patient is a 19-year-old woman with severe vaginal bleeding. As part of the SAMPLE history, it is particularly important to ask the patient if she

a. feels dizzy.

b. has vomited.

c. may be pregnant.

d. has ingested poison.

125. All of the following are examples of indirect medical direction EXCEPT

a. continuing education classes taught by physicians.

b. contact between physicians and EMTs in the field.

c. design of EMS systems by physicians.

d. quality improvement efforts by physicians.

126. You should allow family members to remain with a patient EXCEPT when

a. the patient is in the process of dying.

b. the patient has gruesome injuries.

c. they want to reassure the patient.

d. they interfere with patient care.

127. Appropriate stress management techniques include maintaining a healthy lifestyle, striking a balance between work and leisure activities, and, if necessary

a. getting counseling.

b. taking sick leave.

c. using sedatives to sleep.

d. moving to a different home.

128. To be effective at preventing the spread of disease, hand washing should last for at least

a. five to ten seconds.

b. ten to 15 seconds.

c. 15 to 30 seconds.

d. 30 seconds to one minute.

129. In which of the following situations is the wearing of gloves only a sufficient body substance isolation protection?

a. when assisting in childbirth

b. when suctioning the airway

c. when stopping minor bleeding

d. when treating patients with tuberculosis

130. A standard of care is the
  a. highest level of care an EMT can legally provide.
  b. list of skills EMTs are required to perform in your state.
  c. national description of all procedures the EMTs may perform.
  d. minimum level of care that is normally provided in your locality.

131. A patient who claims that his injuries became more severe because an EMT did not perform at an acceptable level is relying on the legal concept of
  a. negligence.
  b. duty.
  c. damage.
  d. proximate cause.

132. Which situation might constitute legal abandonment of a patient?
  a. You leave your patient because the fire in an adjacent building reaches the room you are in.
  b. You begin CPR on a patient and ask a bystander to continue while you assess another patient.
  c. Your patient states that she does not want treatment and signs a statement to that effect.
  d. You transport a patient to the hospital and leave him in the care of a nurse who signed your patient care report.

133. Your patient is an adult male who was found in a state of collapse. He has no identification, and no one else is nearby. When you care for this patient, you are acting under the legal doctrine of
  a. cxpressed consent.
  b. eminent domain.
  c. advance directives.
  d. implied consent.

134. Your patient is a 25-year-old male who has had two seizures within the last hour. He shows no signs of drug or alcohol use. He now states that he feels fine and refuses both transport and further treatment. You should
  a. carefully document every attempt you make to provide care.
  b. obtain an order for tranquilizers from the medical direction physician.
  c. call for police backup to help you restrain the patient.
  d. leave the patient immediately to avoid being sued for battery.

135. In most states, you must report to the authorities any situation in which you
  a. treat a patient who dies.
  b. release confidential information.
  c. suspect abuse or neglect.
  d. treat a minor.

136. The power-lift position refers to a position in which you
  a. lift a patient as high as you possibly can.
  b. squat down, lock your back, and use your knees to lift.
  c. bend at the waist and jerk the patient up quickly.
  d. lift a one-rescuer stretcher by yourself.

137. Whenever it is necessary to carry out an emergency move of a patient, it is important to
  a. pull the patient along the line of the body's long axis.
  b. immobilize the patient to a long spine board before the move.
  c. complete the detailed assessment before the move.
  d. have at least two EMTs lift the patient off the ground.

138. The first step in a rapid extrication of a patient from a car is to
   a. apply a cervical immobilization collar.
   b. place the end of the long backboard on the seat.
   c. rotate the patient until his or her back is in the open doorway.
   d. move all of the extremities into a neutral position.

139. Which piece of equipment is used most often during rescue operations?
   a. basket stretcher
   b. stair chair
   c. flexible stretcher
   d. scoop stretcher

140. Which patient should be placed in the recovery position?
   a. a pregnant woman who has been in a car accident
   b. a conscious cardiac patient complaining of shortness of breath
   c. an unresponsive patient who has a suspected spine injury
   d. a child in respiratory distress with a rate of 6/min

141. Which of the following is an example of correct language to use in a radio report?
   a. "Patient appears to have tied one on."
   b. "Patient doesn't look very good—it may be shock."
   c. "Patient states that the pain is crushing his chest."
   d. "Patient seems to have suffered a myocardial infarction."

142. A standard medical report includes all the following information EXCEPT
   a. chief complaint.
   b. patient's date of birth.
   c. assessment findings.
   d. description of care provided.

143. Which of the following is an example of an effective way to communicate with an elderly patient?
   a. "Sir, I'm going to try to make you comfortable until we get to the hospital."
   b. "You just sit down here on this nice, comfortable chair and don't worry."
   c. "I will try to talk very slowly so you can understand me."
   d. "Sir, I'll make sure I explain everything I'm doing to your son."

144. When healthcare professionals speak of trending, they are referring to
   a. new styles and methods of care delivery.
   b. the tendency of depressed patients to refuse treatment.
   c. a general change in the nation's health status.
   d. a comparison of a patient's present and past condition.

Questions 145 through 150 refer to the following scenario:

You respond to a dispatch of an "unknown medical event." As you arrive on the scene, an elderly gentleman greets you at the door and motions you to step inside. You are directed to the rear of the house, where an elderly woman presents to you sitting on the bed. She appears to be in severe respiratory distress.

145. What should you do first?
   a. Perform a global assessment to determine if she is "big sick" or "little sick".
   b. Immediately place the patient on a nasal cannula.
   c. Assess for scene hazards.
   d. Get the patient's name and date of birth, before she gets any worse.

146. After completing your first task, what should you do next?
   a. Establish the patient's baseline vital signs.
   b. Establish a SAMPLE history.
   c. Perform an initial assessment.
   d. Perform a focused assessment.

147. When should you place the patient on oxygen?
   a. after the focused assessment
   b. during the initial assessment
   c. after taking baseline vital signs
   d. after medical command gives you permission

148. Which of the following signs would you assess for first?
   a. lung sounds
   b. abdominal tenderness
   c. presence of pedal pulses
   d. swelling in her fingers

149. Which of the following questions would you NOT ask during your OPQRST of the present illness?
   a. When did begin having trouble breathing?
   b. Does anything else cause you pain or discomfort?
   c. Does anything make the breathing easier or worse?
   d. Do you have any respiratory problems?

150. After a few minutes of supplemental oxygen therapy, the patient states that she feels much better. What would you do now?
   a. Discontinue the oxygen, since she feels better.
   b. Perform a reassessment of her vital signs.
   c. Have her sign a refusal of care form.
   d. Contact her private physician.

▶ Answers

1. b. This patient's vital signs are all within the normal range for his age.

2. a. Signs of labored respirations, or increased effort of breathing, include use of accessory muscles to breathe, grunting, and stridor. Stridor is a loud, high-pitched sound heard on respirations that usually indicates an upper-airway obstruction. Agonal respirations are gasping slow respirations that happen for some patients as they are dying.

3. d. This low resting pulse may be normal for a healthy athlete. To be sure, ask the patient if he knows what his normal resting pulse rate is.

4. c. The color, temperature, and condition of the skin allows you to form an indirect assessment of the patient's perfusion, or circulatory status.

5. d. You assess the size and reactivity of a patient's pupils to determine if there is a possibility of head injury.

6. b. A single blood pressure reading, unless it is extremely high or extremely low, is not in itself significant. Blood pressure readings are most useful in establishing a trend that can signal changes in the patient status. Blood pressure varies constantly during the day by 20 mm Hg or more during sleep, work, and relaxation activities. Assessment of BP by palpation is useful when the patient is in a very noisy environment, making auscultation difficult.

7. c. Chances are, this patient is experiencing sudden ventricular fibrillation that may be most likely reversed with defibrillation attempt.

8. c. In determining the mechanism of injury for a fall and therefore how serious the injuries are likely to be, it is most important to determine the height of the fall.

9. d. Children are likely to suffer serious injury in lower-speed collisions than adults; none of the other choices represents a serious mechanism of injury.

10. c. In order to accurately assess the patient's airway, breathing, and circulation status, all external compressions or ventilations must be stopped.

11. d. The jugular veins are normally somewhat distended while a patient is lying down; flat veins signify blood loss.

12. a. You still must perform an initial assessment and confirm that the patient is not breathing and has no pulse, regardless of which type of AED you use. In addition both types of AED, interpret the patient's EKG rhythm, not the operator.

13. c. In addition to evaluating for specific injuries (DCAP-BTLS), check the extremities for sensation, motor function, and the presence of distal pulses.

14. d. This patient has no significant mechanism of injury. If vital signs and a SAMPLE history disclose no abnormal findings, you need only perform a focused assessment. If you are ever unsure, however, you should perform a very thorough assessment, like a rapid trauma assessment to look for hidden injuries.

15. a. The T in the OPQRST acronym stands for Time, or the duration of the problem.

16. c. An AED should only be applied when the patient does not have a pulse nor respirations.

17. b. Reassess a stable patient every 15 minutes while en route to the receiving facility.

18. a. Although interacting with the patient continuously will keep you informed about his or her level of anxiety and allow you to observe skin color and pupils, the main purpose is to assess changes in mental status and patency of airway.

19. c. The P in the SAMPLE history stands for Pertinent past medical history, so you would ask the patient about previous episodes of chest pain.

20. c. The patient probably does not have a "shockable" rhythm. Therefore, the AED will not deliver an electrical shock. However, you do want to confirm whether the patient has a pulse before resuming CPR.

21. c. If a patient's respiratory rate is irregular, count for one full minute; otherwise, count for 30 seconds and multiply by two to obtain the respiratory rate.

22. a. Wheezing indicates that smaller airways and bronchioles are constricted, usually because of infection or allergy. Fluid is only one of the possible reasons, bronchial constriction is another cause.

23. b. This patient's pulse and respiratory rate are both elevated.

24. d. If a patient does not respond to verbal stimuli, assess whether he or she is responsive to painful stimuli by pinching the skin on the shoulder. You should never break the skin or provide a stimulus that could result in excessive movements from the patient.

25. c. Patients who are having difficulty breathing are priority patients, as are patients who are unstable or who give a poor general impression, are having complications of childbirth, or who have signs and symptoms of shock.

26. a. The purpose of the detailed physical examination, which is performed while en route to the hospital on all trauma patients, as well as unresponsive medical patients, is to reveal hidden injuries.

27. c. Paradoxical motion, the movement of one portion of the chest wall in the opposite direction from the rest of the chest during respirations, indicates serious injury to the chest wall.

28. d. The *glottis* is the opening between the pharynx and the trachea.

29. b. Shallow breathing, or inadequate tidal volume, is a sign of inadequate breathing, as are difficulty breathing, shortness of breath, irregular rhythm, cyanosis, and change in breathing rate.

30. d. An AED will deliver a shock only to patients experiencing ventricular fibrillation or ventricular tachycardia.

31. d. EMTs should administer high-flow oxygen to all patients who show signs and symptoms of respiratory distress.

32. d. The AED determined that the patient's rhythm switched to something other than ventricular fibrillation, and therefore, it no longer requires a shock. However, you must check if the patient has a pulse and is spontaneously breathing.

33. a. The jaw thrust is performed instead of the head-tilt/chin-lift on patients with suspected spinal trauma, since it allows you to open the airway without moving the patient's neck.

34. c. Based on the information provided by the scenario, the patient does not need artificial ventilation. Monitor the patient closely and provide high levels of oxygen.

35. c. Before inserting the catheter, measure the distance between the corner of the patient's mouth and the earlobe, and keep your fingers at that spot on the catheter; insert only to the point where your fingers are.

36. d. If you cannot clear the patient's mouth of secretions, logroll the patient so the secretions can drain out. Never suction for longer than 15 seconds at a time, and oxygenate the patient between suction attempts.

37. a. The position of comfort for most people having trouble breathing is sitting; however, this patient may have low blood pressure, possibly due to a cardiac emergency. In this case, it would be important to ensure that her blood pressure is adequate to support a sudden change in body position.

38. c. This option describes a proper technique; option **a** is incorrect because you would ventilate the patient until the chest rises; option **b** is incorrect because you would form the seal with both hands; option **d** is incorrect because you would ventilate adult patients every five seconds.

39. d. This patient's blood pressure is adequate to support a sitting patient. This patient also requires high-flow oxygen via nonrebreather as part of the treatment plan.

40. c. Although all the options are indications of adequate ventilation, chest rise is considered to be the best indicator.

41. c. Inhalation is an active process that begins when the diaphragm and intercostal muscles contract, increasing the size of the thoracic cavity and pulling air into the lungs.

42. a. Assess breath sounds bilaterally over the midaxillary and midclavicular lines.

43. b. Most prescribed inhalers contain a class of drug called beta-agonist bronchodilators, which work by dilating the bronchioles and thus decreasing resistance.

44. c. Consult medical direction when you encounter a patient who is having difficulty breathing in spite of home administration of oxygen.

45. d. You can help a patient to use a prescribed inhaler if the patient has signs and symptoms of respiratory emergency, if the inhaler was prescribed for that patient, and if the patient is responsive. Be sure and determine if the patient has used the inhaler already and if it helped lessen the distress.

46. b. After removing the oxygen mask, have the patient exhale deeply, and then administer the inhaler immediately.

47. a. To calm a child that is afraid of any oxygen mask, have the parent hold the child on his or her lap and hold the mask in place.

48. c. The normal breathing rate for an adult is between 12 and 20 breaths per minute.

49. a. Reliance on the diaphragm, rather than the intercostal muscles, to expand the chest during inspiration is normal in infants and children.

50. d. You control the flow of oxygen to the patient by adjusting the regulator on the oxygen tank. The size of the tank has no bearing on the flow rate. Oxygen tubing size is standardized. The valve must be in the open position to deliver any oxygen, but it does not change the rate of flow.

51. b. In comparison with an adult, a child has a larger tongue, which can obstruct the airway, and a narrow airway, which can more easily be blocked by secretions.

52. c. Because oxygen tanks contain gas at very high pressure, they can explode if they are dropped or otherwise roughly handled.

53. c. Your legs are generally the strongest part of your body. Keeping your back as straight as possible and using your legs to lift will minimize the potential for injury.

54. c. A respiratory rate of 12–20 BPM is normal; signs of inadequate breathing include cyanosis, increased or decreased breathing rate, shortness of breath, and irregular rhythm.

55. d. This is the correct order for cardiopulmonary circulation.

56. a. Partners who lift in unison will deliver more force, more smoothly, than partners who lift separately. Twisting your back while lifting will increase your chance of injury. You should use your legs as much as possible during lifting techniques, not your back or arms.

57. d. The dorsalis pedis artery, which can be palpated on the anterior surface of the foot, is used to check peripheral pulses.

58. a. The white blood cells make up an important part of the body's immune system.

59. c. The patient's pulse and breathing rate indicate that she is in shock; therefore, the first priority is to treat her for shock and transport her to a hospital.

60. b. *Ischemia* refers to a condition of not receiving enough oxygen.

61. c. O stands for Onset, or when the pain began.

62. a. Signs and symptoms of cardiac compromise include pressure or pain that starts in the chest and radiates, sweating, difficulty breathing, anxiety, irregular pulse rate, abnormal blood pressure, and nausea or vomiting.

63. b. Nitroglycerin is not administered to a patient whose systolic blood pressure is lower than 100. Repeat the blood pressure reading and the order and request that the physician confirm it.

64. d. Before using the AED, you must stop performing CPR in order to verify that the patient is without a pulse.

65. a. If the AED says "no shock advised," you should perform CPR for one minute and then recheck the pulse. If you still detect no pulse at the end of the one minute of CPR, analyze the rhythm once again.

66. b. Patients can go into ventricular fibrillation again after being resuscitated. Continue checking the patient's pulse every 30 seconds during transport.

67. d. In early shock, the body diverts blood flow away from the skin and toward the body's vital organs, resulting in decreased peripheral circulation and cool, clammy skin.

68. b. Capillary refill time is used to determine peripheral perfusion in infants and children only.

69. d. If no traumatic injury mechanism is suspected, keeping the patient flat with legs elevated will promote blood circulation back to the critical organs.

70. a. The most important intervention for shock is to provide a high concentration of oxygen; this helps prevent cells from dying due to lack of oxygen.

71. a. Bleeding from a single site can usually be controlled by concentrated direct applied pressure to that site. Diffuse pressure is reserved for circumstances when concentrated direct pressure is unadvisable, like when controlling bleeding from an open skull fracture. Pressure point pressure and elevation are steps to take if direct pressure is ineffective.

72. b. Because most patients for whom PASG is appropriate also have suspected spinal injury, place the PASG on the long spine board and logroll the patient onto the PASG and the board together.

73. b. The purpose of performing a rapid trauma assessment is to identify major injuries sustained in the "kill zone" areas of the body, such as the head, neck, chest, and abdomen.

74. d. Because the mechanism of injury strongly suggests spinal trauma, you should immobilize the patient on a long spine board, but tilt the board to one side to allow blood to drain. Suction may also be needed to keep the airway clear.

75. b. This mechanism of injury, plus the tender abdomen and signs of shock, strongly suggests that the patient has internal bleeding.

76. a. Paradoxical motion of the chest may indicate broken ribs or flail chest. Softness and distention during assessment generally refers to the abdomen.

77. a. Always open the airway first, regardless of other priorities. Since the patient is bleeding profusely, the second priority is to control the bleeding from the leg wound. Since the patient is showing signs and symptoms of shock, the next priorities are to immobilize the spine and transport rapidly.

78. b. For a sucking chest wound, apply an occlusive dressing that is taped on only three sides. This will allow air to escape from the chest cavity.

79. d. In an adult, full-thickness burns covering more than 10% of the body, or partial-thickness burns covering more than 30% of the body, are considered critical.

80. a. Electrical burns are frequently more serious than they appear from the entrance and exit wounds; you should be alert for the possibility of cardiac arrest and be prepared to use the AED.

81. b. In DCAP-BTLS, the D stands for deformity. Distention may be found on palpation and visualization of the abdomen.

82. a. When a pulse is missing distal to an injury, attempt to align the limb with gentle traction. Bringing the limb into alignment may relieve pressure on the blood vessels and restore circulation.

83. d. One of the most serious problems is possible injury to the spine as a result of the bullet. Any tenderness palpated along the spine will be a critical finding.

84. b. Both life-threatening injuries to the patient must be treated as quickly as possible.

85. b. If the mechanism of injury of the patient's signs and symptoms suggest spinal injury, you must immobilize the neck and spine. Use rolled-up towels if you do not have a cervical collar that fits properly.

86. c. Whiplash injuries result when a passenger in a car that is hit from the rear has his or her neck snapped backward and then forward as a result of the impact.

87. a. To help determine the extent of injuries, ask a patient with suspected spinal trauma to move her fingers and toes; otherwise, the patient should remain immobile.

88. a. Without a serious mechanism of injury being reported, a focused physical assessment of the patient's injuries is appropriate.

89. d. This statement reflects paranoia, a psychotic state in which people imagine that other people are conspiring to harm them.

90. b. You can frequently prevent situations from becoming dangerous by maintaining a calm, professional manner and speaking quietly to a distraught patient.

91. b. The mechanism of injury suggests that you should look through the "kill zone" areas to make sure there are no other underlying injuries.

92. a. Diabetic emergency produces symptoms such as slurred speech, a staggering gait, and altered mental status, which make them appear drunk.

93. c. A patient who is in a postictal state has just had a seizure and appears to be asleep.

94. d. With medical direction, EMTs may administer oral glucose to patients with a history of diabetes and altered mental status.

95. c. Conducting an OPQRST on the pain and finding out the SAMPLE history will gather a lot of information about the patient's complaint.

96. c. The most serious effect of severe allergies is respiratory distress, caused by swelling of the tissues in the respiratory system.

97. b. Since the patient is unresponsive, the most effective method of obtaining information about the patient's condition is through a rapid physical assessment.

98. d. Some poisons can be identified by the unusual breath odors they cause; for example, cyanide causes an odor of bitter almonds. Choice **a** is incorrect because some substances may burn mucous membranes of the mouth but may not burn the skin. Choice **b** is incorrect because, depending upon the substance ingested, vomit may or may not be discolored or bloody. Choice **c** is incorrect because the toxin may or may not cause changes in skin temperature or color; it will depend upon the action of the poison and if it causes shock.

99. c. The other three choices are part of the SAMPLE history. Vital signs include pulse, blood pressure, respirations, skin signs, and pupil reactivity to light.

100. c. When toxins come in contact with the eye, irrigate the eye with clean water for 20 minutes, preferably while en route to the hospital.

101. d. Since the patient is unresponsive, it will not be possible to elicit a medical history directly. An early set of vital signs may help determine the underlying cause of the patient's condition.

102. a. Evaporation occurs when a liquid, such as sweat, turns into a gas. Heat loss from radiation occurs as heat leaves the body and travels directly into the still air. Conduction heat loss from direct transfer of heat from the body into an object in contact with the body. Convection heat loss occurs as moving air (wind) travels over the skin, taking heat with it.

103. d. Because of the great risk of spinal injury with this type of trauma, the EMT's first action should be to immobilize the patient while still in the water; the second step is to attend to the airway.

104. c. Calm the toddler by allowing her to remain with her parent and by explaining what you are doing in simple language. Warn her if something will hurt, and if possible, perform painful procedures (sometimes BP assessment is painful) at the end of your assessment. Also, keep all your equipment out of sight until you are ready to use it so she can't get all worked up about it. Kids have incredible imaginations and will invent all sorts of painful scenarios as they look at your equipment and supplies. Sometimes you can let the child briefly examine a piece of equipment before you use it or pretend to use it on the parent to help calm her down.

105. b. When suctioning infants and children, be sure not to stimulate the back of the throat, which can lead to bradycardia. Administer oxygen before and after suctioning, suction for no more than 10 to 15 seconds at a time, and set the vacuum pump at 80–120 Hg.

106. a. The blow-by method refers to holding the mask near the patient's face without attaching it. This is the preferred oxygen-delivery method for infants and children, unless the patient is in severe respiratory distress, because it is less stressful to the child.

107. d. An infant who is responsive to voice, or to verbal stimuli, would turn in the direction of the parent's voice.

108. a. When inserting an airway in an infant or child, use a tongue depressor and avoid rotating the airway.

109. b. A child with a complete airway obstruction would either be gasping or would be making no attempt to breathe; he or she would be unable to cough, wheeze, or speak.

110. c. Back blows, chest thrusts, and ventilation are performed on infants with complete airway obstructions; care for a child with partial obstruction consists of placing the child in a position of comfort and transporting rapidly.

111. d. To perform abdominal thrusts on a child, place one fist between the umbilicus and the xiphoid process, place the other fist on top of the first, and give five inward, upward thrusts.

112. c. In cases of child abuse, different people frequently give different accounts of the same accident, or parents may appear unconcerned.

113. a. Shock in children is most frequently associated with fluid loss due to vomiting and diarrhea or to blood loss.

114. c. It is normal for the amniotic sac to rupture and the fluid it contains to drain out of the woman's vagina before delivery.

115. a. If the mother's abdomen feels hard during the contractions, they are strong, and birth is more likely to happen quickly.

116. d. The average length of labor for a first baby is approximately 12 to 18 hours, but the length of labor varies greatly among individual women.

117. b. If the cord is wrapped around the infant's neck and it cannot be placed back over the head, the infant is in danger of suffocation. Immediately clamp the cord in two places and carefully cut between the clamps. Never pull on the umbilical cord as this can cause uterine inversion, which is a life-threatening emergency.

118. b. The mother will feel contractions before the placenta delivers. Prepare to wrap it in a towel and place it in a plastic bag for delivery to the hospital along with the mother and infant.

119. c. The baby's head is usually born face down in the vertex position, and the head rotates just after it emerges from the birth canal.

120. b. This infant would receive one point for skin color (Appearance), one point for Pulse rate, zero for Grimace, one point for Activity, and one point for Respirations.

121. c. An infant normally starts breathing independently within about 20 to 30 seconds after birth; if it does not, provide tactile stimulations.

122. a. A prolapsed cord is an emergency condition in which the umbilical cord is the presenting part; in this position, the cord can be compressed by the baby's head, preventing it from supplying oxygen to the infant during delivery. If the infant is still inside the mother, transport her immediately in either the kneeling, knee-chest position, or Trendelenburg's position with the hips elevated. Keep the cord warm by wrapping it in sterile saline soaked dressings. A gloved hand can be placed into the vagina to lift the head off the umbilical cord.

123. d. A limb presentation, in which an arm or leg is the presenting part, is a true emergency situation that cannot be managed in the field. Place the mother with her pelvis elevated, exert gentle pressure on the baby's body, and transport the mother in this position. Breech, meconium, and multiple births can all be handled in the field. Call for ALS assistance for each of these emergencies and expect fetal distress in the newborn(s).

124. c. Determine if the patient may be pregnant, and if so, treat her like a pregnant woman—administer oxygen and transport her on her left side.

125. b. Indirect medical direction includes all involvement by physicians with EMS systems except direct supervision of EMTs in the field.

126. d. Always allow family members to stay with a patient except if their presence interferes with necessary care.

127. a. Effective stress management techniques include making various lifestyle changes that promote health, seeking a healthy balance between work and recreation, changing one's work schedule if necessary, and seeking professional counseling help.

128. b. Hand washing should last for at least ten to 15 seconds to effectively stop the spread of disease.

129. c. Gloves alone are sufficient protection when your patient has minor bleeding; for severe bleeding, or childbirth, a gown, mask, and eyewear should be worn as well. For treating tuberculosis, a special respiratory mask should be worn as the contagion is airborne.

130. d. A standard of care for any locality is the minimum acceptable level of care normally provided there. All care providers, including EMTs, are legally held to this standard.

131. a. Negligence occurs when a patient is hurt or injured because you did not perform at an acceptable level. In order to prove negligence, a patient must prove that you legally had a duty to provide care, that you did not provide required care, that some kind of damage occurred, and that your actions caused the damage.

132. b. Abandonment may occur if you stop caring for a patient without his or her consent, and without transferring care to personnel of the same or higher level. For patient **a**, personal safety takes priority over patient care. If a conscious capable adult patient has signed a refusal (and he or she heard about risks/benefits first), you have not committed abandonment, ruling out case **c**. To avoid abandonment when dealing with hospitals, hospital personnel must assume care of patient before you can leave, and this occurred in case **d**.

133. d. Implied consent means that you assume that any rational person would consent to care under the circumstances.

134. a. Refusal of treatment requires that the patient be fully aware of the consequences of refusing care. Document all attempts made to change the patient's mind by you and other caregivers.

135. c. Certain situations, such as when you use restraints, witness a crime, or suspect criminal behavior, must be reported to authorities, although specific requirements differ from state to state.

136. b. In the power lift, you squat down, lock your back to keep it straight, and use your knees to lift the required weight.

137. a. An emergency move is carried out when the patient is in immediate danger. Because there is no time to protect the spine before an emergency move, you should try to protect the spine by dragging the patient in a straight line, either by pulling on his or her clothing or by placing the patient on a blanket and dragging the blanket.

138. a. Before beginning the actual extrication, the first step is to check and open the airway if necessary. You need to attempt to apply a cervical collar before performing the move. If it is a true emergency (scene is very unstable and dangerous) and you cannot do this, make every effort to keep the head and neck in a neutral alignment while you move the patient. If you can slide the patient on to a long board, it will make moving him or her easier because you can keep him or her in alignment easier.

139. a. The basket stretcher, because it is constructed so that patients can be securely strapped into it, is the preferred piece of equipment for rescue operations.

140. c. Use the recovery position for a patient who is breathing spontaneously but who is unresponsive or likely to vomit and aspirate material into the airway. You should not use it for a spinal injured patient until he or she is properly immobilized. Patient **a** should be placed in the left lateral recumbent position once he or she is immobilized. Patient **b** should be assisted into the position of comfort with the recovery position used if the mental status decreases (and he or she is still breathing adequately.) Patient **d** needs bag-valve-mask ventilation.

141. c. In radio reports, as in written documentation, use simple, clear language that is free of judgments (patients **a** and **b**), conclusions, and diagnoses (patient **d**).

142. b. Most standard prehospital care reports include the patient's age but not the exact date of birth. Other relevant information includes age, gender, chief complaint, pertinent history, mental status, vital signs and assessment findings, care already given, and estimated travel time.

143. a. Speak to elderly patients respectfully, directly, and clearly, and do not assume that they can't understand the situation.

144. d. Trending refers to a comparison of a patient's past and present condition. Trending is always more significant than a single set of vital signs.

145. c. Always first ensure the safety of yourself and your crew before entering the scene.

146. c. An initial assessment will determine the initial, most serious life threats first.

147. b. If the patient is having respiratory distress, provide oxygen immediately after assessing her respiratory effort.

148. a. Since her chief complaint appears to be respiratory distress, listening to lung sounds early would provide some information about her respiratory system.

149. d. This is a good question to ask during the SAMPLE history taking.

150. b. An ongoing assessment is important to perform, so you can spot trends in the patient's condition.

EMT-Basic Practical Skills Exam

CHAPTER SUMMARY

This chapter presents the National Registry's EMT-Basic practical skills examination, which is used by many states and forms the basis for the practical exam in many other states. Being familiar with what will be expected of you—and knowing how the practical exam is scored—will help your self-confidence when you take the practical exam.

During your EMT-Basic training, you practiced various techniques and skills under a variety of conditions. But during a practical examination for certification, conditions have to be standardized as much as possible. The procedural guidelines that your examiners will be following will be sequential and often stringent. You have to do things in a particular order, just as you are told. This means that testing can be stressful. Proper preparation can help you overcome this stress.

The National Registry of Emergency Medical Technicians (NREMT) requires successful completion of a state-approved practical examination that meets the NREMT's minimum standards. The following 13 skills are tested because they are directly related to the potential loss of life or limb.

1. Patient Assessment/Management–Trauma
2. Patient Assessment/Management–Medical
3. Cardiac Arrest Management
4. Airway, Oxygen, Ventilation Skills/Bag-Valve-Mask–Apneic with Pulse
5. Spinal Immobilization–Supine Patient
6. Spinal Immobilization–Seated Patient
7. Immobilization Skills–Long Bone
8. Immobilization Skills–Joint Injury
9. Immobilization Skills–Traction Splinting
10. Bleeding Control/Shock Management
11. Airway, Oxygen, Ventilation Skills/Upper Airway Adjuncts and Suction
12. Airway, Oxygen, Ventilation Skills/Mouth-to-Mask with Supplemental Oxygen
13. Airway, Oxygen, Ventilation Skills/Supplemental Oxygen Administration

The National Registry developed a sample practical examination to help states develop their EMT-Basic practical exam. Many states have adopted this sample exam as their skills certification examination. Whether your state uses the NREMT exam or has developed its own EMT-Basic skills exam, the NREMT exam that follows will help you prepare for your practical examination. *However, you should become familiar with your state's examination, local scope of practice, and treatment protocols before you take the exam.*

The skills examination consists of six stations. Five of these stations are mandatory stations, and one is a random skill station. The stations and time limits are listed in the table on this page.

NREMT PRACTICAL SKILLS EXAM		
STATION	**SKILLS TESTED**	**TIME**
Station 1	Patient Assessment/Management–Trauma	10 min.
Station 2	Patient Assessment/Management–Medical	10 min.
Station 3	Cardiac Arrest Management/AED	15 min.
Station 4	Bag-Valve-Mask–Apneic with Pulse	10 min.
Station 5	Spinal Immobilization–Supine or Seated	10 min.
Station 6	Random Skill:	
	Long Bone Immobilization Skills	5 min.
	Joint Injury Immobilization Skills	5 min.
	Traction Splinting Immobilization Skills	10 min.
	Bleeding Control/Shock Management	10 min.
	Upper Airway Adjuncts and Suction	5 min.
	Mouth-to-Mask with Supplemental Oxygen	5 min.
	Supplemental Oxygen Administration	5 min.

You will not be told which random skill you will be tested on before the examination. Many examiners will have you blindly select from skills listed on separate cards, or the coordinator may select one skill to administer to all candidates.

This chapter contains the NREMT sample practical examination and the instruction to the candidates. Generally, you can fail up to three skills and retest those skills on the same day. Retests are proctored by a different examiner. Please refer to "Candidate General Instructions" on page 152 for more detailed information.

It may be helpful to the examiner during the examination process if you talk aloud while performing each skill. The examiner can then not only see what you are doing, but he or she can also hear what you are thinking as you go through the process. This might also help you stay on track during the skills exam, as it might jog your memory of a missing or out-of-sequence step.

Instructions for each station are listed with the skill assessment sheet, along with the minimum score for each station. In addition, failure to perform critical criteria, listed at the bottom of each skill assessment sheet, constitutes failure of that station. All the necessary equipment will be provided for you at each station. You must follow proper body substance isolation procedures for every skill.

Before you begin each station, ask any questions that you have; you will not be permitted to ask questions during the assessment. Remember, good communication and critical-thinking skills are vital to successfully completing any practical examination.

Remember this: "Practice makes perfect" applies perfectly to the skills exam portion of any EMT-Basic testing process. The more times you can rehearse these skills, the more comfortable you will be when performing them in front of an examiner. This translates directly to the field setting where you can be confident that your skills will be competent when the patient needs them the most!

▶ EMT-Basic Practical Examination

Candidate General Instructions

Welcome to the EMT-Basic practical examination. I'm *name and title*. By successfully completing this examination process and receiving subsequent certification, you will have proven to yourself and the medical community that you have achieved the level of competency assuring the public receives quality prehospital care.

I will now read the roster, for attendance purposes, before we begin the orientation. Please identify yourself when your name is called.

The skill station examiners utilized today were selected because of their expertise in the particular skill station. Skill station examiners observe and record your expected appropriate actions. They record your performance in relationship to the criteria listed on the evaluation instrument.

The skill station examiner will call you into the station when it is prepared for testing. No candidate, at any time, is permitted to remain in the testing area while waiting for his or her next station. You must wait outside the testing area until the station is open and you are called. You are not permitted to take any books, pamphlets, brochures, or other study material into the station. You are not permitted to make any copies or recordings of any station. The skill station examiner will greet you as you enter the skill station. The examiner will ask your name. Please assist him or her in spelling your name so that your results may be reported accurately. Each skill station examiner will then read aloud "Instructions to the Candidate" exactly as printed on the instruction provided to him or her by the examination coordinator. The information is read to each candidate in the same manner to ensure consistency and fairness.

Please pay close attention to the instructions, as they correspond to dispatch information you might receive on a similar emergency call and give you valuable information on what will be expected of you during the skill station. The skill station examiner will offer to repeat the instructions and will ask you if the instructions were understood. Do not ask for additional information. Candidates sometimes complain that skill station examiners are abrupt, cold, or appear unfriendly. No one is here to add to the stress and anxiety you may already feel. It is important to understand that the examiners have been told they must avoid casual conversation with candidates. This is necessary to assure fair and equal treatment of all candidates throughout the examination. We have instructed the skill station examiners not to indicate to you, in any way, a judgment regarding your performance in the skill station. Do not interpret any of the examiner's remarks as an indication of your overall performance. Please recognize the skill station examiner's attitude as professional and objective, and simply perform the skills to the best of your ability.

Each skill station is supplied with several types of equipment for your selection. You will be given time at the beginning of the skill station to survey and select the equipment necessary for the appropriate management of the patient. Do not feel obligated to use all the equipment. If you brought any of your own equipment, I must inspect and approve it before you can enter the skill station.

As you progress through the practical examination, each skill station examiner will be observing and recording your performance. Do not let his or her documentation practices influence your performance in the station.

If the station has an overall time limit, the examiner will inform you of this when reading the instructions. When you reach the time limit, the skill station examiner will instruct you to stop your performance. However, if you complete the station before the allotted time, inform the examiner that you are finished. You may be asked to remove equipment from the patient before leaving the skill station.

You are not permitted to discuss any specific details of any station with each other at any time. Please be courteous to the candidates who are testing by keeping all excess noise to a minimum. Be prompt in reporting to each station so that we may complete this examination within a reasonable time period.

Failure of three or less skill stations entitles you to a same-day retest of those skills failed. Failure of four or more skill stations constitutes a failure of the entire practical examination, requiring a retest of the entire practical examination. Failure of a same-day retest entitles you to a retest of those skills failed. This retest must be accomplished at a different site with a different examiner. Failure of the retest at the different site constitutes a complete failure of the practical examination, and you will be required to retest the entire practical examination.

The results of the examination are reported as pass/fail of the skill station. You will not receive a detailed critique of your performance on any skill. Please remember that today's examination is a formal verification process and was not designed to assist with teaching or learning. The purpose of this examination is to verify achievement of the minimal DOT competencies after the educational component has been completed. Identifying errors would be contrary to the principle of this type of examination, and could result in the candidate "learning" the examination while still not being competent in the necessary skill. It is recommended that you contact your teaching institution for remedial training if you are unsuccessful in a skill station.

If you feel you have a complaint concerning the practical examination, a formal complaint procedure does exist. You must initiate any complaint with me today. Complaints will not be valid after today and will not be accepted if they are issued after you learn of your results or leave this site. You may file a complaint for only two reasons:

1. You feel you have been discriminated against. Any situation that can be documented in which you feel an unfair evaluation of your abilities occurred may be considered discriminatory.
2. There was an equipment problem or malfunction in your station.

If you feel either occurred, you must contact me immediately to initiate the complaint process. You must submit the complaint in writing. The examination coordinator and the medical director will review your concerns.

I am here today to assure that fair, objective, and impartial evaluations occur in accordance with the guidelines contained in this guide. If you have any concerns, notify me immediately to discuss your concerns. I will be visiting all skill stations throughout the examination to verify adherence to these guidelines. Please remember that if you do not voice your concerns or complaints today before you leave this site or before I inform you of your results, your complaints will not be accepted.

The skill station examiner does not know or play a role in the establishment of pass/fail criteria, but he or she is merely an observer and recorder of your actions in the skill station. This is an examination experience, not a teaching or learning experience.

Does anyone have any questions concerning the practical examination at this time?

Points to Remember
1. Follow instructions from the staff.
2. During the examination, move only to areas directed by the staff.
3. Give your name as you arrive at each station.
4. Listen carefully as the testing scenario is explained at each station.
5. Ask questions if the instructions are not clear.
6. During the examination, do not talk about the examination with anyone other than the skill station examiner, programmed patient, and when applicable, the EMT assistant.
7. Be aware of the time limit, but do not sacrifice quality performance for speed.
8. Equipment will be provided. Select and use only what is necessary to care for your patient adequately.

▶ Patient Assessment/Management— Trauma

Instructions to the Candidate

Minimum Score: 30

This station is designed to test your ability to perform a patient assessment of a victim of multisystems trauma and "voice" treat all conditions and injuries discovered. You must conduct your assessment as you would in the field including communicating with your patient. You may remove the patient's clothing down to shorts or swimsuit if you feel it is necessary. As you conduct your assessment, you should state everything you are assessing. Clinical information not obtainable by visual or physical inspection will be given to you after you demonstrate how you would normally gain that information. You may assume that you have two EMTs working with you and that they are correctly carrying out the verbal treatments you indicate. You have ten minutes to complete this skill station. Do you have any questions?

Sample Trauma Scenario

The following is an example of an acceptable scenario for this station. It is not intended to be the only possible scenario for this station. Variations of the scenario are possible and should be used to reduce the possibility of future candidates knowing the scenario before entering the station. If the scenario is changed, the following four guidelines must be used.

1. A clearly defined mechanism of injury must be included. The mechanism of injury must indicate the need for the candidate to perform a rapid trauma assessment.
2. There must be a minimum of an airway, breathing, and circulatory problem.
3. There must be an additional associated soft tissue or musculoskeletal injury.
4. Vital signs must be given for the initial check and one recheck.

Trauma Situation #1: Patient Assessment/Management Mechanism of Injury

You are called to the scene of a motor vehicle crash where you find a victim who was thrown from a car. You find severe damage to the front end of the car. The victim is found lying in a field 30 feet from the upright car.

Injuries

The patient will present with the following injuries. All injuries will be moulaged. Each examiner should program the patient to respond appropriately throughout the assessment and assure the victim has read the "Instructions to Simulated Trauma Victim" that have been provided.

1. unresponsive
2. left side flail chest
3. decreased breath sounds, left side
4. cool, clammy skin; no distal pulses
5. distended abdomen
6. pupils equal
7. neck veins flat
8. pelvis stable
9. open injury of the left femur with capillary bleeding

Vital Signs

1. Initial vital signs—BP, 72/60; P, 140; RR, 28
2. Upon recheck—if appropriate treatment: BP, 86/74; P, 120; RR, 22
3. Upon recheck—if inappropriate treatment: BP, 64/48; P, 138; RR, 44

Patient Assessment/Management—Trauma

Start Time: _____

Stop Time: _____   Date: _____

Candidate's Name: _____

Evaluator's Name: _____

		Points Possible	Points Awarded
Takes, or verbalizes, body substance isolation precautions		1	
SCENE SIZE-UP			
Determines the scene is safe		1	
Determines the mechanism of injury		1	
Determines the number of patients		1	
Requests additional help if necessary		1	
Considers stabilization of spine		1	
INITIAL ASSESSMENT			
Verbalizes general impression of the patient		1	
Determines responsiveness/level of consciousness		1	
Determines chief complaint/apparent life threats		1	
Assesses airway and breathing	Assessment	1	
	Initiates appropriate oxygen therapy	1	
	Assures adequate ventilation	1	
	Injury management	1	
Assesses circulation	Assess/controls major bleeding	1	
	Assesses pulse	1	
	Assesses skin (color, temperature, and condition)	1	
Identifies priority patients/makes transport decision		1	
FOCUSED HISTORY AND PHYSICAL EXAMINATION/RAPID TRAUMA ASSESSMENT			
Selects appropriate assessment *(focused or rapid assessment)*		1	
Obtains, or directs assistance to obtain, baseline vital signs		1	
Obtains SAMPLE history		1	
DETAILED PHYSICAL EXAMINATION			
Assesses the head	Inspects and palpates the scalp and ears	1	
	Assesses the eyes	1	
	Assesses the facial areas including oral and nasal areas	1	
Assesses the neck	Inspects and palpates the neck	1	
	Assesses for JVD	1	
	Assesses for trachael deviation	1	
Assesses the chest	Inspects	1	
	Palpates	1	
	Auscultates	1	
Assesses the abdomen/pelvis	Assesses the abdomen	1	
	Assesses the pelvis	1	
	Verbalizes assessment of genitalia/perineum as needed	1	
Assesses the extremities	1 point for each extremity includes inspection, palpation, and assessment of motor, sensory, and circulatory function	4	
Assesses the posterior	Assesses thorax	1	
	Assesses lumbar	1	
Manages secondary injuries and wounds appropriately		1	
1 point for appropriate management of the secondary injury/wound			
Verbalizes reassessment of the vital signs		1	

Critical Criteria   **Total:**   **40**

____ Did not take, or verbalize, body substance isolation precautions

____ Did not determine scene safety

____ Did not assess for spinal protection

____ Did not provide for spinal protection when indicated

____ Did not provide high concentration of oxygen

____ Did not find, or manage, problems associated with airway, breathing, hemorrhage, or shock (hypoperfusion)

____ Did not differentiate patient's need for transportation versus continued assessment at the scene

____ Did other detailed physical examination before assessing the airway, breathing, and circulation

____ Did not transport patient within (10) minute time limit

▶ Patient Assessment/Management— Medical

Instructions to the Candidate

Minimum Score: 22

This station is designed to test your ability to perform a patient assessment of a patient with a chief complaint of a medical nature and "voice" treat all conditions discovered. You must conduct your assessment as you would in the field including communicating with your patient. You may remove the patient's clothing down to shorts or swimsuit if you feel it is necessary. As you conduct your assessment, you should state every-thing you are assessing. Clinical information not obtainable by visual or physical inspection will be given to you after you demonstrate how you would normally gain that information. You may assume that you have two EMTs working with you and that they are correctly carrying out the verbal treatments you indicate. You have ten minutes to complete this skill station. Do you have any questions?

When assessing the signs and symptoms of the patient, the candidate must gather the appropriate information by asking the questions listed on the skill sheet. The number of questions required to be asked differs based on the scenario and the chief complaint. The point for *"Signs and Symptoms (Assess history of present illness)"* is awarded based on the following criteria:

Respiratory	five or more questions asked, award one point
	four or less questions asked, award no point
Cardiac	five or more questions asked, award one point
	four or less questions asked, award no point
Altered Mental Status	six or more questions asked, award one point
	five or less questions asked, award no point
Allergic Reaction	four or more questions asked, award one point
	three or less questions asked, award no point
Poisoning/Overdose	five or more questions asked, award one point
	four or less questions asked, award no point
Environmental Emergency	four or more questions asked, award one point
	three or less questions asked, award no point
Obstetrics	five or more questions asked, award one point
	four or less questions asked, award no point
Behavioral	four or more questions asked, award one point
	three or less questions asked, award no point

Each candidate is required to complete a full patient assessment. The candidate choosing to transport the victim immediately after the initial assessment must be instructed to continue the focused history and physical examination and ongoing assessment en route to the hospital.

NOTE: The preferred method to evaluate a candidate is to write the exact sequence the candidate follows during the station as it is performed. You may then use this documentation to fill out the evaluation instrument after the candidate completes the station. This documentation may then be used to validate the score on the evaluation instrument if questions arise later.

Patient Assessment/Management—Medical

Start Time: _____

Stop Time: _____ Date: _____

Candidate's Name: _____

Evaluator's Name: _____

		Points Possible	Points Awarded
Takes, or verbalizes, body substance isolation precautions		1	
SCENE SIZE-UP			
Determines the scene is safe		1	
Determines the mechanism of inquiry/nature of illness		1	
Determines the number of patients		1	
Requests additional help if necessary		1	
Considers stabilization of spine		1	
INITIAL ASSESSMENT			
Verbalizes general impression of the patient		1	
Determines responsiveness/level of consciousness		1	
Determines chief complaint/apparent life threats		1	
Assesses airway and breathing	Assessment	1	
	Initiates appropriate oxygen therapy	1	
	Assures adequate ventilation	1	
Assesses circulation	Assesses/controls major bleeding	1	
	Assesses pulse	1	
	Assesses skin (color, temperature, and condition)	1	
Identifies priority patients/makes transport decision		1	
FOCUSED HISTORY AND PHYSICAL EXAMINATION/RAPID ASSESSMENT			
Signs and symptoms (*Assess history of present illness*)		1	

Respiratory	Cardiac	Altered Mental Status	Allergic Reaction	Poisoning/ Overdose	Environmental Emergency	Obstetrics	Behavioral
*Onset?	*Onset?	*Description of the episode?	*History of allergies?	*Substance?	*Source?	*Are you pregnant?	*How do you feel?
*Provokes?	*Provokes?	*Onset?	*What were you exposed to?	*When did you ingest/become exposed?	*Environment?	*How long have you been pregnant?	*Determine suicidal tendencies.
*Quality?	*Quality?	*Duration?	*How were you exposed?	*How much did you ingest?	*Duration?	*Pain or contractions?	*Is the patient a threat to self or others?
*Radiates?	*Radiates?	*Associated symptoms?	*Effects?	*Over what time period?	*Loss of consciousness?	*Bleeding or discharge?	*Is there a medical problem?
*Severity?	*Severity?	*Evidence of trauma?	*Progression?	*Interventions?	*Effects— general or local?	*Do you feel the need to push?	*Interventions?
*Time?	*Time?	*Interventions?	*Interventions?	*Estimated weight?		*Last menstrual period?	
*Interventions?	*Interventions?	*Seizures?					
		*Fever?					

	Points Possible	Points Awarded
Allergies	1	
Medications	1	
Past pertinent history	1	
Last oral intake	1	
Event leading to present illness (rule out trauma)	1	
Performs focused physical examination (*assesses affected body part/system or, if indicated, completes rapid assessment*)	1	
Vitals (*obtains baseline vital signs*)	1	
Interventions (*obtains medical direction or verbalizes standing order for medication interventions and verbalizes proper additional intervention/treatment*)	1	
Transport (re-evaluates the transport decision)	1	
Verbalizes the consideration for completing a detailed physical examination	1	
ONGOING ASSESSMENT (VERBALIZED)		
Repeats initial assessment	1	
Repeats vital signs	1	
Repeats focused assessment regarding patient complaint or injuries	1	

Critical Criteria   Total: **30**

____ Did not take, or verbalize, body substance isolation precautions when necessary

____ Did not determine scene safety

____ Did not obtain medical direction or verbalize standing orders for medical interventions

____ Did not provide high concentration of oxygen

____ Did not find or manage problems associated with airway, breathing, hemorrhage, or shock (hypoperfusion)

____ Did not differentiate patient's need for transportation versus continued assessment at the scene

____ Did detailed or focused history/physical examination before assessing the airway, breathing, and circulation

____ Did not ask questions about the present illness

____ Administered a dangerous or inappropriate intervention

► Sample Medical Scenarios

Altered Mental Status

When you arrive on the scene, you meet a 37-year-old male who says his wife is a diabetic and isn't acting normal.

Initial Assessment

Chief Complaint:	"My wife just isn't acting right. I can't get her to stay awake. She only opens her eyes then goes right back to sleep."
Apparent Life Threats:	Depressed central nervous system, respiratory compromise
Level of Responsiveness:	Opens eyes in response to being shaken
Airway:	Patent
Breathing:	14 and shallow
Circulation:	120 and weak
Transport Decision:	Immediate

Focused History and Physical Examination

Description of Episode:	"My wife took her insulin this morning like any other morning, but she has had the flu and has been vomiting."
Onset:	"It happened so quickly. She was just talking to me and then she just went to sleep. I haven't really been able to wake her up since."
Duration:	"She's been this way for about 15 minutes now. I called you right away. I was really scared."
Associated Symptoms:	"The only thing that I can think of is that she was vomiting last night and this morning."
Evidence of Trauma:	"She didn't fall. She was just sitting on the couch and fell asleep. I haven't tried to move her."

Interventions:	"I haven't done anything but call you guys. I know she took her insulin this morning."
Seizures:	None
Fever:	Low grade fever
Allergies:	Penicillin
Medications:	Insulin
Past Medical History:	Insulin dependent diabetic since 21 years of age
Last Meal:	"My wife ate breakfast this morning."
Events Leading to Illness:	"My wife has had the flu and been vomiting for the past 24 hours."
Focused Physical Examination:	Complete a rapid assessment to rule out trauma.
Vitals:	RR, 14; P, 120; BP, 110/72

Allergic Reaction

You arrive to find a 37-year-old male who reports eating cookies he purchased at a bake sale. He has audible wheezing and is scratching red, blotchy areas on his abdomen, chest, and arms.

Initial Assessment

Chief Complaint:	"I'm having an allergic reaction to those cookies I ate."
Apparent Life Threats:	Respiratory and circulatory compromise
Level of Responsiveness:	Awake, very anxious, and restless
Airway:	Patent
Breathing:	26, wheezing, and deep
Circulation:	No bleeding, pulse 120 and weak, cold and clammy skin
Transport Decision:	Immediate transport

Focused History and Physical Examination

History of Allergies:	"Yes. I'm allergic to peanuts."
When Ingested:	"I ate cookies about 20 minutes ago and began itching all over about five minutes later."
How Much Ingested:	"I only ate two cookies."
Effects:	"I'm having trouble breathing, and I feel lightheaded and dizzy."
Progression:	"My wheezing is worse. Now I'm sweating really badly."
Interventions:	"I have my epi-pen upstairs, but I'm afraid to stick myself."
Allergies:	Peanuts and penicillin
Medications:	None
Past Medical History:	"I had to spend two days in the hospital the last time this happened."
Last Meal:	"The last thing I ate were those cookies."
Events Leading to Illness:	"None, except I ate those cookies."
Focused Physical Examination:	Not indicated (award point)
Vitals:	RR, 26; P, 120; BP, 90/60

Poisoning/Overdose

You arrive on the scene where a 3-year-old girl is sitting on her mother's lap. The child appears very sleepy and doesn't look at you as you approach.

Initial Assessment

Chief Complaint:	"I think my baby has swallowed some of my sleeping pills. Please don't let her die!"
Apparent Life Threats:	Depressed central nervous system and respiratory compromise
Level of Responsiveness:	Responds slowly to verbal commands
Airway:	Patent
Breathing:	18 and deep
Circulation:	120 and strong
Transport Decision:	Immediate

Focused History and Physical Examination

Substance:	"My baby took sleeping pills. I don't know what kind they are. They just help me sleep at night."
When Ingested:	"I think she must have got them about an hour ago when I was in the shower. Her older sister was supposed to be watching her."
How Much Ingested:	"My prescription was almost empty. There couldn't have been more than four or five pills left. Now they're all gone. Please do something."
Effects:	"She just isn't acting like herself. She's usually running around and getting into everything."
Allergies:	None
Medications:	None
Past Medical History:	None
Last Meal:	"She ate breakfast this morning."
Events Leading to Illness:	"She just swallowed the pills."
Focused Physical Examination:	Complete a rapid trauma assessment to rule out trauma.
Vitals:	RR, 18; P, 120; BP, 90/64.

Environmental Emergencies

You arrive on the scene as rescuers are pulling a 16-year-old female from an ice-covered creek. The teenager has been moved out of the creek onto dry land, is completely soaked, and appears drowsy.

Initial Assessment

Chief Complaint:	"I saw something in the water below the ice. When I tried to get it out, the ice broke."
Apparent Life Threats:	Generalized hypothermia
Level of Responsiveness:	Responsive, but slow to speak
Airway:	Patent
Breathing:	26 and shallow
Circulation:	No bleeding; pulse, 110 and strong; pale, wet skin still covered in wet clothing
Transport Decision:	Immediate transport

Focused History and Physical Examination

Source:	"I fell in the creek when the ice broke. I tried to get out, but the current was too strong. Thank God you came."
Environment:	"The water was up to my neck. I could stand up, but I couldn't get out of the water."
Duration:	"I think I was in the water for ten minutes before they pulled me out. It felt like an hour."
Loss of Consciousness:	"I feel sick, but I never passed out."
Effects:	Lowered body temperature, slow speech patterns, "I can't stop shivering."

Allergies:	None
Medications:	None
Past Medical History:	None
Last Meal:	"I ate lunch at school three hours ago."
Events Leading to Illness:	"I thought the ice would hold me."
Focused Physical Examination:	Complete a rapid assessment to rule out trauma.
Vitals:	RR, 26; P, 110 and strong; BP, 120/80

Obstetrics

You arrive on the scene where a 26-year-old female is lying on the couch saying, "The baby is coming and the pain is killing me!"

Initial Assessment

Chief Complaint:	"I'm nine months pregnant and the baby is coming soon."
Apparent Life Threats:	None
Level of Responsiveness:	Awake and alert
Airway:	Patent
Breathing:	Panting, rapid breathing during contractions
Circulation:	No bleeding, pulse 120, skin is pale
Transport Decision:	Unknown

Focused History and Physical Examination

Are You Pregnant:	See chief complaint (award point if mentioned in general impression).

How Long Pregnant:	See chief complaint (award point if mentioned in general impression).
Pain or Contractions:	"My pain is every 2–3 minutes, and it lasts 2–3 minutes."
Bleeding or Discharge:	None
Do You Feel the Need to Push:	"Yes, every time the pain begins."
Crowning:	Present (award point if identified in focused physical exam)
Allergies:	None
Medications:	None
Past Medical History:	"This is my third baby."
Last Meal:	"I ate breakfast today."
Events Leading to Illness:	"The contractions started a few hours ago and have not stopped."
Focused Physical Examination:	Assess for crowning, bleeding, and discharge.
Vitals:	RR, 40 during contractions; P, 120; BP, 140/80

Behavioral

You arrive on the scene where you find a 45-year-old male in the custody of the police. He is unable to stand and smells of beer. He appears to be dirty, and you notice numerous rips and tears in his clothes.

Initial Assessment

Chief Complaint:	"Nothing is wrong with me except these cops won't leave me alone. I only drank two beers."
Apparent Life Threats:	None
Level of Responsiveness:	Responds slowly with slurred speech to verbal questions
Airway:	Patent
Breathing:	16 and effortless
Circulation:	No bleeding, pulse 100, warm skin, and red nose
Transport Decision:	Delayed

Focused History and Physical Examination

How Do You Feel:	"I'm a little sick, otherwise, I just want to go to sleep."
Suicidal tendencies:	"No, I ain't going to kill myself."
Threat to others:	"Hey man, I ain't never hurt anyone in my life."
Is There a Medical Problem:	"My wife says I'm an alcoholic, but what does she know?"
Interventions:	"Yeah, I took three aspirins because I know I'm going to have one heck of a headache in the morning."
Allergies:	None
Medications:	None
Past Medical History:	"I've been in the hospital four time with those DTs."
Last Meal:	"Man, I haven't eaten since yesterday."
Events Leading to Illness:	"I don't care what these cops say, I didn't fall down. I was just taking a nap before going home."
Focused Physical Examination:	Complete a rapid assessment to rule out trauma.
Vitals:	RR, 16; P, 100; BP, 90/60

▶ Cardiac Arrest Management

Instructions to the Candidate

Minimum Score: 15

This station is designed to test your ability to manage a prehospital cardiac arrest by integrating CPR skills, defibrillation, airway adjuncts, and patient/scene management skills. There will be an EMT assistant in this station. The EMT assistant will only do as you instruct him or her. As you arrive on the scene, you will encounter a patient in cardiac arrest. A first responder will be present performing single-rescuer CPR. You must immediately establish control of the scene and begin resuscitation of the patient with an automated external defibrillator. At the appropriate time, the patient's airway must be controlled, and you must ventilate or direct the ventilation of the patient using adjunctive equipment. You may use any of the supplies available in this room. You have fifteen minutes to complete this skill station. Do you have any questions?

Cardiac Arrest Management

Start Time: _____

Stop Time: _____   **Date:** _____

Candidate's Name: _____

Evaluator's Name: _____

	Points Possible	Points Awarded
ASSESSMENT		
Takes, or verbalizes, body substance isolation precautions	1	
Briefly questions the rescuer about arrest events	1	
Directs rescuer to stop CPR	1	
Verifies absence of spontaneous pulse (**skill station examiner states "no pulse"**)	1	
Directs resumption of CPR	1	
Turns on defibrillator power	1	
Attaches automated defibrillator to the patient	1	
Directs rescuer to stop CPR and ensures all individuals are clear of the patient	1	
Initiates analysis of the rhythm	1	
Delivers shock (up to three successive shocks)	1	
Verifies absence of spontaneous pulse (**skill station examiner states "no pulse"**)	1	
TRANSITION		
Directs resumption of CPR	1	
Gathers additional information about arrest event	1	
Confirms effectiveness of CPR (ventilation and compressions)	1	
INTEGRATION		
Verbalizes or directs insertion of a simple airway adjunct (oral/nasal airway)	1	
Ventilates, or directs ventilation of, the patient	1	
Assures high concentration of oxygen is delivered to the patient	1	
Assures CPR continues without unnecessary/prolonged interruption	1	
Re-evaluates patient/CPR in approximately one minute	1	
Repeats defibrillator sequence	1	
TRANSPORTATION		
Verbalizes transportation of patient	1	
Total:	**21**	

Critical Criteria

____ Did not take, or verbalize, body substance isolation precautions

____ Did not evaluate the need for immediate use of the AED

____ Did not direct initiation/resumption of ventilation/compressions at appropriate times

____ Did not assure all individuals were clear of patient before delivering each shock

____ Did not operate the AED properly (inability to deliver shock)

____ Prevented the defibrillator from delivering indicated stacked shocks

► Airway, Oxygen, Ventilation Skills/ Bag-Valve-Mask—Apneic with Pulse

Instructions to the Candidate

Minimum Score: 8

This station is designed to test your ability to ventilate a patient using a bag-valve mask. As you enter the station, you will find an apneic patient with a palpable central pulse. There are no bystanders, and artificial ventilation has not been initiated. The only patient management required is airway management and ventilatory support. You must initially ventilate the patient for a minimum of 30 seconds. You will be evaluated on the appropriateness of ventilator volumes. I will then inform you that a second rescuer has arrived and will instruct you that you must control the airway and the mask seal while the second rescuer provides ventilation. You may use only the equipment available in this room. You have five minutes to complete this station. Do you have any questions?

Airway, Oxygen, Ventilation Skills/Bag-Valve-Mask—Apneic Patient

Start Time: _____

Stop Time: _____   **Date:** _____

Candidate's Name: _____

Evaluator's Name: _____

	Points Possible	Points Awarded
Takes, or verbalizes, body substance isolation precautions	1	
Voices opening the airway	1	
Voices inserting an airway adjunct	1	
Selects appropriately sized mask	1	
Creates a proper mask-to-face seal	1	
Ventilates patient at no less than 800 ml volume	1	
(The examiner must witness for at least 30 seconds)		
Connects reservoir and oxygen	1	
Adjusts liter flow to 15 liters/minute or greater	1	
The examiner indicates arrival of a second EMT. The second EMT is instructed to ventilate the patient while the candidate controls the mask and the airway.		
Voices re-opening the airway	1	
Creates a proper mask-to-face seal	1	
Instructs assistant to resume ventilation at proper volume per breath	1	
(The examiner must witness for at least 30 seconds)		
Total:	**11**	

Critical Criteria

_____ Did not take, or verbalize, body substance isolation precautions

_____ Did not immediately ventilate the patient

_____ Interrupted ventilations for more than 20 seconds

_____ Did not provide high concentration of oxygen

_____ Did not provide, or direct assistant to provide, proper volume/breath (more than two ventilations per minute are below 800 ml)

_____ Did not allow adequate exhalation

▶ Spinal Immobilization—Supine Patient

Instructions to the Candidate

Minimum Score: 10

This station is designed to test your ability to provide spinal immobilization on a patient using a long spine immobilization device. You arrive on the scene with an EMT assistant. The assistant EMT has completed the scene size-up as well as the initial assessment, and no critical condition was found that would require intervention. For the purpose of this testing station, the patient's vital signs remain stable. You are required to treat the specific problem of an unstable spine using a long spine immobilization device. When moving the patient to the device, you should use the help of the assistant EMT and the evaluator. The assistant EMT should control the head and cervical spine of the patient while you and the evaluator move the patient to the immobilization device. You are responsible for the direction and subsequent action of the EMT assistant. You may use any equipment available in this room. You have ten minutes to complete this skill station. Do you have any questions?

Spinal Immobilization
Supine Patient

Start Time: _____

Stop Time: _____   Date: _____

Candidate's Name: _____

Evaluator's Name: _____

	Points Possible	Points Awarded
Takes, or verbalizes, body substance isolation precautions	1	
Directs assistant to place/maintain head in the neutral in-line position	1	
Directs assistant to maintain manual immobilization of the head	1	
Reassesses motor, sensory, and circulatory function in each extremity	1	
Applies appropriately sized extrication collar	1	
Positions the immobilization device appropriately	1	
Directs movement of the patient onto the device without compromising the integrity of the spine	1	
Applies padding to voids between the torso and the board as necessary	1	
Immobilizes the patient's torso to the device	1	
Evaluates and pads behind the patient's head as necessary	1	
Immobilizes the patient's head to the device	1	
Secures the patient's legs to the device	1	
Secures the patient's arms to the device	1	
Reassesses motor, sensory, and circulatory function in each extremity	1	
Total:	**14**	

Critical Criteria

____ Did not immediately direct, or take, manual immobilization of the head

____ Released, or ordered release of, manual immobilization before it was maintained mechanically

____ Patient manipulated, or moved excessively, causing potential spinal compromise

____ Patient moves excessively up, down, left, or right on the patient's torso

____ Head immobilization allows for excessive movement

____ Upon completion of immobilization, head is not in the neutral position

____ Did not assess motor, sensory, and circulatory function in each extremity after immobilization to the device

____ Immobilized head to the board before securing the torso

▶ Spinal Immobilization– Seated Patient

Instructions to the Candidate

Minimum Score: 9

This station is designed to test your ability to provide spinal immobilization of a patient using a half-spine immobilization device. You and an EMT assistant arrive on the scene of an automobile crash. The scene is safe, and there is only one patient. The assistant EMT has completed the initial assessment, and no critical condition requiring intervention was found. For the purpose of this station, the patient's vital signs remain stable. You are required to treat the specific, isolated problem of an unstable spine using a half-spine immobilization device. You are responsible for the direction and subsequent actions of the EMT assistant. Transferring and immobilizing the patient to the long spine board should be accomplished verbally. You have ten minutes to complete this skill station. Do you have any questions?

Spinal Immobilization
Seated Patient

Start Time: _____

Stop Time: _____   Date: _____

Candidate's Name: _____

Evaluator's Name: _____

	Points Possible	Points Awarded
Takes, or verbalizes, body substance isolation precautions	1	
Directs assistant to place/maintain head in the neutral in-line position	1	
Directs assistant to maintain manual immobilization of the head	1	
Reassesses motor, sensory, and circulatory function in each extremity	1	
Applies appropriately sized extrication collar	1	
Positions the immobilization device behind the patient	1	
Secures the device to the patient's torso	1	
Evaluates torso fixation and adjusts as necessary	1	
Evaluates and pads behind the patient's head as necessary	1	
Secures the patient's head to the device	1	
Verbalizes moving the patient to a long spine board	1	
Reassesses motor, sensory, and circulatory function in each extremity	1	
Total:	**12**	

Critical Criteria

_____ Did not immediately direct, or take, manual immobilization of the head

_____ Released, or ordered release of, manual immobilization before it was maintained mechanically

_____ Patient manipulated, or moved excessively, causing potential spinal compromise

_____ Device moved excessively up, down, left, or right on the patient's torso

_____ Head Immobilization allows for excessive movement

_____ Torso fixation inhibits chest rise, resulting in respiratory compromise

_____ Upon completion of immobilization, head is not in the neutral position

_____ Did not assess motor, sensory, and circulatory function in each extremity after voicing immobilization to the long board

_____ Immobilized head to the board before securing the torso

▶ Immobilization Skills— Long Bone

Instructions to the Candidate

Minimum Score: 7

This station is designed to test your ability to properly immobilize a closed, nonangulated long bone injury. You are required to treat only the specific, isolated injury to the extremity. The scene size-up and initial assessment have been completed, and during the focused assessment, a closed, nonangulated injury of the _____ (radius, ulna, tibia, fibula) was detected. Ongoing assessment of the patient's airway, breathing, and central circulation is not necessary. You may use any equipment available in this room. You have five minutes to complete this skill station. Do you have any questions?

Immobilization Skills
Long Bone

Start Time: _____

Stop Time: _____   Date: _____

Candidate's Name: _____

Evaluator's Name: _____

	Points Possible	Points Awarded
Takes, or verbalizes, body substance isolation precautions	1	
Directs application of manual stabilization of the injury	1	
Assesses motor, sensory, and circulatory function in the injured extremity	1	
Note: The examiner acknowledges "motor, sensory, and circulatory function are present and normal."		
Measures the splint	1	
Applies the splint	1	
Immobilizes the joint above the injury site	1	
Immobilizes the joint below the injury site	1	
Secures the entire injured extremity	1	
Immobilizes the hand/foot in the position of function	1	
Reassesses motor, sensory, and circulatory function in the injured extremity	1	
Note: The examiner acknowledges "motor, sensory, and circulatory function are present and normal."		
Total:	**10**	

Critical Criteria

_____ Grossly moves the injured extremity

_____ Did not immobilize the joint above and the joint below the injury site

_____ Did not reassess motor, sensory, and circulatory function in the injured extremity before and after splinting

► Immobilization Skills–
Joint Injury

Instructions to the Candidate

Minimum Score: 6

This station is designed to test your ability to properly immobilize a noncomplicated shoulder injury. You are required to treat only the specific, isolated injury to the shoulder. The scene size-up and initial assessment have been accomplished on the victim, and during the focused assessment, a shoulder injury was detected. Ongoing assessment of the patient's airway, breathing, and central circulation is not necessary. You may use any equipment available in this room. You have five minutes to complete this skill station. Do you have any questions?

Immobilization Skills
Joint Injury

Start Time: _____

Stop Time: _____   **Date:** _____

Candidate's Name: _____

Evaluator's Name: _____

	Points Possible	Points Awarded
Takes, or verbalizes, body substance isolation precautions	1	
Directs application of manual stabilization of the shoulder injury	1	
Assesses motor, sensory, and circulatory function in the injured extremity	1	
Note: The examiner acknowledges "motor, sensory, and circulatory function are present and normal."		
Selects the proper splinting material	1	
Immobilizes the site of the injury	1	
Immobilizes the bone above the injured joint	1	
Immobilizes the bone below the injured joint	1	
Reassesses motor, sensory, and circulatory function in the injured extremity	1	
Note: The examiner acknowledges "motor, sensory, and circulatory function are present and normal."		
Total:	**8**	

Critical Criteria

_____ Did not support the joint so that the joint did not bear distal weight

_____ Did not immobilize the bone above and below the injured site

_____ Did not reassess motor, sensory, and circulatory function in the injured extremity before and after splinting

▶ Immobilization Skills– Traction Splinting

Instructions to Candidate

Minimum Score: 10

This station is designed to test your ability to properly immobilize a mid-shaft femur injury with a traction splint. You will have an EMT assistant to help you in the application of the device by applying manual traction when directed to do so. You are required to treat only the specific, isolated injury to the femur. The scene size-up and initial assessment have been accomplished on the victim, and during the focused assessment, a mid-shaft femur deformity was detected. Ongoing assessment of the patient's airway, breathing, and central circulation is not necessary. You may use any equipment available in this room. You have ten minutes to complete this skill station. Do you have any questions?

Immobilization Skills
Traction Splinting

Start Time: _____

Stop Time: _____   Date: _____

Candidate's Name: _____

Evaluator's Name: _____

	Points Possible	Points Awarded
Takes, or verbalizes, body substance isolation precautions	1	
Directs application of manual stabilization of the injured leg	1	
Directs the application of manual traction	1	
Assesses motor, sensory, and circulatory function in the injured extremity	1	
Note: The examiner acknowledges "motor, sensory, and circulatory function are present and normal."		
Prepares/adjusts splint to the proper length	1	
Positions the splint next to the injured leg	1	
Applies the proximal securing device (e.g...ischial strap)	1	
Applies the distal securing device (e.g...ankle hitch)	1	
Applies mechanical traction	1	
Positions/secures the support straps	1	
Re-evaluates the proximal/distal securing devices	1	
Reassesses motor, sensory, and circulatory function in the injured extremity	1	
Note: The examiner acknowledges "motor, sensory, and circulatory function are present and normal."		
Note: The examiner must ask the candidate how he or she would prepare the patient for transportation.		
Verbalizes securing the torso to the long board to immobilize the hip	1	
Verbalizes securing the splint to the long board to prevent movement of the splint	1	
Total:	**14**	

Critical Criteria

_____ Loss of traction at any point after it was applied

_____ Did not reassess motor, sensory, and circulatory function in the injured extremity before and after splinting

_____ The foot was excessively rotated or extended after splint was applied

_____ Did not secure the ischial strap before taking traction

_____ Final immobilization failed to support the femur or prevent rotation of the injured leg

_____ Secured the leg to the splint before applying mechanical traction

Note: If the Sagar splint or the Kendricks Traction Device is used without elevating the patient's leg, application of annual traction is not necessary. The candidate should be awarded one (1) point as if manual traction were applied.

▶ Bleeding Control/Shock Management

Instructions to the Candidate

Minimum Score: 7

This station is designed to test your ability to control hemorrhage. This is a scenario-based testing station. As you progress throughout the scenario, you will be given various signs and symptoms appropriate for the patient's condition. You will be required to manage the patient based on these signs and symptoms. A scenario will be read aloud to you, and you will be given an opportunity to ask clarifying questions about the scenario; however, you will not receive answers to any questions about the actual steps of the procedures to be performed. You may use any of the supplies and equipment available in this room. You have ten minutes to complete this skill station. Do you have any questions?

Scenario (Sample) Bleeding Control/Shock Management

You respond to a stabbing and find a 25-year-old male victim. Upon examination, you find a two-inch stab wound to the inside of the right arm at the anterior elbow crease (antecubital fascia). Bright-red blood is spurting from the wound. The scene is safe, and the patient is responsive and alert. His airway is open, and he is breathing adequately. Do you have any questions?

Bleeding Control/Shock Management

Start Time: _____

Stop Time: _____   Date: _____

Candidate's Name: _____

Evaluator's Name: _____

	Points Possible	Points Awarded
Takes, or verbalizes, body substance isolation precautions	1	
Applies direct pressure to the wound	1	
Elevates the extremity	1	
Note: The examiner must now inform the candidate that the wound continues to bleed.		
Applies an additional dressing to the wound	1	
Note: The examiner must now inform the candidate that the wound still continues to bleed. The second dressing does not control the bleeding.		
Locates and applies pressure to appropriate arterial pressure point	1	
Note: The examiner must now inform the candidate that the bleeding is controlled.		
Bandages the wound	1	
Note: The examiner must now inform the candidate the patient is now showing signs and symptoms indicative of hypoperfusion.		
Properly positions the patient	1	
Applies high-concentration oxygen	1	
Initiates steps to prevent heat loss from the patient	1	
Indicates the need for immediate transportation	1	
Total:	**10**	

Critical Criteria

_____ Did not take, or verbalize, body substance isolation precautions

_____ Did not apply high-concentration oxygen

_____ Applied a tourniquet before attempting other methods of bleeding control

_____ Did not control hemorrhage in a timely manner

_____ Did not indicate a need for immediate transportation

▶ Airway, Oxygen, Ventilation Skills/Upper Airway Adjuncts and Suction

Instructions to the Candidate

Minimum Score: 9

This station is designed to test your ability to properly measure, insert, and remove an oropharyngeal and a nasopharyngeal airway, as well as suction a patient's upper airway. This is an isolated skills test comprised of three separate skills. You may use any equipment available in this room. You have five minutes to complete this station. Do you have any questions?

Airway, Oxygen, and Ventilation Skills/Upper Airway Adjuncts and Suction

Start Time: _____

Stop Time: _____   Date: _____

Candidate's Name: _____

Evaluator's Name: _____

OROPHARYNGEAL AIRWAY	Points Possible	Points Awarded
Takes, or verbalizes, body substance isolation precautions	1	
Selects appropriately sized airway	1	
Measures airway	1	
Inserts airway without pushing the tongue posteriorly	1	
Note: The examiner must advise the candidate that the patient is gagging and becoming conscious.		
Removes the oropharyngeal airway	1	
SUCTION		
Note: The examiner must advise the candidate to suction the patient's airway.		
Turns on/prepares suction device	1	
Assures presence of mechanical suction	1	
Inserts the suction tip without suction	1	
Applies suction to the oropharynx/nasopharynx	1	
NASOPHARYNGEAL AIRWAY		
Note: The examiner must advise the candidate to insert a nasopharyngeal airway.		
Selects appropriately sized airway	1	
Measures airway	1	
Verbalizes lubrication of the nasal airway	1	
Fully inserts the airway with the bevel facing toward the septum	1	
Total:	**13**	

Critical Criteria

_____ Did not take, or verbalize, body substance isolation precautions

_____ Did not obtain a patent airway with the oropharyngeal airway

_____ Did not obtain a patent airway with the nasopharyngeal airway

_____ Did not demonstrate an acceptable suction technique

_____ Inserted any adjunct in a manner dangerous to the patient

▶ Airway, Oxygen, Ventilation Skills/Mouth-to-Mask with Supplemental Oxygen

Instructions to the Candidate

Minimum Score: 6

This station is designed to test your ability to ventilate a patient with supplemental oxygen using a mouth-to-mask technique. This is an isolated skills test. You may assume that mouth-to-barrier device ventilation is in progress and that the patient has a central pulse. The only patient management required is ventilator support using a mouth-to-mask technique with supplemental oxygen. You must ventilate the patient for at least 30 seconds. You will be evaluated on the appropriateness of ventilatory volumes. You may use any equipment available in this room. You have five minutes to complete this station. Do you have any questions?

Airway, Oxygen, Ventilation Skills/Mouth-to-Mask with Supplemental Oxygen

Start Time: _____

Stop Time: _____   Date: _____

Candidate's Name: _____

Evaluator's Name: _____

	Points Possible	Points Awarded
Takes, or verbalizes, body substance isolation precautions	1	
Connects one-way valve to mask	1	
Opens patient's airway or confirms patient's airway is open (manually or with adjunct)	1	
Establishes and maintains a proper mask-to-face seal	1	
Ventilates the patient at the proper volume and rate *(800–1200 ml per breath/10–20 breaths per minute)*	1	
Connects the mask to high concentration of oxygen	1	
Adjusts flow rate to at least 15 liters per minute	1	
Continues ventilation of the patient at the proper volume and rate *(800–1200 ml per breath/10–20 breaths per minute)*	1	
Note: The examiner must witness ventilations for at least 30 seconds.		
Total:	**8**	

Critical Criteria

_____ Did not take, or verbalize, body substance isolation precautions

_____ Did not adjust liter flow to at least 15 liters per minute

_____ Did not provide proper volume per breath *(more than 2 ventilations per minute were below 800 ml)*

_____ Did not ventilate the patient at a rate of 10–20 breaths per minute

_____ Did not allow for complete exhalation

▶ Airway, Oxygen, Ventilation Skills/Supplemental Oxygen Administration

Instructions to the Candidate

Minimum Score: 11

This station is designed to test your ability to correctly assemble the equipment needed to administer supplemental oxygen in the prehospital setting. This is an isolated skills test. You will be required to assemble an oxygen tank and a regulator and administer oxygen to a patient using a nonrebreather mask. At this point, you will be instructed to discontinue oxygen administration by the nonrebreather mask and start oxygen administration using a nasal cannula because the patient cannot tolerate the mask. Once you have initiated oxygen administration using a nasal cannula, you will be instructed to discontinue oxygen administration completely. You may use only the equipment available in this room. You have five minutes to complete this station. Do you have any questions?

Airway, Oxygen, Ventilation Skills/Supplemental Oxygen Administration

Start Time: _____

Stop Time: _____   Date: _____

Candidate's Name: _____

Evaluator's Name: _____

	Points Possible	Points Awarded
Takes, or verbalizes, body substance isolation precautions	1	
Assembles the regulator to the tank	1	
Opens the tank	1	
Checks for leaks	1	
Checks tank pressure	1	
Attaches nonrebreather mask to oxygen	1	
Prefills reservoir	1	
Adjusts liter flow to 12 liters per minute or greater	1	
Applies and adjusts the mask to the patient's face	1	
Note: The examiner must advise the candidate that the patient is not tolerating the nonrebreather mask. The medical director has ordered you to apply a nasal cannula to the patient.		
Attaches nasal cannula to oxygen	1	
Adjusts liter flow to six (6) liters per minute or less	1	
Applies nasal cannula to the patient	1	
Note: The examiner must advise the candidate to discontinue oxygen therapy.		
Removes the nasal cannula from the patient	1	
Shuts off the regulator	1	
Relieves the pressure within the regulator	1	
Total:	**15**	

Critical Criteria

_____ Did not take, or verbalize, body substance isolation precautions

_____ Did not assemble the tank and regulator without leaks

_____ Did not prefill the reservoir bag

_____ Did not adjust the device to the correct liter flow for the nonrebreather mask (*12 liters per minute or greater*)

_____ Did not adjust the device to the correct liter flow for the nasal cannula (*6 liters per minute or less*)

State Certification Requirements

CHAPTER SUMMARY
This chapter outlines EMT-Basic certification requirements for all 50 states, the District of Columbia, Puerto Rico, and the U.S. Virgin Islands. It also lists state EMT agencies you can contact for more information about certification requirements.

The table on pages 186–188 shows some of the minimum requirements you must meet to be certified as an EMT-Basic in the 50 states, the District of Columbia, Puerto Rico, and the U.S. Virgin Islands. The next few paragraphs explain the entries on the table. After the table is a state-by-state list of EMT agencies, which you can contact for more specific information.

You should know that some minimum requirements are pretty standard and so are not listed on the table. For instance, you must be physically, mentally, and emotionally able to perform all the tasks of an EMT. Usually, you are required to have a high school diploma or GED before you begin training. You must have a clean criminal record. And, of course, you must successfully complete an EMT-Basic training program that meets the standards set by the U.S. Department of Transportation.

The minimum age for most states is 18 years old; however, you should check age specifications with the EMT agency in your state. Some states allow you to begin a training program before you reach this minimum age, often requiring permission a parent or guardian's permission.

The first entry, **Minimum Hours of Training,** lists the number of hours this state or territory considers sufficient for EMT-B training. Courses that meet the requirements will typically cover both the DOT/NHTSA approved curriculum and locality-specific protocols. Be sure to check with the licensing agency in the area where you intend to work to make sure your course meets the requirements. Note that in some states, such as California, the locality-specific requirements are just that: The requirements for EMT-B certification in Los Angeles differ from the requirements in San Diego and Santa Clara. You should also check with your licensing agency to see how much time you have between finishing your training course and fulfilling all the other requirements for certification—including passing the written and practical exams.

States use their own written and practical skills exams, exams from the National Registry of EMTs, or a combination of both. The entry under **Training Accepted** will be "State," meaning the state has its own exam; "NREMT" for National Registry; or an entry indicating a combination of both exams. Even when the state has its own exam, you'll find it's pretty similar to the National Registry exam, and therefore to the exams in this book (except for state- or locality-specific scopes of practice and protocols). After all, the federal government mandates the curriculum of EMT courses nationwide. You can expect exams based on similar curricula to be similar.

Some states' exam will require you to go through *their* certification process; others will accept the National Registry Exams, if you are already certified by the NREMT. Similarly, some states will accept your certification from out of state, some will accept it if you take their exam, and some will require that you be cer-

tified through the National Registry if you are transferring in from out-of-state. In most cases, a state that accepts out-of-state certification will insist that your training program and your exam meet or exceed its standards, so sometimes, it will come down to whether the state you're coming from is deemed to have done so. Some states have additional certification requirements for transferring EMTs, such as background investigation, being a state resident, being employed with an EMS agency in that state, or taking a refresher course. If you are certified in another state, you will need to show proof of certification when applying in a different state. Some states have what is known as "legal recognition," which means they will recognize and accept your training for a limited time period, often one year. This is similar to a temporary certification. During this period of legal recognition, you apply for official certification and fulfill the necessary requirements. Once the process is complete, your certification will be good for as long as that state allows. You should check with the appropriate state's EMS office for more detail.

The last column, **Recertification**, indicates the number of years from your initial certification to the time when you will have to be recertified. Recertification usually requires a given number of hours of continuing education, demonstration of your continuing ability to perform the necessary skills, or both—but you'll find out all about that once you're certified in the first place.

STATE	MINIMUM HOURS OF TRAINING	TRAINING ACCEPTED	RECERTIFICATION
Alabama	172	NREMT	2 years
Alaska	128	State	2 years
Arizona	115	NREMT	2 years
Arkansas	120	State and NREMT	2 years
California	110	State or NREMT	4 years
Colorado	110	State	3 years

STATE	MINIMUM HOURS OF TRAINING	TRAINING ACCEPTED	RECERTIFICATION
Connecticut	120	NREMT	2 years
Delaware	110	NREMT	1 years
District of Columbia	140	State	2 years
Florida	110	State or NREMT	2 years
Georgia	N/A	State	2 years
Hawaii	315	NREMT	2 years
Idaho	110	NREMT	3 years
Illinois	110	State	4 years
Indiana	144.5	State	2 years
Iowa	128	State	2 years
Kansas	150	State	1 years
Kentucky	120	State and NREMT	2 years
Louisiana	140	State and NREMT	2 years
Maine	111	State	3 years
Maryland	131	State	3 years
Massachusetts	110	State	2 years
Michigan	194	State	3 years
Minnesota	130	NREMT	2 years
Mississippi	110	NREMT	2 years
Missouri	110	State	5 years
Montana	110	NREMT	2 years
Nebraska	110	NREMT	3 years
Nevada	110	State	2 years
New Hampshire	110	State and NREMT	2 years
New Jersey	120	State	3 years
New Mexico	120	State	2 years
New York	130	State	3 years

STATE	MINIMUM HOURS OF TRAINING	TRAINING ACCEPTED	RECERTIFICATION
North Carolina	148	State	4 years
North Dakota	110	NREMT	2 years
Ohio	130	NREMT	3 years
Oklahoma	148	NREMT	2 years
Oregon	140	NREMT	2 years
Pennsylvania	123.5	State	3 years
Rhode Island	122	State and NREMT	3 years
South Carolina	139	State	3 years
South Dakota	110	NREMT	2 years
Tennessee	150	NREMT	2 years
Texas	140	State	4 years
Utah	120	State	3 years
Vermont	110	State and NREMT	2 years
Virginia	120	State	4 years
Washington	110	State	3 years
West Virginia	110	NREMT	3 years
Wisconsin	120	NREMT	2 years
Wyoming	120	NREMT	2 years
Puerto Rico	110	State	2 years
U.S. Virgin Islands	140	NREMT	With NREMT

▶ State EMT Agencies

The following is a list of the agencies that control EMT certification in each state, with their addresses and phone numbers. You can contact those offices for more information on their certification requirements. Visit the NREMT website (www.nremt.org/EMTServices/emt_cand_state_offices.asp) for up-to-date links to state EMS websites.

ALABAMA

Emergency Medical Services
Department of Public Health
201 Monroe Street
Montgomery, AL 36104
Telephone: 334-206-5383

ALASKA

Department of Health and Social Services
Division of Public Health
Community Health and EMS Section
PO Box 110616
Juneau, AK 99811-0616
Telephone: 907-465-3027

ARIZONA

Bureau of EMS
150 North 18th Avenue, Suite 540
Phoenix, AZ 85007-3248
Telephone: 602-364-3150

ARKANSAS

Division of EMS-State Department of Health
4815 West Markham Street, Slot 38
Little Rock, AR 72205-3867
Telephone: 916-322-4336

CALIFORNIA

EMS Authority, State of California
1930 9th Street, Suite 100
Sacramento, CA 95814
Telephone: 916-322-4336

COLORADO

Colorado Department of Public Health &
    Environment, EMS Division
4300 Cherry Creek Drive South
Denver, CO 80246-1530
Telephone: 303-692-2980

CONNECTICUT

Division of Health Systems Regulation
PO Box 340308, 410 Capital Avenue
Hartford, CT 06134-0308
Telephone: 860-509-7975

DELAWARE

Division of Public Health,
    Department of Health and Social Services
Office of EMS, Blue Hen Corporate Center
655 Bay Road, Suite 4-H
Dover, DE 19901
Telephone: 302-739-6637

DISTRICT OF COLUMBIA

Emergency Health and Medical Services
864 New York Northeast Suite 5000
Washington, DC 20001
Telephone: 202-671-4222

FLORIDA

Bureau of EMS
4052 Bald Cypress Way, Bin C18
Tallahassee, FL 32399-1738
Telephone: 850-245-4073

GEORGIA
Office of EMS/Trauma
2600 Skyland Drive, Lower Level
Atlanta, GA 30319
Telephone: 404-679-0547

HAWAII
State Department of Health,
    Emergency Medical Services
3627 Kilauea Avenue, Room 102
Honolulu, HI 96816
Telephone: 808-733-9210

IDAHO
Idaho EMS Bureau
590 West Washington Street
Boise, ID 83720-0036
Telephone: 208-334-4000

ILLINOIS
Division of EMS, State Department of Public Health
525 West Jefferson Street
Springfield, IL 62761
Telephone: 217-785-2080

INDIANA
State EMS Commission
302 West Washington, Room E208 IGCS
Indianapolis, IN 46204-2258
Telephone: 317-233-6545

IOWA
Iowa Department of Public Health, Bureau of EMS
401 SW 7th Street, Suite D
Des Moines, IA 50309
Telephone: 515-725-0326

KANSAS
Board of EMS
LSOB, Suite 1031, 900 Southwest Jackson
Topeka, KS 66612
Telephone: 785-296-7296

KENTUCKY
Kentucky Board of EMS,
    Commonwealth of Kentucky
2545 Lawrenceburg Road
Frankfort, KY 40601
Telephone: 502-564-8963

LOUISIANA
DHH-OPH, Bureau of EMS
8919 World Ministry Avenue
    Main Administration Building, Suite A
Baton Rouge, LA 70810
Telephone: 225-763-5700

MAINE
Maine EMS
16 Edison Drive
Augusta, ME 04330
Telephone: 207-626-3860

MARYLAND
Maryland Institute for EMS Services
653 West Pratt Street
Baltimore, MD 21201-1536
Telephone: 410-706-3666

MASSACHUSETTS
Department of Public Health, Office of EMS
56 Roland Street, Suite 100
Boston, MA 02129-1235
Telephone: 617-284-8300

MICHIGAN
Michigan Department of Community Health
Division of EMS and Trauma Services
Lewis Cass Building, 6th Floor,
    320 South Walnut Street
Lansing, MI 48913
Telephone: 517-241-0179

MINNESOTA

MN EMS Regulatory Board
2829 University Avenue, Southeast Suite 310
Minneapolis, MN 55414-3222
Telephone: 612-627-6000

MISSISSIPPI

Mississippi Department of Health
PO Box 1700,
  570 East Woodrow Wilson, Annex 309
Jackson, MS 39215-1700
Telephone: 601-576-7380

MISSOURI

Department of Health & Senior Services,
  Bureau of EMS
PO Box 570, 912 Wildwood Drive
Jefferson City, MO 65102
Telephone: 573-751-6356

MONTANA

EMS & Trauma Systems Program,
  MT Department of Public Health &
  Human Services
PO Box 202951
Helena, MT 59620-2951
Telephone: 406-444-3895

NEBRASKA

State Department of Health, Division of EMS
301 Centennial Mall South, 3rd Floor
Lincoln, NE 68508-2529
Telephone: 402-471-2159

NEVADA

Department of Human Resources, Office of EMS
1550 East College Parkway, Suite 158
Carson City, NV 89706
Telephone: 775-687-4475

NEW HAMPSHIRE

Department of Safety, Bureau of EMS
33 Hazen Drive
Concord, NH 03305
Telephone: 603-271-4568

NEW JERSEY

New Jersey Department of Health &
  Senior Services, Office of EMS
PO Box 360, 50 East State Street
Trenton, NJ 08625-0360
Telephone: 609-633-7777

NEW MEXICO

EMS Bureau, Department of Health
2500 Cerrillos Road
Sante Fe, NM 87505
Telephone: 505-476-7701

NEW YORK

State Department of Health, EMS Bureau
433 River Street, Suite 303
Troy, NY 12180-2299
Telephone: 518-402-0996

NORTH CAROLINA

Office of EMS, Department of Health &
  Human Services
701 Barbour Drive, PO Box 29530
Raleigh, NC 27603
Telephone: 919-855-3935

NORTH DAKOTA

Division of Emergency Medical Services,
  ND Department of Health
600 East Boulevard Avenue, Department 301
Bismarck, ND 58505-0200
Telephone: 701-328-2388

OHIO

Ohio Department of Public Safety
PO Box 182073
Columbus, OH 43218-2073
Telephone: 614-466-9447

OKLAHOMA

EMS Division, State Department of Health
1000 Northeast 10th Street
Oklahoma City, OK 73117-1299
Telephone: 405-271-4027

OREGON

Emergency Medical Services & Trauma Systems,
    Health Department
800 Northeast Oregon Street, #607
Portland, OR 97232-2162
Telephone: 503-731-4011

PENNSYLVANIA

Division of EMS, Pennsylvania Department of Health
PO Box 90
Harrisburg, PA 17108
Telephone: 717-787-8740

RHODE ISLAND

Division of EMS, Rhode Island Department of Health
3 Capitol Hill, Suite 306
Providence, RI 02908-5097
Telephone: 401-222-2401

SOUTH CAROLINA

Emergency Medical Services Section,
    Department of Health and Environmental Control
2600 Bull Street
Columbia, SC 29201
Telephone: 803-545-4204

SOUTH DAKOTA

South Dakota Department of Health
Emergency Medical Services
118 West Capitol Avenue
Pierre, SD 57501-2000
Telephone: 605-773-4031

TENNESSEE

Division of EMS, Tennessee Department of Health
Cordell Hull Building, 425 Fifth Avenue North,
    1st Floor
Nashville, TN 37247-0701
615-741-2584

TEXAS

EMS & Trauma Systems Coordination Office
Department of State Health Services
1100 West 49th Street
Austin, TX 78756-3199
Telephone: 512-834-6700

UTAH

Bureau of EMS, Department of Health
PO Box 142004
Salt Lake City, UT 84114-2004
Telephone: 801-538-6435

VERMONT

EMS Division, Department of Health
PO Box 70, 108 Cherry Street, Room 201
Burlington, VT 05402
Telephone: 802-863-7310

VIRGINIA

Division of EMS, Department of Health
109 Governor Street, James Madison Building,
    Suite UB-55
Richmond, VA 23219
Telephone: 800-523-6019 or 800-864-7600

WASHINGTON

EMS and Trauma Prevention, ET-40,
    Department of Health
PO Box 47853
Olympia, WA 98504-7853
Telephone: 360-236-2828

WEST VIRGINIA

Office of EMS, State Department of Health
350 Capitol Street, Room 515
Charleston, WV 25301
Telephone: 304-558-3956

WISCONSIN

Bureau of EMS & Injury Prevention
DHFS-P.H., PO Box 2659, 1 West Wilson, Room 118
Madison, WI 53701-2659
Telephone: 608-266-1568

WYOMING

EMS Program, State of Wyoming
Hathaway Building, 4th Floor
Cheyenne, WY 82002
Telephone: 307-777-7955

PUERTO RICO

Puerto Rico Emergency Medical Services
State Emergency Medical System
PO Box 2161
San Juan, PR 00922-2161
809-766-1733

U.S. VIRGIN ISLANDS

Division of Emergency Medical Services
48 Sugar Estate
Charlotte Amalie, USVI 00802
340-776-8311

NOTES

NOTES

NOTES

NOTES